Swift to Wrath

Edited by WILLIAM D. CARRIGAN

and CHRISTOPHER WALDREP

Swift to Wrath

Lynching in Global Historical Perspective

University of Virginia Press   *Charlottesville and London*

University of Virginia Press
© 2013 by the Rector and Visitors of the University of Virginia
All rights reserved
Printed in the United States of America on acid-free paper

First published 2013
9 8 7 6 5 4 3 2 1

LIBRARY OF CONGRESS CATALOGING-IN-PUBLICATION DATA

Swift to wrath : lynching in global historical perspective / edited by William D.
Carrigan and Christopher Waldrep.
     pages   cm
  Includes bibliographical references and index.
   ISBN 978-0-8139-3414-3 (cloth : alk. paper) — ISBN 978-0-8139-3415-0 (e-book)
  1. Lynching—History. I. Carrigan, William D., 1970– II. Waldrep, Christopher,
1951–
   HV6455.S95 2013
   364.1'34—dc23   2012041252

Let every man be swift to hear, slow to speak, slow to wrath.
—James 1:19

Contents

Swift to Wrath

Introduction

WILLIAM D. CARRIGAN AND CHRISTOPHER WALDREP

A FUNNY THING HAPPENED to this book on its way to publication. When we began collecting the essays that make up this volume, we had three goals. First, we hoped to encourage scholars to study the spread of the American word *lynching* throughout the world, analyzing the reasons for its adoption in other nations and the evolution of the word's meanings in those disparate cultures. We next wanted to refute the popular notion that the various acts of collective violence called lynching in American history are unique or exceptional to the history of the United States, thereby encouraging historians to expand chronologically and geographically the study of the practice of "lynching." Third, we sought to collect concrete examples of these new historical approaches, providing a sample of the diverse methods that historians might employ in the study of lynching in the future.

The process of writing a book includes subjecting the manuscript to critical evaluation by scholars before publication, and for this book, this part of the process taught us a great deal. So many scholars have written about lynching all over the world that anyone with basic access to a good library can easily learn that lynching is not uniquely American. Latin America has produced a particularly hardy band of lynching researchers, but India, Africa, and China have too. So why didn't we know about this work when we began this project? The answer is simple: as historians, we focused on history writing, and most of the work done on lynching outside the United States has been done by sociologists and, especially, anthropologists, very often focused on lynching not as history but as a current and ongoing phenomenon. These scholars have done courageous work, going into rough neighborhoods where lynching is common to interview the lynchers and their victims. Their insightful writing challenges our preconceptions to teach us a great deal, but it is not often historical. "Anthropological inquiry often starts with current events and the ethnographically visible," the anthropologist Paul Farmer recently wrote. He makes a point we think needs to be repeated and emphasized: it can be hard to study lynching historically because suggesting a historical context for atrocities seems to excuse them. But, he concludes, it should be done anyway.[1]

We think that Farmer is right and that there is value in studying lynching historically and globally. We make no claim that the essays in this book represent any kind of geographically comprehensive survey of world lynching. We were, however, interested in being chronologically and geographically expansive, demonstrating to readers and students of lynching that there are more options for the historical study of lynching than is traditionally perceived. The recent work by sociologists and anthropologists who employ the word *lynching* to describe mob behavior in a variety of settings underscores the need to proceed historically. Especially scholarly investigators of collective violence should keep in mind the rhetorical challenges the word *lynching* poses; the word has a history that changes over time for political reasons.

We also learned to stop thinking about lynching as a kind of exceptionalism, as uniquely American. It's questionable whether American lynch mobs have encouraged lynching in other countries with their behavior, but American lynching rhetoric has doubtlessly influenced mob violence in other countries. Some anthropologists explicitly compare lynchings in other countries with that in the American South. Carlos M. Vilas begins his magisterial essay about Mexican lynching with words designed to recall Billie Holiday's 1939 American lynching ballad: "Extraños frutos colgaban de los árboles esa mañana de domingo en Zapotitlán" (Strange fruit hung from the trees on that Sunday morning in Zapotitlan).[2] In their article about contemporary lynching in Bolivia, Daniel M. Goldstein and Fatimah Williams Castro recognize that "the term 'lynching' (lincganuebti) is a cognate from English, derived from forms of popular justice-making in early U.S. history."[3] Christopher Krupa explicitly compares contemporary Bolivian lynching with the American variety, urging anthropologists to more closely follow American scholars' policy of identifying with the victims rather than the perpetrators.[4] Anthropologists who differentiate modern lynching from its American antecedents still implicitly or explicitly judge the violence against an American model. Latin American lynching, Leigh Binford and Nancy Churchill write, is "quite different" from American lynching in that it lacks the support of law enforcement.[5]

Paul Brass warns against the "post-hoc labeling" common to anthropology.[6] This wise warning can be difficult to heed, not just for anthropologists, but for historians, geographers, sociologists, and those outside the academy as well. At Amsterdam's famed art museum, the Rijksmuseum, visitors may view *The Bodies of the De Witt Brothers,* a painting attributed to Jan de Baen, ca. 1672–75. The label accompanying the painting, written in Dutch, ends with the word *gelyncht.* It is that last word that grabs the attention of an American tourist wandering down the long row of paintings and stops his or her progress through the gallery. In 1672 mobs blamed Johan de Witt when French and English troops swept through the republic in the Franco-Dutch

Jan de Baen, *The Bodies of the De Witt Brothers,* ca. 1672–1675.
(Rijksmuseum, Amsterdam, Holland)

War. He resigned his position as pensionary (similar to prime minister), but it was not enough. A mob killed not only Johan but his brother Cornelius as well, mutilating their bodies, cutting off the genitalia, noses, and fingers before carving deeper into their bodies for souvenirs, later sold on the street, and displaying the remains on a gallows.

In 1672 no one in Holland knew the word *gelyncht* because the Americans would not invent the word lynching for another century. Yet from the vantage point of the twenty-first century, the Dutch curators working at the Rikjsmuseum thought the word *lynching* perfectly appropriate. What did they have in mind? A neutral, descriptive phrase relating an event without comment? Hardly: they clearly disapprove of the killings, calling the mob "frenzied." The display of the butchered men, even the painting by an artist, recalls similar displays of African Americans and photography James Allen collected from America's lynching era and published in his book *Without Sanctuary: Lynching Photography in America*. The Dutch art historians apparently thought there was something American-like in the killing of the de Witt brothers.[7]

The difficulties that surround the word *lynching* are both similar to and different from the troubles facing an attempt to define any term. All human language is fraught with a certain degree of instability, but we do believe that in particular times and places some words become more politicized, less stable, and rhetorically more contested than other words. In the last two centuries, the American word *lynching* has been a case in point. However, we believe this rhetorical history, far from a hindrance to the study of collective violence, is especially promising for historians interested in understanding the minds of mob members, their defenders, and their critics.

The historical work that has been done on the behavior of lynch mobs in the United States over the past quarter century has been very illuminating. Thorough investigation of newspapers, government documents, court records, and other sources, historians have created a much richer understanding of acts of extralegal violence in the nineteenth- and early twentieth-century United States. Although we believe that attention to the social reality is vital, we also conclude that at times there has been too much weight given to statistical details and not enough emphasis on the cultural world in which the acts of collective violence flourished.

A core assumption that we hold is that people care very deeply about crime and its punishment and take particular pains to defend their own views and criticize those who conceive of it differently. Thus rhetorical debates over how one defines legal and extralegal collective violence are a particularly good window for studying popular attitudes toward not only ethnic, racial, and religious minorities but also the law and the state itself. The study of this discourse of extralegal violence is, of course, much broader than the study of the American word *lynching*, but there are intriguing advantages to the study of "lynching." Unlike other terms that are sometimes used to describe collective violence, like *riot* or *rioting*, *lynching* has a relatively recent origin in a discrete geographic area, 1780s Virginia. This makes studying the spread of this word both within the United States and abroad far easier than related terms. Compounding this advantage is the fact that the word has had for more than a century a particularly potent political value and thus appears more frequently in surviving historical records than related terms like *vigilantism*. In short, we encourage historians to study the discourse over extralegal violence broadly but recommend the study of "lynching" in particular because of its methodological benefits.

As an aid to those who might be interested in using the word *lynching* as a means of studying the attitudes of ordinary people toward the state as well as their attitudes toward "lynching" violence in the United States, we have

GLOBAL SPREAD OF LYNCHING LANGUAGE

Country or region	Word(s)	Estimated date of entry
United States	Lynch law, lynching	1780s
Great Britain	Lynch law, lynching	1830s
France	La loi de Lynch, lynchage	1830s
Mexico	Ley de lynch, linchar, linchamiento	By the 1850s
Italy	Linciaggio	By the 1890s
Slovakia	Lynčovat'	1890s
Germany	Lynchjustiz, lynchend	By 1900
USSR/Russia	Linchevat', sudom Lincha	1920s
Japan	Rinchi	1920s

Sources: Most of these terms come from the essays in this volume, but see also *Il Progresso Italo-Americano*, 22 March 1891; and Thomas Lindenberg, "Die 'verdiente Tracht Prugel,' Ein kurzes Kapitel uber das lynchen in Wilheminischen Berlin," in *Physische Gewalt: Studien zur Geschichte der Neuseit*, ed. Thomas Lindenberger and Alf Ludtke (Frankfurt: Suhrkamp, 1995), 190–212. We thank Manfred Berg for the latter reference. William D. Carrigan and Christopher Waldrep, eds., "Swift to Wrath: Lynching in Global Perspective" (no series)

created a table that summarizes this volume's attempt at tracing the spread of the word to other countries. One can note that it was transmitted first to those countries with close connections to the United States: Great Britain, France, and Mexico. During America's rise to power in the twentieth century, the word spread further, being introduced into eastern Europe and Asia.

The best historical scholarship on lynching has long been sensitive to issues of public discourse, but we believe that this approach can be further expanded by attention to the rhetoric of lynching, both in essays specifically focused on the practice of lynching (part 1) and in studies that are largely centered on how non-Americans have grappled with the international meaning of lynching (part 2).

Part 1 of the volume takes on the task of studying the practice of lynching in a world context. These essays confound the popular perception that Americans were alone in their lynching behavior, but this is not the primary purpose of this section. Instead, these essays suggest a wide range of approaches to studying extralegal collective violence with varying degrees of attention to the rhetoric that is front and center in the essays in part 2. Some scholars of collective violence around the world write about what might be called lynching but carefully avoid the word. To represent this strain of thought we invited Rachel Monaghan to contribute an essay on her work in Northern Ireland. Other scholars feel comfortable using the word to describe lynching outside the United States or, as discussed in William Carrigan and Clive Webb's contribution, on the American borderlands. To represent this strain of scholarship, we solicited essays from Scott Morschauser and Brian Levack. Despite their varied approaches to the use of the term *lynching* and their differing degrees of concern for the relevant rhetorical history of the term, each of these essays opens a new, promising direction in the historical analysis of extralegal violence.

For part 2, we have grouped together four essayists who write about lynching outside the normal rhetoric of Gilded Age American lynching but still explicitly show the influence of American lynching. If this seems "American-centric," we feel that in the case of lynching, this focus is fully justified. Americans have, in fact, invented a powerful word and exported it. We asked each of our authors to think about the rhetoric so that the word is used consciously. We also asked our authors to think historically, to see the word in its historical context, changing over time.

From their essays we can see that lynching has influenced foreigners' perceptions of the United States. In the Gilded Age, Britain revisited and revised its understanding of the nature of the American character in light of lynching violence. In both World War II and the Cold War, the enemies of the United States used lynching as a foreign policy weapon to attack Americans' pretense to moral rectitude. Americans' capacity for lawless violence has played an important role in shaping the image of the United States around the world.

These essays, we hope, will help readers and future researchers appreciate the power that the word has and the strengths and weaknesses that come with that power. On the one hand, the word can make narratives of violence more dramatic, as many journalists and scholars can attest in their more candid moments. On the other hand, there is a less often recognized downside. Using the word *lynching* to describe mob violence can obscure historical context, even imply that neither time nor geography matters by suggesting that there is a universal human behavior that can be objectively understood outside time and space. It is in this false objectivity that *lynching* carries its greatest rhetorical power. Just using the word *lynching,* or some variant or cognate, often makes a claim hidden under the guise of objectivity.

One Hawaiian scholar not represented in our collection unconsciously demonstrated this point when she described the "lynching" of Kamanawa II and Lonopuakau in 1840. Although RaeDeen Keahiolalo-Karasuda calls the hangings lynchings, she also acknowledges that they "marked the start of a codified legal system" in Hawai'i. She quotes a newspaper at length: "The accused were allowed to challenge the jury, which consisted of twelve of the most intelligent Hawaiians, all of high rank. They were allowed to select counsel." To Keahiolalo-Karasuda, Hawai'i is not now legitimately a state and never legitimately belonged to white people. She calls these legal executions lynchings because the Americans could not legitimately govern Hawai'i; she uses the word to make a judgment.[8] Making the rhetorical decision to call Kamanawa's death a lynching allows the author to compare the colonizers of Hawai'i to Gilded Age lynch mobs. Labeling a violent act a lynching is often a political act.

In sum, the use, adoption, and transformation of the rhetoric of lynching to other societies is a window into the minds of people in distant societies and the scholars who study them. Why do they adopt the term—or avoid it? How does the meaning of the word get transformed over time in that society? What contextual factors explain such transformations? These questions should open windows into the minds of ordinary people on such critical issues as the role of law in their society and their attitudes toward their own government.

It is the particular essays, the concrete examples from our third stated goal, that are the keys to this volume. For scholars interested in the behavior of mobs, the essays in part 1 illustrate several models for how to study the practice of extralegal collective violence outside of the American South. Sociologists and anthropologists, particularly those working in Latin America, have shown how mob violence can feel empowering both to the individuals in the mob and to their communities. That important contemporary work has much to teach us. The essays in part 1 look at earlier episodes to find historical parallels and context for the mob violence that continues today.

For scholars interested in exploring the public discourse that has surrounded extralegal collective violence, the essays in part 2—through their analyses of the rhetorical history of the American word *lynching*—chart a fruitful direction. As our introductions to each of the sections make clear, there are strengths and weaknesses in either confronting or sidestepping the troublesome issue of the varying words that people have used to describe that violence. In the final analysis, we hope that this volume will help a wide range of scholars and students as they explore the important and illuminating history of collective violence.

NOTES

The volume editors would like to thank the members of Rowan University's work-in-progress seminar for their valuable comments on an early draft of this introduction. They would also like to thank the anonymous peer reviewers of the book proposal and the first draft of the volume for their insightful and useful suggestions.

1. Paul Farmer, "An Anthropology of Structural Violence," *Current Anthropology* 45 (June 2004): 305–17.

2. Carlos M. Vilas, "(In)Justicapormanopropia: Linchamientos en el Mexico Contemporaneo," *Revista Mexicana de Sociologia* 63 (January–March, 2001): 131.

3. Daniel M. Goldstein and Fatimah Williams Castro, "Creative Violence: How Marginal People Make News in Bolivia," *Journal of Latin American Anthropology* 11 (November 2006): 401n8.

4. Christopher Krupa, "Histories in Red: Ways of Seeing Lynching in Ecuador," *American Ethnologist* 36 (February 2009): 25.

5. Leigh Binford and Nancy Churchill, "Lynching and States of Fear in Urban Mexico," *Anthropologica* 51 (2009): 302.

6. Paul R. Brass, *The Production of Hindu-Muslim Violence in Contemporary India* (Seattle: University of Washington Press, 2003), 386.

7. Herbert H. Rowen, *John de Witt: Statesman of the "True Freedom"* (Cambridge: Cambridge University Press, 1986), 218; James Allen et al., *Without Sanctuary: Lynching Photography in America* (Santa Fe, NM: Twin Palms, 2000).

8. RaeDeen Keahiolalo-Karasuda, "A Genealogy of Punishment in Hawai'i: The Public Hanging of Chief Kamanawa II," accessed March 12, 2011, http://www.ksbe .edu/spi/Hulili/Hulili_vol_6/7_A_Genealogy_of_Punishment_in_Hawai'i.pdf.

PART 1

The Practice of Lynching

From the Ancient Middle East to Late Twentieth-Century Northern Ireland

F OR THIS SECTION WE HAVE CHOSEN essayists who demonstrate that crowd
violence occurs in a variety of geographies and times. Clearly a lot of
lynching-like violence has happened in many places, some of it authorized
by governments, some of it carried out by government agents, some of it carried out by criminal gangs. But just as clearly governments had a stake in
suppressing news of violence they considered anarchic. Utilizing the methods employed by ancient historians to eke out meaning from scant source
material, Scott Morschauser traces threads in ancient mob violence, finding,
for example, that mobs often made special targets of outsiders. Unavoidably,
this research takes Morschauser into the difficult terrain of distinguishing
mob violence from warfare. He finds that nothing makes mob violence more
likely than rebellions, wars, and dynastic struggles, "liminal situations."
Morschauser's discussion of the formation of law in the Fertile Crescent suggests something fundamental to all human society throughout time: assertions of power of private groups undermine community stability.

Brian Levack offers a comprehensive survey of witch lynchings from the
fifteenth century to the present. Levack is interested in the common features
of these illegal executions of witches. Mobs formed to lynch witches far more
often in small towns and villages than in urban centers, he finds. In addition,
local officials often promoted lynching by signaling toleration or even en-
couragement of the violence. Finally, popular doubts about the competence
and efficacy of the formal criminal justice system seems to have been necessary before lynchings could occur. Levack, in other words, charts the cultural
and social structure of societies likely to carry out lynchings. The structure
he outlines is hardly unique to the United States—it can be found anywhere
in the world.

William D. Carrigan and Clive Webb study the 1928 extralegal execution
of Rafael Benavides in Farmington, New Mexico. They argue that his killing
proved to be a turning point in the history of anti-Mexican mob violence in
the American Southwest. Prior to Benavides's murder, public opinion had
been shifting on the relative value of lynching to the social order. Whereas
once it had been as an essential remedy to the unstable conditions of the
frontier, it was—in an era of more powerful legal institutions—increasingly
seen as an embarrassing symbol of the West's lack of modernization. Criti-

cism of the Benavides lynching from many quarters—from New Mexico's Spanish-speaking population, from Anglo editors, and from the Mexican government—forced New Mexicans and other westerners to reevaluate what they thought about lynching and vigilantism. The murder of Benavides thus tipped the balance of public opinion and became the last episode of its kind.

Joël Michel considers mob violence in France, observing that the structural forces usually understood as foundational for a lynching culture did not exist. The French have a strong police apparatus and no hesitation about using it. As a result, there have been few acts of violence that might be called lynchings in France since the 1860s. Nonetheless, Michel argues that France had a lynching spirit not so different from the Americans. Until 1940, French authorities staged public executions as lynching-like spectacles, complete with jeering crowds. In World War II French mobs attacked collaborators, especially women, who collaborated "horizontally" with German soldiers. In these incidents, mobs formed and performed summary justice. Yet most French saw these mobbings as acts of war and did not consider them "lynchings." Michel concludes that the horrific mob spectacles in Mississippi and Texas would be impossible in Europe in peacetime.

Rachel Monaghan looks at paramilitary "punishments" in Northern Ireland after 1973. She finds that Northern Ireland has a long history of informal justice, a history of violence closely associated with community cohesiveness and approval. Throughout Irish history violent organizations have formed to solicit community support and approval, establishing informal justice systems. These groups punished disloyalty but also such "normal" crimes as vandalism, rape, and mugging. In some cases they acted when they judged the formal criminal justice system ineffective or overly lenient.

These essays demonstrate just how pervasive mob violence has been in human history, and they provide several models for how scholars might fruitfully study lynching-like violence across time and space.

"Vengeance Is Mine"

"Lynching" in the Ancient Near East?

Scott Morschauser

FOR MANY READERS OF THE BIBLE, the following passage is most disturbing:

> "Let seven of Saul's sons be given to us, so that we may hang them up before the Lord." . . . And King David gave them into the hands of the Gibeonites, and they hung them on the mountain before the Lord, and the seven of them perished together.[1]

Not only does the act occur with the full approval of David—the sweet singer of psalms and the "beloved" of God—but regardless of the cause, the execution of his royal predecessor's offspring appears to be nothing less than a "lynching." A group of essentially innocent bystanders is handed over to a band seeking vengeance for past wrongs, with the victims' "crime" being their relation to a long-deceased and now disgraced monarch. Cynics point out that the incident is hardly isolated in Scripture. However, this biblical case points to some of the difficulties one faces in dealing with "vigilantism" in antiquity. There were certainly approved bodies for the punishment of criminals, but sometimes the line that would distinguish legal and extralegal mechanisms for enforcement is unclear. Why would a king abrogate his well-accepted role as executor of justice to nonroyal parties? Moreover, while there are examples of what might be regarded as "frontier" or ad hoc justice, on closer examination, one discovers that ruling authorities have either granted permission to individuals or groups to deal harshly with targeted parties or that such approval is tacitly implied. This suggests that under certain circumstances, the broader community was regarded as a legitimate extension of "official" power, beyond the formal personnel of the courts. Yet this also raises the questions of whether the societies of the ancient Near

East were then plagued by what amounted to uncontrolled and uncontrollable violence, with parties able to take the law into their hands at will. Indeed, Thomas Hobbes's sweeping caricature of premodern existence as being "nasty, brutish, and short"[2] has been quoted approvingly by Enlightenment critics as an apt description of life in the ancient Near East.

At a cursory glance, available evidence does suggest wide-ranging societal violence in the ancient Near East. Apart from ubiquitous texts pertaining to warfare, various sources testify that inhumane practices were standard and acceptable tools of law in antiquity. Literary and pictorial references to the unapologetic torture of criminals and suspects abound, with punishment of those judged guilty assuming macabre forms—beating, bodily mutilation, blinding, forced suicide, drowning, stoning, decapitation, strangulation, hanging, impaling, and burning—sometimes in combination.[3] The official—and very graphic—use of such brutality to dissuade malefactors was strongly sanctioned, especially in religious texts. Cosmogonies of the ancient Near East portrayed the universe as arising out of a bloody conflict between opposing forces, representing the gods of order on the one hand and chaos on the other.[4] The triumph of the former provided the basis for a resulting political cosmology: ruling authorities would justify coercive policies by claiming divine permission to carry on the never-ending battle against contemporary agents of nihilism. Royal imperialism is the prime expression of this ideology, with military campaigns ending in the public execution of captives before cheering throngs, often as the climax to a sacral drama that served to reinforce the nation's foundational myth.[5]

But this worldview also included the upholding of law against domestic malefactors, the important caveat being that the king—or some centralized authority—was to be chief administrator of justice.[6] In actual practice, sentencing of capital cases was reserved with few exceptions for the monarch, who was held responsible for the taking of human life. By extension, rulers who abused subjects at whim or allowed their officials to settle personal scores through physical intimidation were suspected of being illegitimate.[7] Consequently—and perhaps surprisingly to modern assumptions—there is well-attested abhorrence toward vendettas occurring outside approved channels, and a leader who too readily approved of such practices was regarded with suspicion. A lack of judicial restraint was proof that the king was a "bad" or "false shepherd": he was either too weak to maintain order or, worse, willing to abide outrages to his "flock" by others, threatening the land with the very anarchy he was supposed to restrain.[8]

Given this reality, mob violence and "lynching" are rarely mentioned in royal inscriptions of the ancient Near East—the Bible itself being a notable exception. For the most part, official records carved onto stelae and temple walls—or what are termed "display texts"—largely focus on a monarch's positive achievements and gloss over or ignore anything that would mar the portrait of the "just" and "benevolent" sovereign. If societal discord is referred to at all in this type of "public" literature, the phraseology is tendentious, frequently used as a literary device to blacken the name of a predecessor and to serve as a contrast with the idyllic reign of the current leader.

Perhaps more than for the other eras addressed in this volume, the availability of sources for the ancient Near East is thus highly problematic. The propagandistic nature of royal accounts makes it necessary for the scholar of ancient violence to turn to broader avenues to find evidence for vigilantism in antiquity. Unfortunately, despite the survival of thousands of documents pertaining to judicial matters—including law codes and court records—there are few cases that involve the carrying out of "private justice" in any sort of useful detail, apart from the commission of murder itself.[9] There are references to acts of personal "vengeance," but this is a special, technical category that was limited to certain circumstances.[10] For the most part, allusions to mob or group violence are elusive[11] and must be gleaned and teased out from a variety of genres, including ritual and religious texts, letters, and literary writings.

Bearing in mind the interpretative difficulties inherent in these sources, this essay will summarily address the topic of extralegal violence with respect to (1) terminology, (2) some representative cases, (3) the issue of "vengeance," and (4) group violence in the Old Testament.

Terminology

In the ancient Near East, societal lawlessness was generally described by the extraordinarily broad terms "injustice" or "wrongdoing" or it is couched in dramatic phrases such as "fury/uproar," and "violence."[12] Occasionally, "storm" and "flood" metaphors are employed to depict a nation "swept away" by discord and instability, while at times, mayhem could be described in the language of "sickness" and ritual pollution.[13] Less frequent are those cases where strife is portrayed as "brother killing brother," sometimes attributed to the anarchic condition of "each person doing what is right in his (own) eyes."[14] The difficulty is that this otherwise picturesque—and often highly exaggerated—imagery is maddeningly imprecise.[15] "Injustice/wrongdoing" could encompass *anything* that was amiss, while other terminology describes events ranging from foreign invasions to local protests and strikes. To be sure, this sort of language—sometimes encompassing periods of political instability—might well have included acts of revenge and the private settling of scores, but such collateral violence is rarely singled out for mention.

A further problem is that a genuine act of vigilantism in modern eyes might receive no particular designation in a text, being subsumed instead under the umbrella of royal authority. This is probably the case in descriptions of some incidents along border areas, which have been depicted as the prosecution of a full-scale "war," with the limitless host of the king defeating equally numerous hordes that had threatened his realm. Upon closer examination, such events often appear to have been little more than members of an isolated fortress rounding up bands of troublemakers for infringements against local property of the Crown, such as trespassing or cattle rustling.[16] This suggests that local garrisons were given carte blanche to deal with problems on their own. In the same manner, more "literary" reports of assaults against royal personnel—soldiers, officials, envoys—in which travelers are portrayed as having been bushwhacked by groups in foreign territory tend to reflect the viewpoint of the writer. There is little attempt to provide significant details about the mode of attack or to seek the cause of the disruption, other than noting that the action is deemed unwarranted by the author.

Nevertheless, something of the horrific nature of group violence and the fear that it aroused can be gleaned from references to disruptive parties that survive in religious and mythological texts. Harbingers and conveyers of discord are portrayed as "demonic" confederacies, in league with a malign deity or chaotic force.[17] These bands are depicted as being armed with knives, nets, and snares to waylay, mutilate, and kill unsuspecting—and unprotected— travelers, usually at crossroads. Often, they are portrayed as operating at random in areas such as boundary zones or at night, with legal authority weak or absent.[18] These lurid scenarios undoubtedly had real-life parallels, and we see this type of language being adapted elsewhere for mundane usage, whereby "foreigners" and "outsiders" of varying stripes are stereotyped as perpetual "marauders" who refuse to recognize the laws of the state.[19] These supposedly uncivilized "others" hide in bushes or conceal themselves in inaccessible terrain until the opportunity to ambush the itinerants presents itself.[20] That the elite scribes who created these texts have a distinct animus, dismissing any justification for this behavior out of hand, does not negate the fact that a transit through alien climes could truly be hair raising and life threatening.

REPRESENTATIVE CASES

When we get to particular cases, it comes as no shock that extralegal mob violence is generally situated in contexts of (1) individuals or groups passing through foreign territory, (2) periods of domestic political tension, (3) attacks against religious cults and their followers, and (4) resident aliens encountering difficulties from the indigenous populace. In certain incidents, these contexts overlap, with several factors contributing to the violent encounter.

Travelers' Troubles

Despite the use of passports, letters of safe conduct, and conventions of international law to ensure travelers immunity from bodily harm, texts show that victims of random violence tended to be merchants, diplomats, and ambassadors—those whose origins were outside the indigenous community.[21] Although robbery appears to be the primary motive for assaults, political enmity between envoys' sponsors and the place of visit is sometimes indicated, and occasionally blatant xenophobia is the cause.

The latter factor appears to be at work in an incident recorded in a travel account of an Egyptian envoy named Wen-Amun.[22] Near the end of the eleventh century BCE, a ship carrying the diplomat is blown off course, inadvertently taking him from the Lebanese coast to the island of Cyprus. There, for no apparent reason, he is immediately accosted by "townsmen who come out to kill him." Catastrophe is averted only when the harried party shames the head of the city—a princess—into calling off the mob: "I used to hear that although in every town injustice is practiced, in the land of Cyprus, justice is practiced. Is it here (too) that injustice now is always practiced?"[23] The lofty oratory, hinting at the complicity of authorities, is balanced by the implied threat that if Wen-Amun is harmed, the ship's owner would retaliate against Cypriote vessels. The appeal is effective, and the instigators are somehow disciplined, although the exact nature of their censure is not specified.[24]

A more deadly incident illustrating the vulnerability of parties in transit is recorded in an earlier diplomatic letter of the fourteenth century BCE to the Egyptian pharaoh Akhenaton.[25] The king of Babylon complains that his own envoys and merchants had been robbed, killed, and enslaved while passing through Canaan (modern-day Israel), which was under the sovereignty of the Egyptian ruler. The Babylonian monarch identifies the transgressors—a *razzia* (raid) sent by local mayors to harass the entourage—and demands satisfaction from the pharaoh: "Canaan is your country . . . and in your country

I have been despoiled. Bring [them] to account and make compensat[ion] for the money they took away. Put to death the men who put my servants to death, and so avenge their blood. And if you do not put these men to death, they are going to kill again, be it a caravan of mine or your own messengers, and so messengers between us will thereby be cut off."[26]

The reason for the attack—at least from the aggrieved writer's point of view—would appear to be simple banditry sponsored by some petty rulers of Syria-Palestine, as the offending parties are accused of theft and murder in addition to the disruption of international diplomacy. Liability for the outrage is placed in the hands of the regional overlord—the pharaoh—who is held responsible for "avenging" the deaths and enslavement of the seemingly innocent parties. The offended ruler cites the practices of both *lex talionis,* "eye for an eye" retribution, and monetary compensation for damages to his personnel—traits characteristic of Mesopotamian law codes, but not necessarily that of Egyptian jurisprudence.[27] Although the Babylonian king expresses confidence in the pharaoh to set things right in what he regards as a budding international scandal, the outcome of the case is unknown.[28]

Such rhetoric should not be dismissed as posturing, since violence against royal employees in foreign climes could lead to outright war between nations.[29] One of the most notorious incidents in the ancient world—also occurring in the fourteenth century BCE—was the waylaying and killing of a Hittite prince sent to the Nile valley to marry a widowed Egyptian queen. The surviving reports—abstracts from Hittite royal annals and penitential prayers—lack significant details.[30] The relevant passages laconically note that the Hittite prince, coming from Asia Minor, was accosted when his wedding party entered the farthest climes of pharaonic territory—likely somewhere around the Lebanon-Antilibanus region.[31] The outraged father—the Hittite king, Šuppiluliuma—blamed the Egyptians for his son's death despite their protestations of innocence, leading him to break a long-standing treaty between the countries to avenge the murder.[32] We have little detail about the form in which the original assault occurred, but there was little question in the mind of Šuppiluliuma that the motivation was political. By killing the prince, the assassins—whoever they were—successfully thwarted an alliance that would have given the Hittites access to the rival Egyptian empire.

Domestic Strife

The use of violence for internal political ends is likewise documented and includes accounts of assassinations, rebellions, and civil war. Further admonitions in sapiential literature, along with intercessory prayers and loyalty oaths warning against opposing a monarch "in thought, word, or deed," belie assertions that kings always governed with the full devotion and love of their subjects.[33] Nonetheless, sources recording civic disruption are typically spare in particulars, depicting royal opposition in the broadest—and most carica- tured—of terms, describing the opposition as "rebels," "troublemakers," or "children of chaos." To some degree, this anonymity is not unexpected: in the wake of societal upheaval, defeated groups would be subjected to formal execration.[34] Modern scholars conveniently refer to this practice by the Ro- man term *damnatio memoriae*—"the elimination from memory"—whereby public and religious records would be purged of any reference to the guilty parties by name.[35] Keeping this official censorship in mind, the historian is fortunate that any references from the ancient Near East to domestic turmoil have survived at all. Even more startling are those rare instances in which the means and manner of violence have been preserved.

One such incident comes from Egypt, ca. 2000 BCE, and is contained in a wisdom text known as the "Instruction for Merikare."[36] Presented as the last will and testament of an actual king, Khety, it offers advice for his son on how to rule effectively. While the text stresses that a monarch must main- tain the allegiance of his subjects—with appropriate denunciations of dema- gogues and popular factions—there is one section that is remarkable for its apologetic tone. Here, Khety specifically refers to an outrage that occurred during a recent civil war, which had pitted his army against troops from the southern part of the country. The monarch confesses that he prompted his own forces to wreak havoc in the nation's most sacred burial ground: "Lo, a shameful deed occurred in my time; the district of Abydos [the site of the cemetery] was ravaged; Though it happened through my doing, I learned it, after it was accomplished."[37] The king regretfully comments that, as a result, he had received "retribution for what [he] had done."

The incident is fascinating for a number of reasons, not the least of which is that Khety admits his own culpability in the affair. This concession against type suggests that there was something tangible behind the reference, and archeologists have found physical evidence that seems to confirm the king's lament.[38] More pointedly, the desecration of the dead attests to the savagery of the political struggle in Egypt during this period: to destroy a tomb was be- lieved to deny its occupant a meaningful afterlife—demonstrating that vio- lence in antiquity was not restricted to just the living.[39] There does not seem to have been any military purpose behind the act, which was unprecedented in ancient Egyptian warfare: Khety's men do not appear to have been attacking their armed counterparts in the burial ground.[40] Consequently, the king's embarrassing admission suggests that while he may have agreed with the zealotry of his men, he had not sanctioned their target or methods. The sacrilege—too well known to ignore and attaining "proverbial" status—appears to have been committed by out-of-control contingents taking matters into their own hands rather than as an expression of official policy. By the same token, there can be little doubt that the tenor of the times themselves provided the opportunity to perpetrate what was regarded as an extraordinary violation of the laws of god and man.

Political instability is also an obvious factor in a violent proposal contained in a series of letters—likewise from Egypt—dating to the end of the New Kingdom, ca. 1070 BCE.[41] The documents coincide with the last years of the weakened pharaoh, Ramesses XI. The period itself was marked by increasing clashes between mercenary groups of Libyans and Nubians, who were attempting to consolidate their power within the Nile valley in general and in the city of Thebes in particular.[42] In this highly charged atmosphere, one of the leading players of the day, a Libyan general, Piankh, suggests in writing to three accomplices a quick solution for what seems to have become a personal liability: "As for the mention you made of this matter of these two policemen saying: 'They spoke these charges'; join up with Nodjme and Payshuuben as well, and they shall send word and have these two policemen brought to this [my] house and get to the bottom of the charges in short order. If they determine they are true, you shall put them [in] two baskets and they shall be thrown [into] the water by night—but don't let anybody in the land find out!"[43]

In a subsequent dispatch, Piankh spells out precisely what he means— "*kill [them]*"—completely ignoring the matter of the crime's concealment.[44] Savagely ironic is Piankh's observation that the policemen are to be eliminated "if their charges are true," pointing to some unnamed incident threatening his ambitions in the region.[45] Equally striking is the composition of the budding conspiracy: each member of the group was a high official or from the local nobility and was to use his influence to thwart justice at all costs. The reference to "bringing" the policemen to Piankh's house and "getting to the bottom of the charges quickly" probably indicates the issuing of a formal summons as a ruse to extract the needed information from the unsuspecting victims through torture—characteristic of "legal procedure" in Egypt during this time.[46] Ultimately—and cynically—the broken and drowned corpses of the policemen were intended to convey the very public lesson not to oppose the current power broker in Thebes.

Violence against Cults and Their Members

King Khety's acknowledgment of his troops' sacrilege against the Abydene cemetery should not be seen simply as a case of property damage: cults along with their members would have been active at the site and would have suffered from the onslaught. Undoubtedly, the depredations of the Egyptian king's forces were intended to terrify his opponents, but religious installations were also repositories of great wealth. Owing to their magnificence, divine sanctuaries were a prime target of invading armies, rebellious groups, and raiding parties. This is demonstrated by the records of conquering kings who list in detail the human and material plunder captured from these locales. The horrifying impact of such destruction is borne witness to by the lamentations of victims. Representative are the contents of a prayer of a Hittite king, which contains curses against rebellious vassals who seek to "burn the temples of the [Hittite] gods, steal their equipment, destroy their property, and carry off their workers into slavery."[47]

In addition to the scourge of warfare, however, domestic outrages to religious complexes are attested in letters and assorted juridical documents. One such instance is recounted in a fifth-century BCE dispatch from a member of a Jewish colony, garrisoned in Elephantine, at the southernmost part of Egypt. Its purpose was to inform an official of the Persians—the overlords of the Nile valley at that time—that the personnel of a neighboring Egyptian temple had severely damaged the Jewish sanctuary in Elephantine:

> In the month of Tammuz in the fourteenth year of King Darius . . . the priests of the god Khnum in Fort Elephantine, in collusion with Vidranga, the military governor here, said, "Let us get rid of the temple of the God YHW in Fort Elephantine!"
>
> Then that criminal Vidranga wrote a letter to his son Nafaina, commandant at Fort Syene, as follows, "Let the temple in Fort Elephantine be destroyed!" So Nafaina came at the head of some Egyptian and other troops to Fort Elephantine with their pickaxes.
>
> They forced their way into the temple and razed it to the ground, smashing the stone pillars there. The temple had five gateways built of hewn stone, which they wrecked. They set everything else on fire: the standing doors and their bronze pivots, the cedar roof—everything, even the rest of the fittings and

other things. The gold and silver basins and anything else they could find in the temple, they appropriated for themselves![48]

The attack reflects not just the venality of the perpetrators, which included imperial officials, but the growing animosity between the indigenous Egyptians and the Jewish community, which had been composed of resident aliens. Although they had been settled in the Nile valley for centuries, the Jews, now regarded as collaborating with the conquering Persians, were treated by the locals with enmity.[49]

In similar fashion, much earlier Hittite instructions of the Bronze Age contain warnings against potential troublemakers who might interfere with the workings of a shrine and admonish guards "to let no one start a disturbance in the presence of the gods."[50] Admittedly, "disturbance" is a notoriously hazy concept and could include anything from rowdy behavior of all sorts to the theft of offerings and trespassing upon sacred space. However, one crime that would also seem to fall within the confines of the term—as well as the present study—was the physical intimidation of religious workers by local authorities.

In the ancient Near East, cultic personnel were often exempted from communal labor, which was required of citizens as a form of taxation. Typically, infringements against temple employees are characterized as their being illegally "seized" and forced to work on farms or in quarries, contrary to contractual agreement.[51] Notwithstanding that donation decrees establishing the rights of priestly employees carried threats of punishment for their violation, evidence points to frequent infringements of these protections. Letters from cult officials survive, urging that a king bring to justice those who had kidnapped and abused their charges.[52] Again, as in many ancient sources, there is little detail about the makeup or behavior of the parties who actually carried out such press-ganging, but we should not assume that violent coercion was not a component in the crime.

Most of these complaints are directed against wayward administrators and their minions, but there are rare cases where rulers themselves suddenly withdrew their favor from a religious establishment, making it a target of exploitation. For example, at the end of the third millennium BCE, Narim-Sin, the king of the city of Akkad (in modern-day Iraq), was denounced in a later epic poem for his desecration of one of the most important sanctuaries of Mesopotamia.[53] Although the poem is concerned more with the treatment of the actual temple—comparing its destruction to a man "stretched 'neck to ground' like [one] who had been killed [in battle]"—Narim-Sin's aggression would have been understood by contemporaries as including reprisals against the workers of the precinct.[54]

Equally infamous was the "religious revolution" initiated by the previously mentioned Eighteenth Dynasty pharaoh Akhenaton.[55] Attempting to establish worship of a single god throughout the Nile valley, the king outlawed the millennia-old polytheism of Egypt, entailing the suppression and eradication of cults other than those that worshipped the king's personal deity. Both textual and archeological evidence points to these measures being accompanied by the destruction of property and abuse of individuals. Legislation following Akhenaton's death refers to the discredited monarch allowing his troops to wander through the country intimidating the populace at large and confiscating their goods with impunity.[56] What is unusual is that records contemporary with Akhenaton allude to vocal opposition to his programs. In a royal decree, the king—with great indignation—complains that his innovations were being met with a reaction worse than any his predecessors had ever encountered.[57]

The disdain in which this king was held is reflected not only in later historiography but by the fact that Akhenaton's memory was officially suppressed. Following his death, the pharaoh's name was stricken from all public monuments. If he is mentioned at all by later generations, it is by the derogatory epithet "the damned one."[58] This raises the question as to whether such political retribution manifested itself in other forms. More precisely, were living associates of a rejected ruler and his despised regime subject to something like the later Roman practice of "proscription," whereby traitors against the state could be subjected to mob violence?[59] Although there is some evidence to suggest that this was a possibility, the question is difficult to answer. But it leads us to the thorny concept of "vengeance" and what that entailed in the ancient Near East.

VENGEANCE

To a great degree, the formation of law in the Fertile Crescent arose out of a need to inhibit parties from carrying out retribution on their own, which—if unchecked—had the potential of undermining community stability. Despite this danger, legal and extralegal sources demonstrate that under certain circumstances, "private justice" was permitted. That is, retribution for a crime by the injured individuals or groups rather than by the state was sometimes sanctioned.[60] However, the restriction of the custom to clearly defined cases points to a concerted effort to limit the practice. The term that is used for this contingency is translated as the verb *avenge*, with *vengeance* denoting the act itself.[61] Although the practice could be applied to redress particular cases of bodily harm or death, it could also be used for affronts to one's hierarchical status within the family or the viability of society as a whole when an offense had to be redressed expeditiously. The second category primarily applies to the integrity of family relations and involves the dual concept of "honor-shame," while the last contingency pertains to individuals who were regarded as a threat to the welfare of the entire nation, such as traitors, assassins, and blasphemers.

If there is a common thread that runs through the *authorized* practice of vengeance, it seems to be that the crime involved a particularly close relationship between the avenger and the object of his actions: the guilty party may have caused actual physical injury or have perpetrated some act that had damaged the reputation of the victim and family. While the latter is more easily understood in reaction to sexual outrages that were viewed as dishonoring an entire clan, it might be difficult to discern in cases such as the complaint that pharaoh is to "avenge" the murder of the officials of the Babylonian king.[62] However, a crucial aspect of legal custom in the ancient Near East—both domestic and international—was the centrality of "household politics": juridical relations were conceived in familial terms.[63] Thus the relationship of an overlord to a vassal or of a sovereign to his subjects was not predicated solely upon power but was often pictured as a guardian protecting his charges or, more intimately, as a father watching over a son. By logical extension, parity relations were expressed in the related language of "brotherhood."[64] Accordingly, in the previously cited diplomatic furor, the Egyptian king is petitioned to redress an insult committed not against a foreign power but against his putative "sibling."

The rare cases of "vengeance" in ancient Near East law codes themselves largely relate to "family law," where a wronged party—almost always male— is permitted to exact punishment for an outrage to, or by, one of his relatives.[65] Strikingly, a statute of a Hittite code contains a provision for hunting down newlyweds who have married without permission: "If anyone elopes with a woman and an avenger goes after them, if two or three men die, there be no compensation."[66] The implication is that some agent—designated as an "avenger"—was granted latitude to employ deadly force in retrieving errant brides, with the usual penalties for homicide or manslaughter being suspended. Likewise, the same document refers to the humiliating circumstance of a man discovering his wife engaged in intercourse with a partner in his own house: the cuckolded husbanded was permitted to kill both parties in flagrante delicto.[67]

Another area where individual violence was deemed warranted was in cases of lèse-majesté—affronts to the dignity and honor of a king or deity, which amounted to high treason. In an Assyrian treaty of the seventh century BCE, the ruler Esarhaddon admonishes all the inhabitants of his empire—both foreign and domestic—to show absolute loyalty to himself and to his prince heir.[68] Amid the dozens of provisions in the text, there are contingencies that refer to attempts to usurp the Crown. In such scenarios, every Assyrian subject, of any rank, is expected "to seize and kill" plotters who (much as in Roman law) have become public enemies, so as to "eradicate their name and descendants from the country," to foment rebellion if the subversive power is successful, and to do whatever is necessary to avenge "the king of Assyria and his family," "blood for blood."[69]

While attested throughout the ancient Near East, "vengeance" may be best known to the general public from the Bible,[70] which, unlike other ancient sources, furnishes us with evidence of the custom in both legal and narrative contexts. Notwithstanding complicated questions of historicity and literary issues surrounding sources and redaction, the so-called patriarchal records of Genesis offer a vivid glimpse into some of the dynamics of the practice. The archetypal story of Cain and Abel portrays the perilous state of the individual in antiquity who is guilty of manslaughter. Following his commission of fratricide, Cain is "driven out" as a "fugitive and wanderer," at the mercy of others who would act as bounty hunters, looking to kill him on the spot.[71]

The threat posed by such individual retaliation clearly lies behind later statutes that refer to places of sanctuary for "the manslayer who kills any person without intent."[72] In ideal biblical legislation, "cities of refuge" were designated to serve as holding areas until a perpetrator had been tried.[73] If guilty of unintentional or accidental homicide, the accused was to be "rescued" from the "hand of the avenger of blood"[74] and allowed to remain in the protective site without fear of retribution. These constraints, however, were lifted for first-degree murder, where "the avenger of blood . . . when he meets [the murderer], shall put him to death."[75] Likewise, if the latter was found wandering outside the confines of his sanctuary, the aggrieved was permitted to exact vengeance upon the transgressor without liability.[76]

Still, the danger posed by private justice—and the need for its bridling—

is dramatically shown, again, in the early chapters of Genesis. A descendent of Cain, Lamech, is portrayed as boasting about exacting punishment disproportionate to his injury: "I have slain a man for wounding me, a young man for striking me. If Cain is avenged sevenfold, truly Lamech [is avenged] seventy-seven-fold."[77] It is interesting that such spiraling violence is not considered an isolated incident but is cited as a cause for the Great Flood itself,[78] the implication being that excessive private retribution was responsible for the unleashing of civilization-ending chaos. Yet the cautionary tale was to go unheeded, as vengeance persisted in the postdiluvian age.

Extralegal Violence in the Bible

In contrast to other sources from the ancient Near East, biblical accounts are at times relatively detailed in presenting the form and shape of societal violence. More precisely, the records contained in the Old Testament are valuable for supplying the perspectives of groups other than that of royal elites.[79] Undoubtedly, this is due to the fact that throughout much of their history, the Israelites of the Iron Age and their earlier tribal ancestors were immigrants, refugees, or exiles living in the midst of the great powers of the region. Moreover, it is evident that the compilers and redactors who gave canonical form to the biblical texts followed a teleological scheme that was sometimes reflective of parties critical of the governing authorities and some texts were suppressed as a result.[80] In marked contrast to the inscriptions found on the palace walls and temples of the pharaohs of Egypt and the conquering rulers of Mesopotamia, which celebrate the defeat of their enemies, the Old Testament Scriptures preserve the voices of people on the underside of society—the stranger, the sojourner, and those victimized by the mighty.

Indeed, a recurrent theme in the book of Genesis is the vulnerability of wandering bands to the depredations of local inhabitants, typified by the notorious episode surrounding the destruction of the city of Sodom.[81] While the provocation for the disaster ostensibly is the mistreatment of heavenly envoys, the story demonstrates prevailing hostile attitudes toward "strangers" or "sojourners."[82] After being granted permission by an official, Lot, to pass the night within the city's confines, divine visitors find themselves accosted by an angry group of citizens, who threaten them—along with their aforementioned sponsor, himself a resident alien—with bodily harm. Clearly, there is a causal nexus between xenophobia and violence. However, it is worth observing that the biblical narrative further informs us that Sodom had earlier been at conflict with its neighbors.[83] Typically, the city would have been surrounded by a defensive wall to protect against outside attack. Apart from costly and time-consuming siege, the only way to breach such fortifications was by getting infiltrators inside the bulwarks, where they could open the gates to forces hidden in the surrounding countryside. Appropriate concerns over security might help to explain the extreme hostility roused by foreigners appearing in the midst of a populace anxious over warfare.[84]

A close parallel to this scene is to be found later in the book of Judges.[85] Here, a guest worker in the Israelite town of Gibeah offers quarters to an itinerant clergyman and his concubine to pass the night. As the news spreads that newly arrived visitors have been given residence in the town, a band designated by the derogatory phrase "the sons of Belial"—variously rendered as "base men" and "hell-raisers"—surrounds the house.[86] After the owner and his family are threatened with assault for sheltering unknown parties, a deal is made, by which the concubine is to be turned over to the intruders. It is likely that the arrangement involved something along the lines of a hostage exchange: the woman was to be held in the protective custody of the group until the guest's departure the next morning.[87] Once the latter's stay was demonstrated not to be for hostile purposes, the woman was to be restored to her partner—safe and sound—and the pair could continue onward in peace. Instead, the plan goes horribly awry. The townsmen sexually molest the concubine, resulting in her death. The atrocity causes such outrage that a genocidal tribal war is precipitated.[88] As in the earlier events at Sodom, there seems to be a direct linkage between violence and the victims' status as "foreigners."

Centuries later, deported Israelite/Jewish communities express similar anxiety over living as exiles. The book of Esther depicts families scattered throughout the Persian Empire being threatened by royal decrees granting permission to local populations "to destroy, slay, annihilate all Jews, young and old, women and children."[89] Whatever the date and purpose of the text,[90] the episode aptly reflects the uncertainty felt by dispossessed peoples: genial relations were largely dependent upon the whims of governing elites. In similar fashion, the hostile attitude of the instigator of the policy, Haman, and his attempted justification for persecution (they are "scattered . . . and dispersed . . . peoples . . . [whose] laws are different") point to the historical experience of persecution of groups not fully assimilated into an imperial landscape.[91]

By contrast, subject parties could also respond with deadly force when exploited by indigenous authorities. Genesis 34 records an incident in which an Israelite woman, Dinah, is raped by the Canaanite "prince of the land," Shechem, in whose territory the former's kin had been resident aliens.[92] Following the assault, an accommodation is made: the official agrees to marry the woman to maintain peace. Regardless of the agreement, two of Dinah's brothers avenge their sister's mistreatment: they "took their swords; and came upon the city unawares, and killed all the males," while the rest of Dinah's brothers "plundered the city, because their sister had been defiled."[93] Remarkably, while acknowledging indignation over the sexual outrage, the text characterizes the action as unwarranted, having been undertaken without the permission of the tribal leader, Jacob. The patriarch laments: "You have brought trouble on me by making me odious to the inhabitants of the land . . . ; my numbers are few, and if they gather themselves against me and attack me, I shall be destroyed, both I and my household."[94] Notwithstanding Jacob's protest, the perpetrators reply: "Should he treat our sister as a harlot?"[95] In this case, the demands of honor and shame outweigh concerns over personal security.[96]

As with other ancient Near East sources, it is not always easy to distinguish mob violence from genuine warfare during the patriarchal and premonarchial periods, with hostilities often occurring in frontier areas.[97] As early Israelite society is presented as being composed of extended families, cases of border infringement trigger blood libel, with random killings taking place through assassinations, ambushes, and the execution of captives taken in raids.[98] Furthermore, the Bible cites insults and slights as providing fodder for intertribal violence. An example is an episode in Judges 12, where a rival clan threatens to burn alive the war chief Jephtah because he had excluded the group from sharing in plunder taken on a campaign.[99] Within this same book, the vignettes of the brawling judge and warrior Samson very much convey a sense of frontier justice. Following both a failed marriage and his destruction of his adversaries' fields by arson, the targets of Samson's wrath—the Philistines—retaliate by burning Samson's ex-bride and her father to death.[100] This triggers a series of guerrilla actions on Samson's part and reactions by his foes, culminating in the former's own capture, torture, and death.[101] It is intriguing that the Israelite leader—who is portrayed as something of a loose cannon—justifies his violence through an appeal to the concept of "vengeance":[102] by executing his former bride and father-in-law, the Philistines had abrogated Samson's legal role as household disciplinarian.

Significantly, during this period of tribal federation and competition, attacks on religious sites are also reported. In Judges 18, violence is threatened against a household shrine, resulting in the theft of sacred objects as well as the coercion of its cultic personnel to serve another tribe.[103] In the ancient world, the action would have been regarded as a sign that the deity had withdrawn its support from its former hosts and was now favoring its new sponsors. When the aggrieved party objects, he is bluntly warned: "Do not let your voice be heard among us, lest angry fellows fall upon you, and you lose your life with the lives of your household."[104] A generation later, Joshua of Beth-Shemesh is reported as having slain seventy men "because they looked into the ark of the Lord."[105] The offense is presented as a sacrilege, Joshua's victims having transgressed divine space. What is unusual is that this Joshua is nowhere named as an official of any sort: his punishment of the violators is undertaken on his own initiative, out of his offended sense of piety.

The endless cycle of raids, border provocations, and religious retribution points to increasing anarchy, which the redactor of Judges summarizes by saying, "There was no king in Israel; every man did what was right in his eyes."[106] With the Israelites' subsequent adoption of monarchy, we see something of a shift away from mob violence, although blood feuds, assassinations, and the exacting of vengeance continue up to the reign of Solomon and into the period of the Divided Monarchy, often being linked to competition for the throne itself.[107]

However, within David's reign, we find an unusual extension of legal vengeance through what has been termed "scapegoating." Biblical law attests to a process in which an animal—a goat—was chosen by lot and driven off "into the wilderness," bearing upon itself the sins of the people.[108] There are cases where the practice seems to have been applied to individuals and groups who were singled out for violating a taboo that was regarded as threatening community safety.[109] While the purpose of the ritual is often described in terms of "expiation"—the technical phrase for redressing a cultic transgression—the attainment of "satisfaction" appears to be an important component as well. This may be seen in 2 Samuel 21:1–14, where the cause for a national famine during the reign of David is eventually attributed to a sacrilege incurred by the now deceased king Saul. The discredited monarch had earlier persecuted a group of resident aliens who had been employed as religious workers. Saul's violent infringement of their protected status was regarded as the present cause of divine wrath, which is assuaged when David hands over the surviving members of the king's family to the persecuted victims, who hang Saul's sons in revenge.[110]

During the period of the Divided Monarchy, in which the country is split along geographical and tribal lines into two independent nations—Judah in the south and Israel in the north—violence is sometimes depicted as a result of government persecution of prophets who are critical of royal behavior.[111] Prophetic denunciation generally centers on a king's failure to follow the demands of the Mosaic covenant, especially a monarch's tolerance of polytheism and sponsorship of cults other than that of the national deity, Yahweh.

The friction between ruling elites and religious opposition comes to a head during the reign of King Ahab and its immediate aftermath.[112] The relationship between the two parties is represented, on the one hand, by the prophets' adherence to the Israelite deity, Yahweh, and, on the other, by the devotion of Ahab's consort—the Phoenician-born Jezebel—to the Canaanite god, Baal.[113] The books of 1 and 2 Kings portray this queen as "The Idolatress," and she persecutes the holy man Elijah and his followers with genocidal fury.[114] Jezebel's zeal is matched by Elijah's disdain for Baalism, as the prophet slays its cultic followers on Mount Carmel. The tension between the partisans is finally resolved in a military coup, when Ahab's dynastic line is replaced by a usurper, the general Jehu.[115] With prophetic approval, Jehu settles past scores through the mass execution of the supporters of the old regime, including Jezebel herself.[116]

The religious element in this conflict should not be minimized, and there are indications that Jehu's brutal reprisals against the Baal cults was an ideological watershed, reflected by a discernible change in biblical historiography.[117] However, the Old Testament's antipathy toward Jezebel is symbolized not just by her loyalty to a non-Israelite deity but by her perceived willingness to use force to achieve personal and political ends. This is best exemplified by the dramatic vignette of 2 Kings 21:1–16, which relates the death and dispossession of a private citizen, Naboth, at the instigation and connivance of the queen.[118] As the account begins, her husband, King Ahab, wants to exercise what we now might call "eminent domain," desiring Naboth's property to expand his royal gardens. Offers in the form of land exchange or monetary payment come to naught on religious grounds: the territory had been part of Naboth's ancestral tribal allotment. According to the narrative, Naboth's refusal to broker a deal sends the king into a deep depression until Jezebel provides her own solution to the dilemma:

> So [Jezebel] wrote letters in Ahab's name and sealed them with his seal, and she sent the letters to the elders and the nobles who dwelt with Naboth in his city.

And she wrote in the letters, "Proclaim a fast, and set Naboth on high among the people; and set two base fellows opposite him, and let them bring a charge against him saying, 'You have cursed God and the king.' Then take him out, and stone him to death." And the men of [Naboth's] city, the elders and the nobles who dwelt in [Naboth's] city, did as Jezebel had sent word to them. As it was written in the letters which she had sent to them, they proclaimed a fast, and set Naboth on high among the people. And the two base fellows came in and sat opposite him; and the base fellows brought a charge against Naboth, in the presence of the people, saying, "Naboth cursed God and the king." So they took him outside the city, and stoned him to death with stones. Then they sent to Jezebel saying, "Naboth has been stoned; he is dead."[119]

Jezebel's complicity in Naboth's execution on a trumped-up charge will be condemned by Elijah,[120] with the shaping of the episode clearly sympathetic to the prophetic cause. Still, the incident is important, since it describes the process of individual excecration, in which a person is declared a public enemy, and it provides technical terminology regarding legal procedure in ancient Israel.[121] In this case, a fast is ordered (literally, "called") by the local authorities ("the elders" and the "nobles," or "free citizenry") at the instigation of the queen. The ritual entailed public penitence; that is, the populace was atoning for some unknown sin that was harming the entire community. Though not specified here, we read earlier that the northern kingdom had been suffering from a prolonged famine during Ahab's reign.[122] Though chronologically displaced within the biblical narrative, this scene would logically suit such a situation. In fact, Ahab's attempts to expand his grounds suggests an agricultural emergency, requiring every bit of available land to be utilized to make up for shortages. By extension, the procedure also points to the need to identify the source for the current crisis—that is, to find a "scapegoat," which furnishes Jezebel with convenient justification for killing Naboth.

The assignation of this unfortunate role to Naboth is likewise given in detail: (1) He is physically singled out (literally, "made to sit at the head of the people/citizenry"). (2) The accusers literally face the defendant and present the charge. Here, the plaintiffs are "two base fellows," as the translators put it, but the phrase is the pejorative "two men, namely 'sons of Belial.'"[123] (3) The charge is one of "cursing God and the king"—which is euphemistically phrased as "blessing"—and should be seen as the commission of blasphemy and treason, both capital offenses.[124] (4) Sentence is passed and carried out immediately, without an opportunity for the accused to make further appeal. The execution is by stoning the offender to death, a method having implications of communal responsibility.[125] While on the surface the condemnation and punishment of Naboth has the appearance of legal probity—it is under official auspices, and there is a "trial" of sorts, with formal witnesses and charges—its notoriety within the biblical narrative demonstrates that it became emblematic of injustice. While supposedly bolstered by law, the affair is denounced by Elijah as a case of "murder" and "dispossession"—the exaltation of naked power over the powerless and a violation of the very ideals upon which the nation was supposed to have been founded.

The waning of Baalism in Israel and Judah did not halt enmity between kings and prophets. Warnings of divine judgment upon the nation would rouse both royal and popular opposition, which would be manifested by conspiracies against a seer's life, seizure and shaming by mobs, imprisonment, death threats, and, at times, actual execution. This is especially embodied in the tragic figure of Jeremiah, prior to the Babylonian destruction of Jerusalem in the sixth century BCE.[126] His harassment and mistreatment would become the model for the "suffering servant of Yahweh," a typology that would reappear in Jewish and Christian hagiographies in centuries to come.

This survey clearly demonstrates that violence was a reality in the ancient world: a ruler's ferocity in battle was endlessly extolled in epic poems, while the ability to punish domestic miscreants was celebrated in legal decrees. Yet the evidence regarding "vigilantism" or mob violence is frustratingly meager, especially considering the chronological and geographical expanse covered by the term *ancient Near East*. This paucity of evidence is clearly due in part to the vagaries of preservation—only a fraction of the documents from antiquity survives—but also reflects the compositional nature of the surviving texts. Largely coming from elites, "public literature" was hesitant to acknowledge civil unrest or to give credence to individual attempts to punish wrongdoers that bypassed legal authority. Such deviations could have been seen as failure on the part of leadership to fulfill the divine mandates of office and might undermine royal claims of legitimacy.

On the other hand, the scarcity of references to private, popular, or extralegal justice attests to another reality: of all the fears that burdened ancient communities, the most terrible was societal anarchy. Uncontrolled violence, once unleashed, could cast everything—and everyone—back into a state of chaos in which meaningful existence was impossible. This anxiety lies behind the severity of law codes themselves, which sought to maintain and reinforce the idea of life-giving and life-preserving order. This does not mean that things like vendettas did not occur: the reality was likely far more messy than the texts convey.[127] Likewise, one suspects that a king's claims of victory might well have included individual atrocities by soldiers given free range to plunder captured towns or allowed to hunt down troublesome frontier bands.

If there were outbreaks of mob justice in the ancient Near East, as we see in the Greco-Roman world, they have largely been excluded from the record—suffering a kind of *damnatio memoriae*. But it might very well be that "lynchings" are better attested in the later societies of the Hellenic and Hellenistic periods because of the "democratic" nature of their polities. There, we find clear instances where the "people" do assume the role of judge, jury, and executors of vengeance—sometimes authorized, sometimes ad hoc. This is particularly evident in cases of official malfeasance, sacrilege, and treason, where the entire community was put at risk and retaliation could assume brutal and occasionally unbridled form.[128] Moreover, the practice of dictators placing bounties upon members of rival factions—known as "proscription"—during the Roman civil wars of the first century BCE facilitated and fostered vigilantism and gang violence. While a fuller exploration of the topic is beyond the scope of this investigation, it might be argued that some of the biblical examples cited above also exhibit a tendency toward the employment of "communal" or popular violence in the exaction of punishment. This is not entirely surprising, since the Old Testament accounts present ancient Israel as being composed of tribal clans, formed into a "covenantal community," in which all members—individually and collectively—were responsible for observing, and preserving, divine mandates. This "democratic" element is especially evident in incidents where a person or group assumes on its own the task of punishing transgressors who have committed cultic violations, which would have been regarded as placing the entire populace under divine threat.

Still, it might be argued that, apart from authorized "vengeance" itself, instances of vigilantism, vendettas, and mob uprisings in the ancient Near East—when they do occur—appear in what might be termed "liminal" situations.[129] This includes periods of societal stasis: rebellion, civil war, dynastic struggles. Or violence occurs among those who were regarded as "uncivilized" tribal groups or takes place in far-flung areas where vulnerable itinerants were regarded with suspicion by the indigenous populace. If one were to trace a thread linking incidents of extralegal violence from the diverse sources of the ancient Near East, xenophobia is a recurrent element, which should not be dismissed.[130] To enter into an unknown community in the ancient Near East as a "stranger" was, at times, to expose oneself to resentment and hostility, if not mortal danger.[131] Justification for rough treatment might have linkages to religious ideology, which, for the most part, tended to be ethnocentric: the god(s) created and commissioned specific groups to maintain order, while outsiders were remnants and markers of chaos. However, the Hobbesian depiction of the ancient world as a place marked by unbridled violence is itself a fiction of the modern "enlightened" mind. The ancient Near East above all else recognized that in order for society to survive—both domestically and internationally—the use of authorized and controlled force was necessary. By extension, the settling of personal scores outside of legal venues was regarded as a direct threat to a precarious balance achieved over millennia and was suppressed with deadly rigor.

Notes

Because of the interdisciplinary nature of the audience, this essay largely avoids the complex philological and textual problems that accompany the study of ancient inscriptions. For those wanting to pursue such issues, cited sources provide lengthy bibliographies of the referenced documents. For a comprehensive overview of law in the ancient Near East, see the two-volume study edited by Raymond Westbrook, *A History of Ancient Near Eastern Law* (Leiden: Brill, 2003). While one can find "revenge" in Westbrook's index, there are no specific references to "lynching," "mob-violence," "riots," "vendetta," or "vigilantism." There is one mention of "rebellion against authority" (p. 1124), but none of "civil rebellion" (although "treason" is mentioned on p. 1135).

1. 2 Sam. 21:5, 21:9.

2. Thomas Hobbes, *Leviathan,* ed. Marshall Missner (New York: Pearson-Longman, 2008), 83 (13.3.1).

3. For convenient overviews, see Kerry Muhlestein, "Royal Executions: Evidence Bearing on the Subject of Sanctioned Killing in the Middle Kingdom," *Journal of the Economic and Social History of the Orient (JESHO)* 51, no. 2 (2008), 181–208; David Lorton, "The Treatment of Criminals in Ancient Egypt through the New Kingdom," *JESHO* 20, no. 1 (1977), 1–64; and Raymond Westbrook, "Punishments and Crimes," in *Anchor Bible Dictionary (ABD)* 5, ed. David Noel Freedman (New York: Doubleday, 1992), 546–56.

4. Robert A. Oden Jr., "Cosmogony, Cosmology," *ABD* 1:1161–71; Jon Levenson, *Creation and the Persistence of Evil: The Jewish Drama of Divine Omnipotence* (Princeton, NJ: Princeton University Press, 1994), 3–5. Although the biblical accounts of Genesis present the creation of the universe ex nihilo, remnants of the "cosmic battle

pattern" appear throughout the Old Testament (OT). Oden, "Cosmogony, Cosmology," 1164–65; Levenson, *Creation and the Persistence of Evil.*

5. Alan Schulman, *Ceremonial Execution and Public Rewards: Some Historical Scenes on New Kingdom Private Stelae,* Orbis biblicus et Orientalis 75 (Freiburg-Göttingen: Universitätsverlag VandenHoeck-Ruprecht, 1987); Leo Bersani-Ulysse Dutoit, *The Forms of Violence: Narrative in Assyrian Art and Modern Culture* (New York: Schocken, 1985); Mario Liverani, *Prestige and Interest: International Relations in the Near East ca. 1600–1100 B.C.* (Padua: Sargon, 1990), 126–43.

6. The role of the king as warrior and administrator of justice is neatly expressed in the Code of Hammurabi, especially in the prologue and epilogue. See Theophile J. Meek, trans., "The Code of Hammurabi," in *Ancient Near Eastern Texts Relating to the Old Testament (ANET),* 3rd ed., ed. J. B. Pritchard (Princeton, NJ: Princeton University Press, 1969), 161–80.

7. This is aptly expressed in the ancient Egyptian literary text "The Tale of the Eloquent Peasant," where a farmer complains that the king has allowed his steward to rob and assault him without cause. For a translation, see Vincent A. Tobin, trans., "The Tale of the Eloquent Peasant," in *The Literature of Ancient Egypt: An Anthology of Stories, Instructions, and Poetry (LAE),* 3rd ed., ed. William Kelly Simpson (New Haven, CT: Yale University Press, 2003), 25–44. See also Nili Shupak, "A New Source for the Study of the Judiciary and Law of Ancient Egypt: The Tale of the Eloquent Peasant," *Journal of Near Eastern Studies (JNES)* 51 (1992): 1–18. Similarly, in another piece of literature from Egypt, "King Cheops and the Magicians," the monarch (Cheops) is denounced for wanting to execute a prisoner for his own amusement. See Simpson, *LAE,* 13–24, esp. 20.

8. On abuse of power, see Raymond Westbrook, *Studies in Biblical and Cuneiform Law,* Cahiers de la Revue Biblique 26 (Paris: J. Gabalda, 1988), 9–14.

9. See Pamela Barmash, *Homicide in the Biblical World* (Cambridge: Cambridge University Press, 2005), 28–31, 36–43, 105–8, for a discussion of homicide in Mesopotamia.

10. See the discussions of "vengeance" in H. G. L. Peels, *The Vengeance of God: The Meaning of the Root NQM and the Function of the NQM-Texts in the Context of the Divine Revelation in the Old Testament* (Leiden: E. J. Brill, 1995), 43–102; Raymond Westbrook, *Studies in Biblical and Cuneiform Law,* 39–54; Westbrook, "The Trial Scene in the Iliad," *Harvard Studies in Classical Philology* 94 (1992): 53–76; Wayne T. Pitard, "Vengeance," *ABD* 6, 786–87; and Pitard, "Amarna *ekēmu* and Hebrew *nāqam,*" *Maarav* 3 (1982): 5–25.

11. Warfare against foreign enemies and rebellious client states is a different matter and beyond the scope of this paper.

12. For "injustice/wrongdoing" in ancient Egyptian, see Adolf Erman and Hermann Grapow, *Wörterbuch der Aegyptischen Sprache (Wb.)* (Berlin: Akademie-Verlag, 1982), 1:240, l. 15 ('*dj3*); and ibid., "injustice/sin/lie," 1:129, l. 9 (*isft*). In the "Prophecies of Neferty" it is predicted that following a period of civil strife, at the accession of a new king, "justice will come into its place, while chaos/sin is driven out." See Victor A. Tobin, trans., "The Prophecies of Neferty," in *LAE,* 214–20, esp. 220. The

ancient Egyptian term for "fury" or "uproar" is *nšny* (*Wb.* 2:340–41). The quality is often associated with Seth, the god of chaos. The Ancient Egyptian for "violence" is *ḥȝ'yt* (*Wb.* 3:30).

13. On flood imagery in Mesopotamian historiography, see Jean-Jacques Glassner, *Mesopotamian Chronicles,* Writings from the Ancient World (WAW) 19 (Atlanta: Society of Biblical Literature, 2004), 108–9; S. N. Kramer, trans., "Lamentation over the Destruction of Sumer and Ur," in *ANET,* 611–19, where the absence of "law and order" is likened to "the Flood," along with other storm metaphors. Similarly, in the "Chronicle of Prince Osorkon," an Egyptian inscription dating to Dyn. 22, civil war is described as "disturbance" or "cloudburst," with the land fallen into a state of "drowning"; a "great convulsion" (lit. "storm of heaven"); and "uproar." The text states that, as a symptom of the chaos, there was "no restraining one from seizing his fellow." For the inscription, see Robert K. Ritner, *The Libyan Anarchy: Inscriptions from Egypt's Third Intermediate Period,* ed. E. Wente, WAW 21 (Atlanta: Society of Biblical Literature, 2009), 243–65. Note the description of Egypt as "passed-by and sick" during the reign of the "heretic" king, Akhenaton. See John Wilson, trans., "Tutankh-Amon's Restoration after the Amarna Revolution," in *ANET,* 251 and n. 2. In the "Admonitions of an Egyptian Sage"—a piece of "pessimistic literature"—the land is portrayed as being filled with "blood," while the Nile itself "Is blood." Whether the text is making actual historical allusions or is simply heightened metaphor is debated by Egyptologists. See Vincent A. Tobin, trans., "The Admonitions of an Egyptian Sage," in *LAE,* 188–210. See also Barmash, *Homicide,* 94–115.

14. Tobin, "Admonitions," 208; John Wilson, trans., "A Syrian Interregnum," in *ANET,* 260 (P. Harris I, l. 75).

15. Martti Nissinen with contributions by C. L. Seow and Robert K. Ritner, *Prophets and Prophecy in the Ancient Near East,* WAW 12 (Atlanta: Society of Biblical Literature, 2003), 37, cites a Mari letter (no. 15) that describes civic turmoil as "darkness" and "confusion."

16. David Lorton, "The Aswan/Philae Inscription of Thutmosis II," in *Studies in Egyptology Presented to Miriam Lichtheim,* ed. Sarah Israelit-Groll (Jerusalem: Magnes, 1990), 2:668–79. However, in such cases the hanging or impaling of malefactors and the public display of their bodies as trophies of war were characteristic of royal punishment.

17. In ancient Egypt, disruptive parties are characterized sometimes as "confederates of Seth," the god of anarchy, or as "associates of Apophis," the snaky demon of chaos. See H. Te Velde, *Seth, God of Confusion: A Study of His Role in Egyptian Mythology and Religion* (Leiden: E. J. Brill, 1967), 141–51; and Robert K. Ritner, *The Mechanics of Ancient Egyptian Magical Practice,* Studies in Ancient Oriental Civilization 54 (Chicago: Oriental Institute of the University of Chicago, 1993), 111–90. In the OT, like groups are sometimes designated as "the sons of Belial." See Theodore Lewis, "Belial," in *ABD,* 1:654–56.

18. See Erik Hornung, *The Ancient Egyptian Books of the Afterlife,* trans. David Lorton (Ithaca, NY: Cornell University Press, 1999), 63, 87.

19. A typical term of derision in the Bronze Age for such groups was *khabiru,* a

word that likely denoted "refugees" but also "criminals," with some connection to "state-less persons" (e.g., displaced parties and out-of-work mercenaries). See Liverani, *Prestige and Interest*, 103.

20. See Tobin, "Admonitions": "Verily, the roads are avoided and the paths are ambushed, / Men crouch in the bushes until the arrival of a traveler at night / In order to seize his burden and to take what he is carrying; / He is attacked with blows of a cudgel and foully murdered" (19). Likewise, in a somewhat comical description of the passage of an Egyptian official through foreign territory, he is warned about the "Bedouin, hidden under bushes." See John Wilson, trans., "A Satirical Letter," in *ANET*, 475–79. The text appears in Alan Gardiner, *Egyptian Hieratic Texts*, series 1, *Literary Texts of the Old Kingdom* (1911; reprint, New York: Georg Olms, 2007), 25. See also Ferris J. Stephens, trans., "Hymn to the Sun-God," in *ANET*, 387–89, an Assyrian text that contains a list of stereotyped disruptive groups: "the burglar, the thief, the enemy of the king/Sun, the vagabond in the roads of the desert."

21. Raymond Westbrook, "International Law in the Amarna Age," in Raymond Cohen and Raymond Westbrook, *Amarna Diplomacy: The Beginnings of International Relations* (Baltimore: Johns Hopkins University Press, 2000), 28–41, esp. 33–34; Samuel A. Meier, *The Messenger in the Ancient Semitic World* (Atlanta: Scholars, 1988), 89–120; G. H. Oller, "Messengers and Ambassadors in Ancient Western Asia," in *Civilizations of the Ancient Near East*, ed. Jack M. Sasson et al. (New York: Scribner, 1995), 3:1468. Barmash, *Homicide*, 178–201; Liverani, *Prestige and Interest*, 95–105.

22. Edward F. Wente, trans., "The Report of Wenamon," in *LAE*, 116–24. The text is published in Alan H. Gardiner, *Late Egyptian Stories*, Bibliotheca Aegyptiaca 1 (Brussels: Fondation Égyptologique Reine Élisabeth, 1932), 61–76. There is debate over whether the account is an actual travel record or purely "literary" or a mixture of the two.

23. Wente, "Wenamon," 123.

24. One must recognize that the narrative is severely telescoped: if there were precipitating causes for the locals' violent response, they have been completely ignored in the text. However, Wen-Amun's transport by a Lebanese vessel might have had some bearing on his inhospitable treatment.

25. William L. Moran, ed. and trans., *The Amarna Letters* (Baltimore: Johns Hopkins University Press, 1992), 16–17 (EA 8).

26. Ibid., 16.

27. See Westbrook, "International Law," 35–36.

28. Moran, *Amarna Letters*, 16–17. For other incidents of this nature, see Barmash, *Homicide*, 109–10, on a similar complaint by a Babylonian king to a Hittite ruler; and Liverani, *Prestige and Interest*, 97–100.

29. On the care taken to prevent war between "great powers" in the Late Bronze Age, see Cohen and Westbrook, *Amarna Diplomacy*, 225–36.

30. Itamer Singer, trans., "Mursili's 'Second' Plague Prayer to the Storm-God of Hatti," in *Hittite Prayers*, WAW 11 (Atlanta: Society of Biblical Literature, 2002), 57–61; H. G. Gütterbock, "Mursili's Accounts of Suppiluliuma's Dealings with Egypt," *Revue Hittite et Asianique* 66 (1960): 57–63.

31. Singer, *Hittite Prayers,* 58.

32. Billie Jean Collins, *The Hittites and Their World,* Archeological and Biblical Studies 7 (Atlanta: Society of Biblical Literature, 2007), 48–49; Theo P. J. van den Hout, "Der Falke und das Kücken: Der neue Pharao und der Hethitsche Prinze?" *Zeitschrift für Assyriologie* 84 (1994), 60–88.

33. For example, note a passage from an ancient Egyptian text of the Middle Kingdom, "The Loyalist Instruction": "[The king] is Vengeance against the one who transgresses his decree, while the one who would hate him is laden with poverty. Fight on behalf of his name, give reverence to the oath to him, that you have no part in the deed of assassins [lit. "daggers"]. The beloved of the king shall receive funerary honors, but there is no tomb for the one who would rebel against his Majesty: his corpse shall be as refuse, tossed to the water." The text is in Kurt Sethe, *Aegyptische Lesestücke zum Gebrauch im akademischen Unterricht,* 2nd. ed. (Leipzig: J. C. Hinrischs'sche Buchhandlung, 1928), 68. A translation is William Kelly Simpson, "The Loyalist Instruction from the Sehetepibre Stela," in *LAE,* 172–74. On conspiracies and usurpations in ancient Egypt, see Naguib Kanawati, *Conspiracies in the Egyptian Palace: Unis to Pepy I* (London: Routledge, 2003), 9–24, 183–85.

34. Ritner, *Mechanics,* 141, 200.

35. Note the objection to the term by Edward Champlin in *Nero* (Cambridge: Belknap, 2003), 29–30.

36. See Victor A. Tobin, trans., "The Teaching for Merikare," in *LAE,* 152–65. For the text with translation and commentary, see Joachim Friedrich Quack, *Studien zur Lehre für Merikare,* Göttinger Orientforschungen 1, series 4: Egypt, 23 (Wiesbaden: Otto Harrasowitz, 1992).

37. Quack, *Studien,* 191–92; Tobin, "Teaching," 163. The grammar is difficult, but it seems as if the king is stating that he had enacted a policy whose repercussions were unanticipated.

38. R. B. Parkinson, *Poetry and Culture in Middle Kingdom Egypt: A Dark Side to Perfection* (London: Continuum, 2002), 251.

39. On the desecration of corpses in the ancient Near East, see T. M. Lemos, "Shame and Mutilation of Enemies in the Hebrew Bible," *Journal of Biblical Literature* (*JBL*) 125, no. 2 (2006): 225–41.

40. Quack rejected the more lurid interpretation of the incident, instead seeing it as referring to the reuse of older building materials from the necropolis. *Studien,* 84–85. However, apart from the information provided in Parkinson, *Poetry and Culture,* curse formulations concerning the desecration of tombs and their contents by "rebels" during this period become much more extensive and more gruesome in their imagery. See Scott Morschauser, *Threat-Formulae in Ancient Egypt: A Study of the History, Structure, and Use of Threats and Curses in Ancient Egypt* (Baltimore: Halgo, 1991), 151–63. The tactic likely was used by both sides.

41. Edward F. Wente, *Letters from Ancient Egypt,* WAW 1 (Atlanta: Scholars, 1990), 183–84 (##301–4).

42. Ritner, *Libyan Anarchy,* 104–5.

43. Wente, *Letters,* 183.

44. Ibid.

45. Ritner links the conspiracy to charges that Piankh was systematically plundering tombs to finance his programs. *Libyan Anarchy,* 104–8.

46. Lorton, "Treatment of Criminals," 25–46.

47. Albrecht Goetze, trans., "Daily Prayers of the King," in *ANET,* 397. Similarly, Singer, *Hittite Prayers,* 40–43 ("Prayer of Arnuwanda and Asmunikal to the Sun-goddess of Arinna about the Ravages of the Kaska"). See also the description of the Babylonian destruction of the temple of Jerusalem in 2 Kings 25:8–21.

48. James Lindberger, *Ancient Aramaic and Hebrew Letters,* 2nd ed., WAW 14 (Atlanta: Society of Biblical Literature, 2003), 72–76, quotation on 75. There are other letters from the colony that refer to riots and hostilities between the Egyptians and Jewish settlers (ibid., 69–70, 71). The assault has both ethnic and religious overtones, with hostility directed at "outsiders" and their beliefs.

49. This was despite the fact that, legally, Egyptians and Jews were regarded as having equal rights under Persian sovereignty. See Raymond Westbrook, "The Character of Ancient Near Eastern Law," in *Ancient Near Eastern Law,* 37–38.

50. Albrecht Goetze, trans., "Instructions for Temple Officials," *ANET,* 207–9; Goetze, trans., "From the Instructions for the Commander of the Border Guards," *ANET,* 211.

51. Morschauser, *Threat-Formulae,* 47; Lorton, "Treatment of Criminals," 25–27.

52. Scott Morschauser, "The Ideological Basis for Social Justice/Responsibility in Ancient Egypt," in *Social Justice in the Ancient World,* ed. K. D. Irani and Morris Silver, Contributions in Political Science 354 (Westport, CT: Greenwood, 1995), 101–13, esp. 108–9; Alan Gardiner, *Late Egyptian Miscellanies,* Bibliotheca Aegyptiaca 7 (Brussels: Édition de la Fondation Égyptologique Reine Élisabeth, 1937), 123–24; Wente, *Letters,* 25, 74, 115.

53. S. N. Kramer, trans., "The Curse of Agade: The Ekur Avenged," in *ANET,* 646–51. See also Glassner, *Mesopotamian Chronicles,* 108–109, on the historiography of the composition.

54. Kramer, "Curse," 648–49. There was likely a political motivation behind the action, since the cult had been critical of the king.

55. The inscriptions are translated in William J. Murnane, *Texts from the Amarna Period in Egypt,* WAW 5 (Atlanta: Scholars, 1995); for a convenient historical overview, see ibid., 1–15.

56. Ibid., 235–40(the "Edict of Horemheb").

57. Ibid., 78. See also William J. Murnane and Charles C. van Siclen III, *The Boundary Stelae of Akhenaten* (London: Kegan Paul International, 1993), 41, 166–68, who speculate that the problems were generated by the king's sudden withdrawal of patronage from the royal necropolis in Thebes, which was compounded by the de facto movement of the capital from Thebes to Amarna. For a similar case from eighth century BCE Babylon, see Glassner, *Mesopotamian Chronicles,* 300–313 ("Chronographic Document Concerning Nabû-šuma-Iškun").

58. Murnane, *Texts from the Amarna Period,* 240–42.

59. The classic case is given in Tacitus, *Annals* bk. 6, chap. 29, para. 1. See J. A.

Crook, *Law and Life of Rome* (Ithaca, NY: Cornell University Press, 1967), 275. The participation of the "mob" seems to have been largely posthumous, following the execution of a guilty party by legal authorities.

60. The "avenger" was to be the agent of justice *on behalf of* the legal authorities.

61. Pitard, "Vengeance," 786, notes additional terminology, e.g., "to requite," "save," "contend."

62. EA 8.

63. Westbrook, "International Law," 31–33.

64. Ibid., 40. See also Scott M. Hahn, *Kinship by Covenant: A Canonical Approach to the Fulfillment of God's Saving Promises,* Anchor Yale Bible Reference Library (New Haven, CT: Yale University Press, 2009), 59–60.

65. In some Mesopotamian law codes, punishments for familial infractions are assigned to the wronged party. For example, see Theophile J. Meek, "The Middle Assyrian Laws," in *ANET,* 180–88. In this code—dating to the twelfth century BCE—the right of *patria potestas* (paternal authority) is exercised by a husband who is to prosecute and "inflict the (proper) punishment" upon a wife who has stolen his goods and sold them to an outsider. This includes the husband's "cutting off the ears of his wife" if "she has sold his property to slaves"; if she has stolen from another household, the owner shall "cut off her nose." In an Ancient Egyptian literary text of the New Kingdom, "The Story of the Two Brothers," a husband kills his wife for attempted infidelity and falsely accusing another of rape, casting her body to the dogs, thereby denying her a ritual burial. See Edward F. Wente, trans., "The Story of the Two Brothers," in *LAE,* 80–90, esp. 83.

66. Albrecht Goetze, trans., "The Hittite Laws," in *ANET,* 188–96, quotation on 190.

67. Ibid. , 196.

68. Erica Reiner, trans., "The Vassal-Treaties of Esarhaddon," in *ANET,* 534–41.

69. Ibid., 535–36, 536, 536–37.

70. Likely through the declaration "Vengeance is mine, I will repay, says the Lord" (Rom. 12:19). It is interesting that the Pauline verse is composed of two OT passages: Deut. 32:35, in a curse against rebellious Israel, "Vengeance is mine, and recompense for the time when their foot shall slip"; and Lev. 19:18, "You shall not take vengeance or bear any grudge against the sons of your own people, but you shall love your neighbor as yourself. I am the Lord."

71. Gen. 4:14. On the story from a legal standpoint, see Barmash, *Homicide,* 12–19.

72. Num. 35:11.

73. Num. 35:12.

74. Num. 35:24–25; on the term "blood avenger," see Barmash, *Homicide,* 20–27, 50–52.

75. Num. 35:19; Barmash, *Homicide,* 71–93. The cases involved killing with a deadly instrument (iron, wood, or stone) or from personal motive ("hatred," "enmity") or by stealth (Num. 35:16–18, 35:20–21).

76. Num. 35:26.

77. Gen. 4:23–24.

78. Gen. 6:11. The Hebrew term חמס (*khamas*), "violence," can also designate general "lawlessness." See E. A. Speiser, *Genesis: A New Translation with Introduction and Commentary,* Anchor Bible 1 (Garden City, NY: Doubleday, 1964), 51; and Ziony Zevit, "The Search for Violence in Israelite Culture and the Bible," in *Religion and Violence: The Biblical Heritage,* ed. David A. Bernat and Jonathan Klawans, Recent Research in Biblical Studies 2 (Sheffield: Phoenix, 2007), 16–37, esp. 18–19.

79. The assignation of dates to OT sources, the origin of those sources, and proposed stages of editing are extraordinarily complex—and highly debated—issues. For a general overview of the problem, see John Barton, "Source Criticism (OT)," in *ABD* 6:162–65; and Barton, "Redaction Criticism (OT)," in *ABD* 5:644–47.

80. This is especially the case in the so-called Deuteronomistic History, which basically comprises the narrative accounts of Joshua through 2 Kings. Here, Israel's history is largely seen through the lens of fidelity to the Mosaic covenant as presented in the book of Deuteronomy, which likely reflects the influence of "prophetic" circles. Again, the dating of sources, authorship, and identification of redactional layers have been debated, with some scholars opting for "pre-exilic editions" and others arguing that the Deuteronomistic History was entirely exilic (post–586 BCE). See the summaries of Steven L. McKenzie, "Deuteronomistic History," in *ABD* 2:160–68; and Moshe Weinfeld, "Deuteronomy, Book of," ibid., 2:168–83.

81. Gen. 19:1–29. Guarantees for the safety of transient groups were dependent upon the permission of local officials (Gen. 20:15), marked by the making of a covenant or treaty that delineated the respective parties' access to territory and resources (Gen. 21:25–32, 23:17–20) to prevent the outbreak of hostilities. Similar arrangements are attested in cases of intermarriage regarding the disposal of tribal property and dowry goods (Gen. 31:49–52), disputes over which could lead to interfamilial or intertribal violence (see Gen. 27:41). An interesting feature of the Genesis texts is that confrontations are described as taking place on a level below that of the "officiating parties," e.g., the men of the local ruler quarrel with the men of the patriarch.

82. Scott Morschauser, "'Hospitality,' Hostiles and Hostages: On the Legal Background to Genesis 19:1–9," *Journal for the Study of the Old Testament* 27, no. 3 (2003): 461–85. For a convenient overview of the history of the interpretation of the episode, see M. Mulder, "Sodom and Gomorrah," in *ABD* 6:102–3.

83. Gen. 14:1–4, 14:8–11.

84. Morschauser, "Hospitality," 464–67.

85. Judg. 19:1–30, esp. 19:16–28.

86. See T. J. Lewis, "Belial," in *ABD* 1:654–56. The term "sons of Belial," follows other ancient Near East usage, referring to individuals or groups considered to be subverting legitimate authority or to those who would instigate apostasy and idolatry, threatening societal order.

87. Morschauser, "Hospitality," 480–82.

88. Judg. 20:1–44. The point is important to note, since some commentators see the Gibeah and Sodom episodes as providing blatant approval of brutality toward

women: both stories end in the destruction of the groups that would perpetrate such behavior. See, for example, Phyllis Trible, *Texts of Terror: Literary-Feminist Readings of Biblical Narratives* (Philadelphia: Fortress, 1984), 65–91.

89. Esther 3:12–14. This will be countered by an imperial decree supposedly allowing threatened Jewish communities to use preemptive violence themselves (Esther 8:9–11), an event that forms the basis for the Festival of Purim.

90. See Carey A. Moore, "Esther, Book of," in *ABD* 2:633–43.

91. Esther 3:8. Similar charges against Jews are offered in Dan. 3:12, 6:13, resulting in the persecution of the denounced parties. Likewise, Neh. 2:19 refers to accusations of "rebellion" being brought to the Persians by opponents of Jerusalem Jews who want to rebuild the destroyed temple. See Moore, "Esther," 641, on possibly dating Esther (or a redaction of it) to the Hellenistic period, when episodes of anti-Semitism become more marked. See Steven Weitzmann, "Plotting Antiochus' Persecution," *JBL* 123, no. 2 (2004): 219–34, on anti-Semitism continuing into the Roman period. On anti-Semitism and Rome, see Martin Goodman, *Rome and Jerusalem: The Clash of Ancient Civilizations* (New York: Alfred A. Knopf, 2007), 424–87, 551–57.

92. Gen. 34:1–31.

93. Gen. 34:25, 34:27.

94. Gen. 34:30.

95. Gen. 34:31.

96. Zevit, "Search for Violence," classifies the act as "illegal homicide" (Heb. רצח [*rtzkh*]) (20). However, see Philip Carl Salzmann, *Culture and Conflict in the Middle East* (Amherst, NY: Humanity Books, 2003), 101–30, on "tribal honor" in "legitimizing" the modern use of violence in avenging sexual wrongs.

97. Zevit, "Search for Violence," includes in his discussion illegal homicide, warfare, religious zealotry, human sacrifice, and the problematic issue of "mandated genocide" in combat (19–34). For the latter, which is designated in the OT as the *khērem* ("the ban") (חרם), see Philip D. Stern, *The Biblical Kherem: A Window on Israel's Religious Experience*, Brown Judaic Studies 211 (Atlanta: Scholars, 1991).

98. "Pitched battles" are not necessarily involved; cf. Ehud's assassination of the official Eglon (Judg. 3:15–25); the killing of the fleeing general Sisera while asleep by the woman Jael (Judg. 4:17–22); the execution of captured Midianite princes by Gideon's forces (Judg. 7:24–25); Gideon's beheading of Zebah and Zalmunna following their killing of Gideon's relatives (Judg. 8:13–21); Abimelech's hiring mercenaries to kill his enemies (Judg. 9:4–5); and the Shechemites' ambush of Abimelech's forces (Judg. 9:22–27).

99. Judg. 12:1. See Alice Logan, "Rehabilitating Jephtah," *JBL* 128, no. 4 (2009): 665–85, esp. 674–75.

100. Judg. 14:4–6.

101. Judg. 15:8, 15:14–17, 16:21–30. Samson's death, however, results in his pulling down the temple in which he is being mocked upon his own tormentors.

102. Judg. 15:7, 15:11. Samson's insisting on the right to carry out family punishment recalls the Hittite law cited above.

103. Judg. 18:11–20.

104. Judg. 18:25.

105. 1 Sam. 6:19. Note also Judg. 6:25–32, where Gideon, after secretly destroying an altar dedicated to the Canaanite deity, Baal, is singled out by oracular consultation as the guilty party (likely through the casting of lots) and is threatened with death by townsmen (6:30). The incident demonstrates the heated and deadly emotions roused by sacrilege. However, the account is heavily influenced by Deuteronomistic theology and seems to reflect the later religious reforms enacted by King Josiah (2 Kings 23:4–24). Note also king Saul's mass execution of the priesthood and inhabitants at Nob through his officer Doeg the Edomite (1 Sam. 22:16–19). In literary terms, the action serves to highlight Saul's increasing madness. Importantly, the priesthood at Nob had colluded with David, who had been declared a public enemy and traitor by the king.

106. Judg. 21:25.

107. For example, Joab's killing of Abner (2 Sam. 3:6); the assassination of David's remaining opponents (2 Sam. 4:5–8), with the perpetrators themselves being executed, mutilated, and hanged by David in an attempt to deny his complicity in the murders of Saul's family (2 Sam. 4:9–12); Absalom's killing of Amnon for the latter's rape of Tamar, Absalom's sister (2 Sam. 13:29). Note also King Solomon's execution of the prince and claimant to the throne of Israel, Adonijah (1 Kings 2:25), along with his supporter, the general Joab (1 Kings 2:34); the killing of the pro-Saulide priest Shimei (1 Kings 2:46) when he is found outside his place of confinement. These acts, securing Solomon's position, are all committed by the king's agent, Benaiah, who was made commander of the army. However, the premonarchial career of David, while in exile from King Saul (1 Sam. 19:18), is marked by violence. 1 Sam. 25:8–13 recounts David, as head of a paramilitary band, threatening Nabal of Carmel for the latter's refusal to feed his men while engaged in raids. 1 Sam. 27:8–9 summarizes the raids of "David and his men" upon indigenous groups in the south of Judah (Geshurites, Girzites, Amalekites), "attacking" their lands and "leaving neither man nor woman alive" (1 Sam. 27:11). Such ruthlessness is explained as precautionary, so that David's activities could not be reported to his then overlords, the Philistines. Similarly, 1 Sam. 30:1–2 describes an Amalekite raid upon David's residence of Ziklag for plunder and hostages while the latter was away: they "burned it with fire, and had taken captive the women and all who were in it, both small and great; they killed no one, but carried them off and went their way." As a result of the attack, David's own "people spoke of stoning him" (1 Sam. 30:6), indicating dissatisfaction with his leadership. Subsequently, he launches a counterraid against the Amalekites, who are caught unaware while feasting from their plunder (1 Sam. 30:16–20).

108. Lev. 16:10. A person regarded as "tainted" would be chosen to lead the animal. See Raymond Westbrook and Theodore Lewis, "Who Led the Scapegoat in Leviticus 16:21?" *JBL* 127, no. 23 (2008): 417–22.

109. For example, Josh. 7:16–26 (Achan's theft of military spoils dedicated to God, for which he is stoned and burned [7:25]); Judg. 6:25–32 (the ferreting out of Gideon for destroying a Baalist shrine); 1 Sam. 14:40–45 (Saul's son, Jonathan, violates a prebattle oath but eludes punishment).

110. 2 Sam. 21:9. Saul's reasoning was based on "ethnic" considerations: the per-secuted group was composed of Gibeonites. Members of the indigenous populace prior to Israelite settlement, they had been given protection as cult workers (Josh. 9:16–27), whereas other groups were to be eliminated. See also 1 Sam. 8:2 (David's decimation of the Moabites); 1 Kings 11:15–16 (Israel's "slaying" of every male in Edom). On ethnic cleansing, see Zevit, "Search for Violence," 29–34; and John J. Collins, "The Zeal of Phinehas: The Bible and the Legitimation of Violence," *JBL* 122, no. 1 (2003): 3–21. For evaluation of ethnic violence in the Bible in later periods, see Louis H. Feldman, *"Remember Amalek!": Violence, Zealotry, and Group Destruction in the Bible According to Philo, Pseudo-Philo, and Josephus* (Cincinnati: Hebrew Union College Press, 2004), 147–72.

111. 1 Kings 22:24–28 (the beating and imprisonment of Micaiah for opposing the king of Israel); 2 Chron. 24:20–22 (the killing of Zechariah, the son of the high priest, by order of Joash, the king of Judah, for the former's minatory proclamation through "the Spirit of God"); 2 Chron. 16:10 (Hanani, "the seer," is persecuted by king Asa). There is a host of violent incidents surrounding the unstable political situ-ation during this period: 1 Kings 12:18 (the stoning of an official over prohibitive tax policy). However, dynastic struggle is sometimes a precipitating cause: 1 Kings 15:27–29 (the assassination of Nadab and killing of his supporters by the usurper Baasha); 1 Kings 16:10 (the killing of Elah by the usurper Zimri); 2 Kings 11:1 (Queen Athaliah kills the royal family but is herself deposed in a subsequent coup [2 Kings 11:16]); 2 Kings 20:20–21 (the assassination of King Joash); 2 Kings 14:5 (the coup of Amaziah and his own assassination [2 Kings 14:19]); 2 Kings 15:10 (the slaying of Zechariah by Shallum); 2 Kings 15:14 (Shallum's slaying by Menachem); 2 Kings 15:16 (the sack of a city and execution of pregnant women by Menachem's order); 2 Kings 15:23 (Pekahiah is slain by Pekah); 2 Kings 15:30 (Pekah is slain by Hoshea); 2 Kings 24:33 (King Amon of Judah is killed by his retainers); 2 Kings 24:24 ("the people of the land" slay the conspirators against Amon).

112. This essentially encompasses what is known as the "Elijah-Elisha Cycle," contained in 1 Kings 17–19, 21; 2 Kings 1–2, 4–7:2, 8:1–15, 9. See Mordechai Cogan, *I Kings: A New Translation with Introduction and Commentary,* Anchor Bible 10 (New York: Doubleday, 2000), 430–31; Mordechai Cogan and Hayim Tadmor, *II Kings: A New Translation with Introduction and Commentary* Anchor Bible 11 (New York: Dou-bleday, 1988), 27–28, 33–35.

113. Represented by Elijah, Elisha, and the "sons of the prophets." See 1 Kings 18:13, 2 Kings 2:3. 1 Kings 18:19 refers to "the four hundred and fifty prophets of Ba'al and the four hundred prophets of Asherah, who eat at Jezebel's table." That is, she personally sponsored and supported the cults of the Canaanite fertility deities.

114. In 1 Kings 18:13, Jezebel is charged by Elijah with killing "the prophets of the Lord"; in 1 Kings 19:2, the queen swears an oath to kill Elijah.

115. 2 Kings 9:2–10. According to the text, when Jehu is anointed king, he is charged in a divine oracle delivered by an unnamed prophet to "strike down the house of Ahab . . . that I [Yahweh] may avenge on Jezebel the blood of my servants the prophets, and the blood of all the servants of the Lord. For the whole house of

Ahab shall perish; and I will cut off from Ahab every male, bond or free, in Israel. . . . And the dogs shall eat Jezebel in the territory of Jezreel, and none shall bury her" (2 Kings 9:7–8, 9:10). It is to be a total regime change, with all associates of the ousted dynasty purged.

116. Jehu's coup against Ahab's son, Joram, is presented in graphic detail in 2 Kings 9:14 through 10:28, concluding with the terse notice "Thus Jehu wiped out Ba'al from Israel." The Hebrew word for "to wipe out" is *šmd* (שמד), also translated as "to exterminate." This includes the execution of Jezebel (2 Kings 9:33); the slaying of seventy vassals (lit. "sons") of Ahab, i.e., the personal officials of the usurped dynasty (2 Kings 10:7–11), including all of Ahab's "great men, his familiar friends, and his priests" (again, the whole administrative bureaucracy of the preceding regime is forcibly eliminated); and the mass execution of members of the cult of Baal (2 Kings 10:18–28). Zevit, "Search for Violence," regards the violence as "political" rather than "religious" in nature (23), but in the ancient Near East, the two concepts were intertwined.

117. We see a similar policy taken in Judah, at the usurpation of Queen Athaliah, who is killed in a coup (2 Kings 11:16), accompanied by the suppression of the cult of Baal in Jerusalem (2 Kings 11:17–18). On the importance of Jehu, see Winfred Theil, "Jehu," trans. Charles Muenchow, in *ABD* 3:670–73, esp. 672. It should be noted that Jehu's violence was denounced by the eighth–century BCE prophet Hosea in his declaration that Yahweh would "punish the house of Jehu for the blood of Jezreel" (Hosea 1:4). See Zevit, "Search for Violence," 29–32, on the impact of the Deuteronomist on "mandating genocide"; and Collins, "Zeal of Phinehas," 11. For the importance of Deuteronomy to biblical historiography, see Moshe Weinfeld, *Deuteronomy 1–11: A New Translation with Introduction and Commentary*, Anchor Bible 5 (New York: Doubleday, 1991), 13–84, esp. 37–44.

118. See Jerome Walsh, "Naboth," in *ABD* 4:978; and Cogan, *I Kings*, 475–86 on historical and literary issues.

119. 1 Kings 21:8–14.

120. 1 Kings 21:17–24. See Cogan, *I Kings*, 484.

121. Cogan, *I Kings*, 486.

122. 1 Kings 17:1. Cf. 2 Sam. 21:1 for a parallel.

123. As Cogan notes, the designation is that of the redactor. *I Kings*, 479. However, the calling of two witnesses was legally required (Deut. 17:16; Num. 35:30).

124. Cogan suggests that Naboth made an abusive remark against the king that was bolstered by use of the divine name, which would have amounted to perjury. *I Kings*, 480.

125. Ibid. Stoning was used for apostasy, blasphemy, sorcery, violation of the Sabbath, misappropriating goods devoted to Yahweh (*khērem*), juvenile delinquency (a "disobedient son"), and adultery. See Westbrook, "Punishments and Crimes," 555. The practice of stoning does have elements that one often associates with "lynching," since the community itself—or a group claiming to represent it—apparently could carry out the punishment ad hoc. The paradigmatic case is in Num. 15:32–36, where a "man gathering sticks on the Sabbath" is brought before Moses and the "congrega-

tion" of Israel. Through a divine oracle, Moses prescribes that the transgressor be "stoned to death" by the people "outside the camp." The venue is symbolic, representing a kind of exile: by his violation of the holy day, the man had rejected membership in the community. Importantly, however, the individual is not executed without some sort of legal hearing. Westbrook cites an article by J. J. Finkelstein, "The Ox That Gored," *Transactions of the American Philosophical Society* 71 (Philadelphia: American Philosophical Society, 1981): 5–47, esp. 26–29, which asserts that "treason against a superior" is the operating factor in punishment by stoning. Westbrook avers that "sabbath violation . . . fit[s] this category with difficulty" (555). Yet when considered within the covenantal polity of ancient Israel, where Yahweh was suzerain, a transgression of his sacred day could well be seen as a case of lèse-majesté. Indeed, the use of "stones" represents "creation" rising up to punish a malefactor and is akin to elements in biblical curses where "heaven and earth" along with natural elements are invoked to bear witness against a violation of the divine covenant.

126. For prophesying against Judah, Jeremiah is threatened by conspirators (Jer. 11:21) and plotters intent on denouncing him (Jer. 18:18). He is arrested, beaten, and placed in public stocks (Jer. 20:2); charged with blasphemy and treason (Jer. 26:10); imprisoned (Jer. 32:3); and cast into a cistern (Jer. 38:6).

127. A passage from a Neo-Babylonian chronicle that states, "In the month of Tešrit, the twenty-sixth day, the subjects of king Khallušu (Inšušinak I) of Elam revolted against him, lock[ed] him up and killed him," conceals as much as if not more than it reveals. See Glassner, *Mesopotamian Chronicles*, 193–207, quotation at 199.

128. See Sara Forsdyke, "Street Theatre and Popular Justice in Ancient Greece: Shaming, Stoning, and Starving Offenders inside and outside the Courts," *Past & Present* 201 (2008): 3–50; Raymond Westbrook, "Vitae Necisque Potestas," *Zeitschrift für Alte Geschichte* 48, no. 2 (1999): 203–23; Vincent Rosivach, "Execution by Stoning in Athens," *Classical Antiquity* 6, no. 2 (1987): 232–48; Thomas W. Africa, "Urban Violence in Imperial Rome," *Journal of Interdisciplinary History* 2, no. 1 (1971): 3–21.

129. See Liverani, *Prestige and Interest*, 33–105, on the importance of the concept and reality of "border" in the ancient Near East. See also Meir Malul, "*ʾîš ʾittî* (Leviticus 16:21): A Marginal Person," *JBL* 128, no. 3 (2009): 437–42.

130. This might be surprising, considering the somewhat idealistic position taken by some modern scholars that hospitality was a universally observed practice in antiquity: the evidence suggests that the reality was far more complex. See Morschauser, "Hospitality," 463, 470–71.

131. Resident aliens were afforded protections (see Westbrook, "Character of Ancient Near Eastern Law," 37–38), but as the examples show, they were not always followed.

Witch Lynching Past and Present

BRIAN P. LEVACK

OST PEOPLE THINK OF LYNCHING as a distinctly American crime. The term was coined in the United States in the late eighteenth century, and it usually conjures up images of white mobs hanging African Americans or burning them to death. Certainly the scholarly literature on lynching has had an almost exclusively American focus. There is no reason, however, that the word cannot be used to characterize mob violence against subordinate or marginalized groups in other societies. Over the past fifty years, historians have used the term to describe the unlawful execution of people suspected of witchcraft in Europe during the sixteenth and seventeenth centuries, and more recently they have used it to describe similar treatment of suspected witches in Africa and Asia. The purpose of this essay is to show that the public execution of witches without due process of law, which began centuries before the word *lynching* was first used in America, can be properly classified as such. It makes a case for the transformation of the term from a description of a recurrent pattern of collective behavior in America into a broader category of social and extrajudicial action that transcends the boundaries of time and space.

Witch lynchings have occurred since the sixteenth century, when witchcraft was defined as a crime in Europe, and they have continued in some parts of the world to the present day. The word *lynching* carries the primary connotation of mob violence, although the number of participants in such attacks on witches and the extent of their participation (as either ringleaders or supporters) have varied considerably. Witchcraft historians have also used the term *lynching* to describe the summary execution of alleged witches by local judges who, under pressure from the community, refused to follow due process in the prosecution of the alleged offenders.

Witch lynchings share a number of common features. First, they have almost always taken place in villages, rural communities, or small towns—close-knit communities where suspicions and accusations of witchcraft originated. Second, lynch mobs have based their actions on prevailing popular standards of justice, known in Germany as *Volksjustiz*, a term that approximates the meaning of the English phrase "lynch law." Third, witch lynchings have tended to occur when local officials tolerated, encouraged, or actually participated in these illegal executions. If these officials tried to prevent such lynchings, they risked arousing opposition from the community. Finally, witch lynchings, which have always been carried out in summary fashion, have often taken place when it appeared that the regular judicial process would take too long, cost too much, or result in lenient punishments or acquittals.

Witches were people who had allegedly inflicted harm or misfortune on their neighbors by magical means. Because educated theologians and jurists believed that all magic was performed through the power of the devil, they claimed that witches also made pacts with Satan, by which they received their magical powers and pledged themselves to his service, thereby abandoning their Christian faith. This belief that witches concluded pacts with the devil led to a belief, held mainly by educated elites, that witches gathered periodically in large assemblies to worship the devil and engage in a variety of heinous moral acts, including promiscuous sexual activity, naked dancing, the murder of young children, and the consumption of those infants' dismembered bodies. The primary concern of most villagers and uneducated local judges, however, was the harmful magical deeds of the accused witch. Uneducated villagers had little knowledge of or interest in the diabolical interpretations developed by inquisitors and other educated elites. Villagers had relatively little interest in the reports that witches had gathered in nocturnal assemblies except to the extent that the witches used these gatherings to plan further harm on the community. When communities lynched witches, they were therefore wreaking vengeance on alleged miscreants who they believed had destroyed the lives, domestic animals, and livelihood of people in their community.

Almost all cases of witch lynching occurred when villagers or townspeople became convinced that witches had used harmful magic to inflict bodily harm or some other misfortune on themselves or their neighbors. The usual procedure in such cases was for the aggrieved party to bring a complaint before a court. In European countries that had introduced inquisitorial (as opposed to accusatorial) procedure, courts initiated the prosecutions by their own authority, often on the basis of local rumor that a particular person or group of people was responsible for the harm done. The difficulty securing convictions and executions in many witchcraft prosecutions arose when central judicial authorities (those who staffed superior courts), who unlike most local judges had legal training, refused to sanction these local trials on the grounds that they were not observing due process. Central judicial officers, moreover, were not likely to share the commitment of local official to rid their communities of witches, simply because they were not involved in the atmosphere of panic that led to the prosecutions in the first place.

The most common methods of witch lynching were stoning and beating the victims. These were the punishments that angry crowds administered when their intention was to dispatch the victim quickly. In some cases the witch was burned to death, a punishment that mimicked the method of execution reserved for witches in most continental European jurisdictions. Even in imitating this official example, however, the punishment resulted from a rush to judgment. Instead of burning the witch at the stake, which was the practice in formally established jurisdictions, witches who were lynched were burned in their homes or in a community oven. Lynchers, moreover, made no effort to garrote or strangle the witch before the flames consumed their bodies, as was the custom in most northern European jurisdictions. The mercy shown to witches by secular judges in many official witch executions was absent in witch lynchings.

Another method of execution that mimicked a procedure formerly used in criminal trials was drowning. In the Middle Ages, defendants whose guilt was uncertain were often forced to undergo an ordeal by which they would be thrown into a body of water to see whether they floated or sank. Floating, which was interpreted as a sign of rejection by the water (which had been blessed), was seen as proof of guilt, whereas sinking indicated innocence, although in many cases the innocent defendant drowned. In 1215 the Church outlawed all ordeals, including this water test, but the procedure became a popular method of determining a witch's guilt, much to the objection of jurists throughout Europe. In this way "swimming the witch" became a method of lynching. Instead of using it to determine guilt or innocence, it was transformed into a method of drowning the witch, usually by holding the victim under water.

Illegal Execution of Suspected Witches during the Period of the Trials

It is useful to distinguish between witch lynchings that took place during the period when witchcraft was officially a secular crime (a period that had different chronological boundaries in different jurisdictions) and those that occurred after the offense was decriminalized. Those that took place during the earlier period usually occurred when a large number of people in the community did not trust that judicial authorities would bring the alleged culprits to justice or when they resented the fact that the authorities had already failed to do so. After the laws against witchcraft were repealed, witches were lynched mainly because communities felt there was no judicial remedy at hand and that if they did not take action themselves, the witches would go free and continue to present a threat to society.

Denmark. The earliest known lynchings during the period of the trials took place in Denmark in 1543, when fifty-two women were lynched for being witches in Jutland, and peasants throughout the country were reported to have hunted witches "like wolves."[1] These attacks on witches took place in the wake of a period of civil warfare, economic dislocation, and religious reform. These circumstances might help to explain why the community pursued the witches with such determination, but the main reason so many of these executions were illegal was that Danish law was ambiguous regarding the crime of witchcraft. The only national legislation declaring witchcraft to be a crime appeared in the law code of 1521, but this statute was repealed the following year after King Christian II fled the country. When the government enforced a very strict witchcraft law in 1547, the outburst of Danish lynchings came to an end.

France. In the 1580s, at the peak of witch hunting throughout Europe, a series of lynchings took place in the province of Champagne in northeastern France. These incidents illustrate the dynamics of witch lynching throughout Europe during the early modern period. The hunt occurred during a period of widespread famine and economic contraction—circumstances that set the stage for the most intense period of witch hunting throughout the continent.[2] In these circumstances villagers in this region became convinced that witches were responsible for their misfortunes. But the same villagers had little confidence that the established courts would bring the witches to justice. The bishop of Rheims, who had criminal jurisdiction over much of this area, made it clear that all trials would follow due process, which meant that any charges of witchcraft would require solid evidence of *maleficium*, which was extremely difficult to produce. The bishop also ruled that even if the courts did convict the witches who had been accused and arrested, their sentences could be appealed to the Parlement of Paris, which had appellate jurisdiction over a large portion of northern France. The Parlement observed very strict rules of evidence, and it had already acquitted or drastically reduced the sentences of many witches convicted by local courts. Rather than face the prospect that the accused would be set free, and to avoid the high cost of lodging an appeal, local judges ordered the execution of suspected witches without due process. About fifty witches in Champagne were lynched before the archbishop took action, sending a special representative into the villages to order accused witches to be sent to Rheims or Paris for trial. This representative also indicted the local judges who had ordered or tolerated the executions. This investigation by a superior judicial authority saved at least eighteen accused witches from summary execution.[3]

This action greatly restricted but did not put an end to witch lynching in France. During the last great witch panic in France in 1640, lynchings took place along a swath of territory stretching from Languedoc in the southeast to Ardennes in the northeast.[4] These borderlands were most resistant to judicial control from the provincial parlements. After this date, however, both witchcraft prosecutions and lynchings occurred very infrequently, and in 1682 an edict of Louis XIV effectively put an end to all French witchcraft prosecutions.

Spain. Another example of witch lynching during the period of the trials occurred in Spain, where a central judicial institution, the Spanish Inquisition, which had taken the lead in prosecuting witches during the sixteenth century, inaugurated a period of leniency in the prosecution of witches in the wake of a large witch hunt in the Basque country in which more than eighteen hundred people, most of them children, were accused of witchcraft. After the inquisitor Alonso Salazar de Frías had shown this witch hunt to have been a terrible miscarriage of justice, the central tribunal of the Inquisition in Madrid issued a strict set of procedural rules that brought prosecutions by the Inquisition almost to a stop. After that time the Inquisition executed only about fifty witches. Frustrated by such judicial restraints, local communities managed to execute about 250 witches either by proceeding against them in the local courts or by lynching them. In one Spanish village in the early seventeenth century, a witch was lynched as soon as word of her acquittal by the Inquisition reached her home village.[5]

The exact number of Spanish witch lynchings remains unknown, but by all estimates it was substantial. The number of these executions reveals that the central tribunal of the Inquisition in Madrid, *La Suprema*, which was able to control its regional tribunals, could not proceed against either the secular courts or the crowds that took justice into their own hands.[6]

Germany. In the German-speaking lands within the Holy Roman Empire, where central imperial justice was relatively weak, and where small territories and principalities were responsible for more than half of all European witchcraft executions, lynchings were relatively uncommon during the period of the trials. The main reason for this is that German judicial authorities almost always treated witches harshly. The judicial system therefore satisfied the demands of the general population for action against witches. Only toward the end of the period of the trials, when judicial officers throughout Europe were beginning to recommend restraint, did lynchings begin to occur. One of these took place during a witch hunt in the Roman Catholic city of Paderborn in 1657–59. Paderborn was a prince-bishopric, which meant that the bishop exercised secular as well as ecclesiastical jurisdiction. Like many other witch hunts in Europe, these prosecutions began when a group of demoniacs (people allegedly possessed by demons) accused witches of causing their possession by magical means. The prince-bishop, Adolf von der Recke, expressed deep skepticism regarding the authenticity of the possessions and therefore was reluctant to authorize the prosecutions. Eventually he yielded to popular pressure and allowed the trial, which resulted in a number of executions. The more zealous members of the community, however, were not satisfied with these trials and pushed for more vigorous action. When the prince-bishop refused, the people decided to proceed extrajudicially against the witches, who were about to be set free. Local crowds beat ten of the suspected witches to death in the streets.[7]

Scotland. The most notorious case of witch lynching in Scotland occurred in the early eighteenth century at a time when the privy council, after many years of effort, finally managed to secure a measure of control over local justice. The lynching took place after local authorities had been unsuccessful in their efforts to secure the conviction of seven witches accused of bringing about the demonic possession of Patrick Morton, a teenage blacksmith in the fishing burgh of Pittenweem in the shire of Fife. Judicial authorities in this burgh had requested a commission from the Scottish privy council in Edinburgh to try the witches in Pittenweem before members of an ad hoc commission of local dignitaries that would almost certainly have led to their conviction and execution. Having fled from the burgh after her prosecution for witchcraft had failed, Janet Cornfoot was forcibly taken from the nearby village of Leuchars and returned to Pittenweem by two armed men. When she arrived in the town, she was brought to the minister's house and then, since he was not present, to that of one of the bailies (burgh officials who exercised administrative power). The bailies, however, were unable to protect Cornfoot from a group of at least ten people, who seized her and apparently set out to "swim" her. Cornfoot was suspended from a rope extending from a ship's mast to the shore. From this rope she was swung from side to side while people in the crowd threw stones at her. After being cut loose, she was dragged along the shore by her heels. At that point a man placed a door on her chest while her assailants piled stones on top of the door, crushing her to death in a popular version of the judicial procedure known as *peine forte et dure,* which was used in English courts to force an accused criminal to enter a plea. According to one report, which may not be accurate, a man then drove his horse and sledge over Cornfoot's corpse several times.[8]

Like many accused witches who were lynched, Janet Cornfoot fell victim to a community that remained convinced she was guilty but was denied the satisfaction of having her convicted by a legitimate legal tribunal. When the opportunity arose to return her to Pittenweem, her assailants were waiting to give her the rough popular justice they believed she deserved. The responsibility for her murder did not lie entirely with the rabble that strung her up in the harbor. Just as responsible were the members of the town's ruling elite who promoted her prosecution in the first place and then either facilitated or condoned her lynching. It was, after all, the bailies of Pittenweem who failed to protect her from the furious mob. Not surprisingly, when the privy council investigated this gross miscarriage of justice, it recommended the initiation of legal proceedings against not only the people who pelted her with stones and pressed her to death but also the magistrates of the burgh as well.[9] Central authorities in Edinburgh had resisted the determination of local authorities to hold a local trial, but they were not able to prevent the lynching of Janet Cornfoot. Even more indicative of their jurisdictional weaknesses, they were unable to bring the lynchers to justice despite their best intention.

Poland. The lynching of Janet Cornfoot was a relatively isolated incident in the history of Scottish witch hunting. In Poland, however, the number of lynched witches was significantly greater than in Scotland or in any other early modern European state. The exact number of Polish lynchings will never be known. Bohdan B. Baranowski's estimate that Poles lynched as many as five thousand witches (while legally executing about ten thousand) was greatly exaggerated, but Baranowski did nonetheless present evidence that lynching was widespread in Poland.[10] Janusz Tazbir claimed that half the witches executed in Poland were lynched.[11] The main reason for this was the weakness of central state power and authority in a country that suffered peri-odic partitions and resisted the efforts of kings and ministers to implement a program of state building and royal absolutism. Faced with these constraints, the government repeatedly found it was incapable of taking action against witch murderers, leaving it to the local community to take justice into its own hands.

It is unclear whether local judges in Poland tolerated or participated in these lynchings. We do know that in 1690, the local judge in the village of Gnesen did not yield to popular pressure. When this judge acquitted a few accused witches in 1690, the villagers lynched not only the liberated women but also the judge himself.[12]

Witch Lynchings after Decriminalization

Witch trials came to an end at different times in the various countries of Europe, beginning in 1608 in the Dutch Republic (the northern provinces of the Netherlands) and ending in the Swiss canton of Glarus in 1782. Decrimi-nalization occurred either de jure, when legislation or executive edicts de-clared that witchcraft was no longer a crime, or de facto, when jurisdictions simply stopped trying and executing witches.[13] As elsewhere, lynchers in the Dutch Republic took action because they were convinced that their neigh-bors were responsible for their misfortunes and that there was no longer a possibility that the courts would bring them to justice.

Witchcraft scholars disagree whether the lynching of witches increased after decriminalization. It makes sense to assume that the number would rise considerably, since beliefs about witches among the rural population showed little sign of changing and official judicial action was no longer an option. On the other hand, decriminalization was usually accompanied by an increase in state judicial power, and the prospect that central or superior judicial au-thorities might proceed against lynchers could easily have discouraged angry and frustrated villagers from taking justice into their own hands.

The main question regarding the intensity of lynchings before and after decriminalization is not whether the raw numbers increased or decreased but whether there was a sustained pattern of witch lynching in the later pe-

riod. A clear geographical pattern emerges in lynchings after decriminalization. In western and central Europe, where central governments were able to
uphold the rule of law and take swift, decisive judicial action against lynchers, the number of lynchings was kept to a minimum. In those places where
the state had difficulty enforcing its judicial authority in the localities, most
notably in eastern Europe and postcolonial Africa, lynchings either continued to take place in large numbers or, in some places, actually increased.

Western Europe. In western Europe, witch lynchings became relatively infrequent after decriminalization. Isolated incidents took place in all western
European countries and continued into the twentieth century, but the successful prosecution of the people who had incited the lynchings proved to
be an effective deterrent to widespread persecution. In these countries the
state, which during the period of the trials had authorized and in many cases
facilitated witchcraft trials, now reversed its role and emerged as the prosecutor of the witches' assailants.

The success of the Parlement of Paris and to a lesser extent the other
French provincial parlements in controlling local justice provides the most
persuasive explanation why the number of witch lynchings in France declined rather than increased once the trials ended.[14] In the Dutch Republic,
where decriminalization took place earlier than in any other part of Europe,
the prosecution of lynchers at Amsterdam in 1624 and Rotterdam in 1628
and in a village outside Amsterdam in 1746 showed that while popular beliefs
about witches were still alive long after Dutch elites had abandoned them,
the state would not tolerate their illegal expression.[15] A larger number of
lynchings (at least ten) took place in the southern Netherlands, but these
were still infrequent enough to conform to the western/central European
pattern.[16]

Incidents of witch lynching in England illustrate both the durability of
popular beliefs in the period of the Enlightenment and the effectiveness of
the Crown to prosecute these illegal executions after decriminalization. Two
of these lynchings involved the swimming of suspected witches. At Frome,
Somerset, in 1731 a woman died after being subject to the water ordeal with
"200 spectators huzzing and abetting the riot."[17] Twenty years later Ruth
Osborne, a sixty-nine-year-old resident of a workhouse in Tring, Hertford-
shire, drowned when a small group of men submitted her and her husband,
John Osborne, to the water ordeal before a crowd estimated at five thousand
people.[18] Thomas Colley, a local chimneysweep, was tried and executed for
the murder. Since those incidents, which occurred just before and shortly

after the repeal of the English witchcraft statute of 1604 in 1736, only isolated lynchings have occurred in England. In 1808, for example, villagers in Cambridgeshire dragged Ann Izzard, a suspected witch, out of bed and beat her mercilessly with planks of wood. She survived, but a woman who had saved her life was later beaten and died of her wounds. In 1875 a man from Warwickshire attacked Ann Tennant with a pitchfork, intending "to draw her blood in order to break her power over him."[19] The lyncher, James Haywood, who claimed that he considered it his duty to kill witches, was charged with murder but was declared not guilty by reason of insanity. In 2012 two residents of east London, Eric Bikubi and Magalie Bamu, were convicted of the brutal murder of Bamu's fifteen-year-old brother, whom Bikubi had accused of witchcraft and sorcery, claiming that the boy had cast spells on another child in the family.[20]

In Denmark, where the last legal execution took place in 1693 but witchcraft had not yet been decriminalized by statute, a lynching occurred in the village of Øster Grønning in Salling in 1722 when a group of villagers burned Dorte Jensdatter to death in her home for allegedly killing two children and a number of livestock by witchcraft. The Salling district court tried and beheaded two of the ringleaders of this lynching for murder and sentenced one of their accomplices to forced labor for life, while five others were given the much more lenient sentence of doing public penance.[21]

Similar instances of witch lynching can be found throughout the records of western and central Europe in the eighteenth, nineteenth, and twentieth centuries. In 1894 the husbands, relatives, and friends of Bridget Cleary, a young married woman from Clonmell, Tipperary, in Ireland beat and burned her to death on the suspicion that the real Bridget had been taken away by fairies and that a witch had been put in her place.[22] In 1911, in the vicinity of Perugia, Italy, farmers seized an old woman reputed to be a witch and burned her to death in a lime kiln.[23] In 1976 residents of a small German village attacked Elizabeth Hahn, a poor, elderly spinster who was widely suspected of being a witch and keeping familiars in the form of dogs. Her neighbors shunned her, threw rocks at her, threatened to beat her to death, and eventually set fire to her house, badly burning her and killing all of her animals, because they thought she was casting hexes on them.[24] One year later two brothers in a village near Alençon, France, were tried for murdering a village sorcerer who kept a cabin full of magical potions.[25] In all these cases the state took decisive action against the people responsible for the lynchings, thereby minimizing or preventing further extrajudicial efforts to enforce standards of popular justice.

Eastern Europe. In eastern Europe the relative weakness of central or superior state judicial control over local communities, coupled with the strength of popular beliefs about witches, has resulted in far more witch lynchings than in the western and central Europe. In Poland, for example, when witchcraft was decriminalized in 1776, witch lynchings continued to take place as frequently as during the period of the trials.[26] Lynching was also a frequent occurrence in Hungary, especially in those areas that were controlled by the Ottoman Empire.

The most numerous witch lynchings in eastern Europe after decriminalization took place in nineteenth-century Russia, where peasants apparently killed hundreds of people they believed had used witchcraft to cause droughts, famines, crop failures, and in some cases, sexual impotence. Most of these incidents took place between 1870 and 1900, when peasant lawlessness was a severe problem. In 1879 a group of about two hundred peasants in the village of Vrachev burned alive an impoverished woman whom they suspected of causing an outbreak of "falling sickness" in the village.[27]

Many of these lynchings in Russia arose when shriekers—women allegedly possessed by the devil—accused witches of having caused their possession.[28] As in other parts of Europe, lynchings in Russia included water ordeals and severe beatings, but Russian lynchers also mutilated the corpses of their victims and sometimes displayed those parts to discourage further acts of witchcraft.

WITCH LYNCHING BEYOND EUROPE

The witch lynchings that have taken the greatest toll in human life since 1800 have occurred not in Europe but in Africa and Asia. Lynchings in these countries have increased greatly in the closing years of the twentieth century and the first decade of the twenty-first. The strength of traditional beliefs about witches, the difficulty that governments have had punishing offenders, and widespread rural poverty have all contributed to this outbreak of illegal witch hunting in non-Western lands.

Africa. The belief in witches in Africa has a long history, and those beliefs resemble European beliefs about witches in many respects. Witches in Africa, as they were in early modern Europe, are believed to be capable of using magical powers to bring harm to their neighbors and their neighbors' animals and crops. African witches allegedly cause illness and death, especially sudden death, although usually not the deaths of young children. African witches are accused of destroying crops, preventing cows from giving milk, causing women to miscarry, and impeding fertility.[29]

Campaigns to eliminate African witches—known as "witch-cleansing" movements—predated the beginning of European imperial rule in the nineteenth century. There are records of sustained prosecutions among the Malagasy in Madagascar, the Bechuana in Botswana, the Bakweri and the Ndebele in Cameroon, and the Pondo in South Africa in the late nineteenth century, before the onset of European rule.[30] Tribal chieftains sometimes presided over these movements, but without the state apparatus of European countries, the executions bore a closer resemblance to European lynchings than to the trials held in European courtrooms.

There is little question, however, that these witch-cleansing movements increased in frequency after the establishment of European colonial rule. The reason for this increase is ironically that the "enlightened" European rulers, who had already rejected their beliefs about witches, tried to put an end to the witch hunts, a course of action Africans considered to be an assault on their beliefs and traditions. When witches were brought before colonial courts, they were regularly set free on the grounds that the crime could not be proved at law.[31] This refusal to convict witches gave Africans the impression that the law was at the service of the witch rather than the victim. Consequently African communities often took the law into their own hands, trying witches summarily by means of the ordeal and thus rejecting the due process that colonial administrators were trying to enforce.[32]

The emancipation of African colonies from European rule in the second half of the twentieth century has in many ways made the situation worse. Without the restraint imposed by skeptical Western colonial administrators, African communities have experienced a new freedom in pursuing witches. This became evident in South Africa in the late 1980s and early 1990s. In 1957, shortly after South Africa became a republic controlled by Afrikaners, the South African parliament passed the Witchcraft Suppression Act No. 3. The main thrust of the act was to facilitate the prosecution of someone who had killed a witch or had been serving as a witch finder or witch doctor. The act, therefore, which was the work of a white, apartheid government, was based solidly in European skepticism regarding the reality of witchcraft. It was intended to suppress belief in witchcraft.[33] The act reflected the spirit of colonial European rule, professing a disbelief in the reality of witchcraft and prescribing the most serious punishments—imprisonment up to twenty years—not for the witches themselves but for those who attacked them.

During the struggle against the Afrikaner government in the 1980s, the illegal hunting of South African witches in direct violation of the Witchcraft Suppression Act (which was amended in 1970) became more frequent. The African National Congress (ANC), the main resistance organization, did not endorse these witch-cleansing movements, but many black South Africans involved in the resistance began to take illegal action against those whom they suspected of witchcraft. In this way the hunting of witches became politicized, and the Witchcraft Suppression Act became a symbol of white insensitivity to native African culture. The lynching of witches became a means of political mobilization. After resistance meetings and at the urging of local witch-hunting committees, hundreds of people, carrying ANC banners and chanting songs of freedom, would march through villages, pulling accused witches out of their houses, stoning and beating them, and then burning down their houses with them inside.[34]

One of the groups that became involved in this witchcraft eradication campaign during these years was an informal association of male youths known as the Comrades. In 1986 the Comrades attacked more than 150 alleged witches in the Bushbuckridge region of the South African lowveld, killing thirty-six of them.[35] In 1990 a series of unexpected deaths in Green Valley incited groups of the Comrades to conduct another witch hunt, demolishing the homes of suspected witches, whipping some of them, and conducting witch-finding rituals that pressured others to name their accomplices publicly.[36] In the same year, somewhere between three hundred and four hundred accused witches in Venda sought police protection because their houses had been burned down.

The release of Nelson Mandela from prison in 1991 and the establishment of ANC rule in 1994 did not put an end to the witch-cleansing movements, especially since the Witchcraft Suppression Act remained in force. In 1994, just before the elections that brought the ANC to power, sixty witches were killed in the Northern Province. In Zebediela a spate of such lynchings took place within the space of three months in the late 1990s, including the burning to death of twelve alleged witches. The killings have continued into the twenty-first century, although in reduced numbers. In 2003 five family members were arrested for killing an eighty-year-old woman who was believed to be the cause of a young child's death.[37]

The murder of witches in various regions of Tanzania illustrates a second pattern of modern African witch hunting. In August 1999 Tanzania's Criminal Investigations Department reported that in the previous eighteen months more than 350 persons had been killed by angry villagers for using witchcraft to kill their loved ones or inflict curses that made them fail in business or reduce their harvests. Most of the accused witches were old women, some of whose eyes had turned red after years of cooking in the smoke-filled kilns in their huts.[38]

The witch murders in Tanzania have continued into the twenty-first century, as villagers in northern regions along the shores of Lake Victoria have been murdering more than a hundred old women each year for allegedly causing illness, death, or other misfortunes. Those who have survived such attacks, such as the eighty-year-old Magdale Ndila, have suffered blows to the head or the severing of an arm or hand.[39] Traditional healers have often abetted these attacks by suggesting that killing alleged witches would help to remedy medical problems. Deteriorating economic conditions have often aggravated these assaults.[40] In size and motivation modern Tanzanian witch hunts bear a close resemblance to the witch hunts that occurred in early modern Europe. The main difference is that the Tanzanian witch hunts, unlike those in Europe, have lacked any legal authority. In that respect they resemble the lynchings of witches that occurred mainly after the great European witch hunts had ended.

Illegal executions have taken place in other African nations, most notably Kenya, where the killings have also been conducted without any legal sanction. In September 1998, ten elderly suspected witches in Kenya were killed by a local vigilante group in revenge for the abduction of a villager who was forced to exhume a corpse and then eat the decomposing flesh.[41]

New Guinea. Recent lynchings in Africa have their counterpart in the South Pacific island nation of New Guinea, where the *Post-Courier* newspaper reported in January 2009 that more than fifty people had been killed in two Highland provinces in the previous year. In a widely reported case, a group of people in rural Papua New Guinea dragged a woman in her late teens or early twenties to a dumping ground outside the city of Mount Hagen. They stripped her naked, bound her hands and legs, stuffed a cloth in her mouth, tied her to a log, and set her on fire. Such acts of barbarism are not new. A study of Papua New Guinea families conducted in the 1990s revealed that one-third of all adult deaths in the previous forty-two years were collective killings of suspected witches, known in that country as *sangumas*.[42]

Police have not yet been successful in containing or prosecuting this form of collective violence against alleged witches.

One factor contributing to the recent spate of witch lynchings in Papua New Guinea has been the belief that witches, rather than the HIV virus, cause AIDS, which is epidemic in that country. All witch lynchings are based on the belief that witches use their magical powers to cause illness, death, or some personal or communal misfortune. The specific diseases that allegedly cause illness or death vary from place to place and from time to time. In New Guinea the widespread harm caused by AIDS and the fear of its destructive power in a population with little medical knowledge have given a new dimension to traditional beliefs about witches.

India. A number of witch lynchings have taken place in tribal areas of India. In 2003 a mob in the eastern state of Jharkhand burned to death two women accused of witchcraft. The women, who were accused of making a neighbor sick, were dragged into a field, covered with hay and paraffin, and set on fire. In many cases local priests, tribal chiefs, and relatives have identified widows and divorcees as witches so that they could take control of their property.[43] In 2009 a local cleric was the first person to identify five Muslim women in Jharkhand as witches. The women were stripped, beaten, and forced to eat excrement at a local playground. No one in the large mob that witnessed the events came forward to help the victims, but the police eventually took the victims into protective custody and brought charges against eleven villagers. Some of these villagers claimed to be possessed by a holy spirit that allowed them to identify witches, a claim made by many accusers of witches in early modern Europe.[44]

In the northeastern state of Assam more than 500 people were lynched between 2004 and 2009 for allegedly practicing witchcraft, and about 250 suspected witches were killed in neighboring Bengal. Most of the witch lynchings in Assam have come at the hands of Santhal tribesmen, who greatly fear the power of witchcraft to cause harm. Family rivalries often inspire these killings, and the perpetrators usually seize the land of the alleged witches after killing them. The execution of two couples and a teenage girl in two separate incidents in August 2006 conformed to this pattern of violence against families suspected of witchcraft.[45] In 2008 Santhal tribesmen stoned to death four members of a family in a remote village of Assam. Sixty-five-year-old Lakhan Majhi, his wife, his son, and his daughter-in-law were attacked after two hundred of Majhi's neighbors accused him of casting a spell on a villager who died after falling sick.[46]

Baran Choudhury, a Bengal police officer, has blamed powerful people in the community for spearheading these witch lynchings. In some cases village elites target members of isolated families who own some landed property, but in other cases they kill entire families because they have challenged the authority of community elders.[47] In either case the victims of mob violence have occupied positions in their communities similar to those of accused witches in early modern Europe. These suspected witches are either the most vulnerable members of society or individuals who did not conform to prevailing social and cultural norms of their communities.

A global history of witch lynching, both past and present, reveals one clear pattern: the mobs that hanged, burned, stoned, or beat people to death for allegedly practicing witchcraft did so because they believed the witches were responsible for harming them or their neighbors by magical means, not because they had made pacts with the devil or worshipped him in nocturnal assemblies. Judges, inquisitors, and magistrates in early modern Europe often prosecuted witches because they were believed to be servants of Satan, but the villagers who lynched witches did so because they were convinced that the evil people in their midst had caused the misfortunes that had befallen them, their families, and their communities.

Whereas alleged European, African, and Asian witches were lynched because they were believed to have caused harm by magical means, African Americans were hanged or burned to death for a variety of alleged crimes, including rape, theft, and murder, but not for practicing magic. In most other respects, however, witch lynchings have had a great deal in common with the lynching of African Americans. Alleged European, African, and Asian witches who have been lynched, just like the victims of lynching in America, have been subjected to mob violence with the compliance or direction of local judicial authorities; they have been judged in a summary fashion by communal standards of justice without due process of law; and they have fallen victim to these illegal attacks only when higher judicial authorities were unable to exercise effective control over local justice. The lynching of accused witches, just like the lynching of African Americans, has been inspired by the perceived threat represented by subordinate or marginalized segments of the population. These fears were often aggravated by fantasies that these victims had engaged in activities that threatened the very fabric of society.

NOTES

1. Wolfgang Behringer, "Lynching," in *Encyclopedia of Witchcraft: The Western Tradition*, ed. Richard M. Golden (Santa Barbara, CA: ABC-CLIO, 2006), 3:683.

2. Wolfgang Behringer, "Weather, Hunger and Fear: The Origins of the European Witch Prosecutions in Climate, Society and Mentality," *German History* 13 (1995): 1–27.

3. Alfred Soman, "Witch Lynching at Juniville," *Natural History* 95 (1986): 8–15.

4. Behringer, "Lynching," 683. The last legal execution in the region took place in 1625. Soman, "Witch Lynching at Juniville," 15.

5. Gustav Henningsen, "Witch Persecution after the Era of the Witch Trials," *ARV-Scandinavian Yearbook of Folklore* 44 (1988): 103–53.

6. Gustav Henningsen, "La inquisicion y las brujas," in *L'inquisizione: atti del simposio internazionale*, ed. Agostino Borromeo (Vatican City: Biblioteca Apostolica Vaticana, 2003), 567–605.

7. Rainer Decker, *Witchcraft and the Papacy: An Account Drawing on the Formerly Secret Records of the Roman Inquisition*, trans. H. C. Erik Midelfort (Charlottesville: University of Virginia Press, 2008), 172–73.

8. See Brian P. Levack, *Witch-Hunting in Scotland: Law, Politics and Religion* (London: Routledge, 2008), chapter 9.

9. Scottish National Archives, PC1/53, p. 359.

10. Bohdan B. Baranowski, *Procesy czarownic w Polsce w XVII i XVIII wieku* (Lódz: Lódzkie Towarzystwo Naukowe, 1952), 30–31, 175. Baranowski later lowered his estimates. See his afterword to K. Baschwitz, *Czarownice: Dzieje procesów o czary* (Warsaw: Cyklady, 1963), 430. For a denial that there were mass lynchings in Poland, see Michael Ostling, *Between the Devil and the Host: Imagining Witchcraft in Early Modern Poland* (Oxford: Oxford University Press, 2011), 17.

11. Janusz Tazbir, "Hexenprozesse in Polen," *Archiv für Reformationsgeschichte* 71 (1980): 299.

12. Ibid.

13. Brian P. Levack, "The Decline and End of Witchcraft Prosecutions," in *The Eighteenth and Nineteenth Centuries*, ed. Bengt Ankarloo and Stuart Clark, Witchcraft and Magic in Europe (London: Athlone, 1999), 74–78.

14. Marijke Gijswijt-Hofstra, "Witchcraft after the Witch Trials," in Ankarloo and Clark, *Eighteenth and Nineteenth Centuries*, 121–22; Alfred Soman, "La décriminalization de la sorcellerie en France," *Histoire, économie et société* 4 (1985): 198.

15. Behringer, "Lynching," 683.

16. Marie-Sylvie Dupont-Bouchat, "Le diable apprivoisée. La sorcellerie revisitée: magie et sorcellerie au XIX siècle," in *Magie et sorcellerie en Europe du Moyen Âge à nos jours*, ed. Robert Muchembled (Paris: A. Colin, 1994), 235–66; Gijswijt-Hofstra, "Witchcraft after the Witch Trials," 113–16.

17. Owen Davies, *Witchcraft, Magic and Culture, 1736–1951* (Manchester: Manchester University Press, 1999), 90.

18. W. B. Carnochan, "Witch-Hunting and Belief in 1751: The Case of Thomas Colley and Ruth Osborne," *Journal of Social History* 4 (1970–71): 388–403.

19. Owen Davies, *Witchcraft, Magic and Culture, 1736–1951* (Manchester: Manchester University Press, 1999), 41, 111.

20. BBC News, March 1, 2012.

21. Henningsen, "Witch Persecution," 110–19.

22. Patrick Byrne, *Witchcraft in Ireland* (Cork: Mercier, 1967), 56–68; Angela Bourke, *The Burning of Bridget Cleary: A True Story* (New York: Viking, 2000).

23. W. G. Soldan and H. Heppe, *Geschichte der Hexenprozesse,* ed. M. Bauer (Munich: G. Müller, 1912), 2:350.

24. Hans Sebald, *Witchcraft: The Heritage of a Heresy* (New York: Elsevier, 1978), 223.

25. Agence France-Press, May 13, 1977. The case is discussed in Gustav Henningsen, *The Witches' Advocate: Basque Witchcraft and the Spanish Inquisition (1609–1614)* (Reno: University of Nevada Press, 1980), 18.

26. Aldona Christina Schiffmann, "The Witch and Crime: The Persecution of Witches in Twentieth-Century Poland," *ARV-Scandinavian Yearbook of Folklore* 43 (1987): 147–67.

27. Stephen P. Frank, "Popular Justice, Community and Culture among the Russian Peasantry, 1870–1900," *Russian Review* 46 (1987): 260–61. The government brought charges against sixteen of the villagers who had been most responsible for the lynching. Of these, three who confessed were subjected to church penitence; the others went free.

28. Christine D. Worobec, *Possessed: Women, Witches, and Demons in Imperial Russia* (DeKalb: Northern Illinois University Press, 2001), 86–108.

29. Alan Macfarlane, *Witchcraft in Tudor and Stuart England: A Regional and Comparative Study* (New York: Harper and Row, 1970), 214.

30. Stephen Ellis, "Witch-Hunting in Central Madagascar, 1828–1861," *Past & Present* 175 (2002): 90–123; Wolfgang Behringer, *Witches and Witch Hunts: A Global History* (London: Polity, 2004), 198–200.

31. See Richard D. Waller, "Witchcraft and Colonial Law in Kenya," *Past & Present* 180 (2003): 241–75.

32. Cyprian F. Fisiy, "Containing Occult Practices: Witchcraft Trials in Cameroon," *African Studies Review* 41 (1998): 148–51. For a description of a witch-finding movement in Nyasaland and Rhodesia in 1934 and another movement in the late 1940s in West Africa, see Geoffrey Parrinder, *Witchcraft: European and African* (London: Faber and Faber, 1963), 170–80.

33. "Witchcraft Suppression Act No. 3 of 1957," in *Witchcraft Violence and the Law in South Africa,* ed. John Hund (Pretoria: Protea Book House, 2003), 149–50.

34. Johannes Harnischfeger, "Witchcraft and the State in South Africa," in Hund, *Witchcraft Violence and the Law,* 52; A. de V. Minnaar, "Witch Killing with Respect to the Northern Province of South Africa," in *Violence in South Africa: A Variety of Perspectives,* ed. E. Bornman, R. Van Eeden, and M. Wentzel (Pretoria: HSRC, 1998), 175–79.

35. Isak A. Niehaus, "The ANC's Dilemma: The Symbolic Politics of Three Witch-Hunts in the South African Lowveld, 1990–1995," *African Studies Review* 41 (1998): 93–99; Parrinder, *Witchcraft*, 145–47.

36. Niehaus, "The ANC's Dilemma."

37. Harnischfeger, "Witchcraft and the State," 40

38. Reuters, August 3, 1999.

39. BBC News World, October 29, 2002.

40. See R. G. Abrahams, ed., *Witchcraft in Contemporary Tanzania* (Cambridge: Cambridge University Press, 1994).

41. BBC News World, September 5, 1998.

42. Bruce M. Knauft, *From Primitive to Postcolonial in Melanesia and Anthropology* (Ann Arbor: University of Michigan Press, 1999).

43. BBC News, July 3, 2003.

44. BBC News, October 20, 2009. On the role of demoniacs in witch hunting in early modern Europe, see Brian P. Levack, ed., *The Witchcraft Sourcebook* (London: Routledge, 2004), 231–73.

45. BBC News, August 23, 2006.

46. BBC News, June 12, 2008.

47. Ibid.

"This Community Will Not in the Future Be Disgraced"

Rafael Benavides and the Decline of Lynching in New Mexico

WILLIAM D. CARRIGAN AND CLIVE WEBB

A T 11:15 ON THE MORNING of Friday, November 16, 1928, four masked men marched into the San Juan County Hospital in Farmington, a remote town in northern New Mexico. The men seized one of the patients, a Spanish-speaking sheepherder of Mexican descent named Rafael Benavides, and bundled him into the back of a pickup truck. Accompanied by a second vehicle carrying six other men, the kidnappers sped to an abandoned farm two miles north of town. There, they forced their victim to stand on the back of one of the trucks as a rope was tied around his neck and fastened to a locust tree. The vehicle then accelerated forward, snapping Benavides's neck as his body became suspended above the ground.

Less than twenty-four hours earlier, Benavides had been admitted to the hospital with a serious gunshot wound. The injury was inflicted when he attempted to escape a sheriff's posse pursuing him for an assault upon a local farmer's wife. According to the physicians who treated him, Benavides had only hours to live. In their words, the lynching "probably saved the criminal a good deal of suffering." Benavides was thirty-nine years old.[1]

In many respects the lynching of Rafael Benavides conforms to the broader patterns of mob violence throughout the American West and the larger world. The men responsible for his murder acted in open disobedience of the law and with the approval of elements of the community, and no member of the mob was ever brought to justice. A grand jury hearing on the murder occurred on December 4, 1928. Judge Reed Holloman issued a stern instruction to the jurors to set an example, so "that this community will not in the future be disgraced in the eyes of the state and the United States as it recently was." However, although more than fifty witnesses were called to testify, the jury failed to indict a single member of the mob. As one newspaper observed, the authorities had "run against a rock wall" in their efforts to secure a conviction.[2]

The Benavides case is nonetheless of crucial significance. The historian Robert Tórrez believes Benavides to be the last ethnic Mexican lynched in the state of New Mexico.[3] F. Arturo Rosales, one of the foremost experts on anti-Mexican violence, goes further, arguing that Benavides was the last ethnic Mexican lynched in the entire United States.[4] It is impossible to verify these claims for a variety of reasons, including the vexing question of how one defines lynching. Nevertheless, there is little doubt that no later U.S. mob executed an ethnic Mexican with such a public disregard for legal repercussions. The Benavides murder, described by contemporaries as a lynching, therefore represents an important turning point in the history of anti-Mexican violence. Mob violence against persons of Mexican descent was a widespread phenomenon in the American Southwest after the U.S.-Mexican War. Such violence was often committed with the implicit support of law officers and, in many instances, with their direct participation. Benavides was taken by masked intruders from a public place and hanged in broad daylight. The men responsible for the crime were not prosecuted despite the fact that their identities were well known. Although such a series of events had been common in the preceding eight decades, the pattern of mob violence changed after the Benavides lynching. Mexicans continued to live with the danger of mob violence after 1928. However, any attacks against them took place surreptitiously rather than in open defiance of the law, and mobs received more public censure than support.[5]

This essay places the Benavides lynching both in the context of lynching in New Mexico and within the broader framework of the decline and end of mob violence against Mexicans. The collective, extralegal killing of Mexicans was a common occurrence in the borderlands, but patterns of mob violence differed dramatically from region to region, from state to state, and even from country to country. Lynching in New Mexico contrasted sharply with mob violence even in nearby states such as Texas, California, and Arizona, and the United States was far from the only nation to have its legal authorities circumvented by mobs. Many recent Mexican immigrants to New Mexico had experienced mob violence within Mexico, especially during the turbulent decade of the Mexican Revolution. While the local context is crucially important, the Benavides case also provides insights into the larger regional decline of mob violence against Mexicans.

By 1928, northern New Mexico had been firmly controlled by the United States for many decades. However, in the previous century, the sovereignty and control of New Mexico was much in dispute. Spanish-speaking settlers arrived during the seventeenth century. Initially, they entered a region at least partially controlled by Native Americans. Whether under Spanish rule (until 1821), as residents of an independent Mexico (until 1836) or a disputed territory claimed by Mexico and Texas (until 1848), as American citizens living in a U.S. territory (until 1912), or as residents of the state of New Mexico (after 1912), the lives of those Spanish speakers living in and around present-day Farmington changed very little. They raised sheep and saw themselves as "Hispanos" or "Nuevomexicanos," no matter the ruling government of the moment. When Anglos arrived in large numbers at the end of the nineteenth century, they often identified the region's longtime residents as "Mexicans," even though the term was resented by Nuevomexicanos, who were American citizens by virtue of the Treaty of Guadalupe Hidalgo (or by birth after that date).[6]

As for the town of Farmington itself, settlers began to congregate on the future location of the town—some 150 miles north of Santa Fe and 20 miles south of the Colorado border—as early as 1876, but the community was not incorporated as a town until 25 years later. The local economy was based principally upon ranching and agriculture. Limited commercial and industrial development restricted population growth during the early days. By 1910 there were still only 785 people in the town. Although the discovery of oil during the interwar era caused the hurried purchase of land by oil companies, by the late 1920s Farmington had not become a boom town. By 1930, the entire population of San Juan County was only 14,701.[7]

Although the population remained small, there were important differences among the peoples of the region. Some were obvious. The Anglo immigrants were recent arrivals, spoke English, and were Protestant, whereas the Nuevomexicano families had settled earlier, spoke Spanish, and were Catholic. While both groups were principally ranchers, Nuevomexicanos grazed sheep, while the majority of New Mexican Anglos raised cattle.

Yet there were also forces unifying the two groups. Local farmers of both ethnic groups sold their produce to mining camps across the border in Colorado. While the two groups did not identify with each other, they also saw themselves as landowners and distinct from their Navajo neighbors and more recent Mexican immigrants who were contracted as herders and laborers by both Anglo and Nuevomexicano ranchers. And perhaps most important, both groups had experience with disregarding legal procedures and inflicting mob violence.

Lynching-like violence was not something new, and it had not just been brought in by the Anglo settlers who arrived in the region. Spanish speakers, first in the Mexican North and then in the American Southwest, had experience of mob violence, which was, after all, a tool for frontier settlers throughout world history. In 1836, vigilantes in Los Angeles executed Gervasio Alipás for the murder of Domingo Félix, "a great ranchero" whose wife had been seduced by Alipás.[8] Mexican-on-Mexican mob violence did not cease with American conquest in 1848. In 1852, a California mob reported to include "principally Mexicans" hanged three of their countrymen near Santa Cruz for horse theft.[9] In 1871, an Albuquerque mob of masked Spanish speakers hanged Diego Lucero for the murder of Manuel Garcia y Gallegos.[10] In 1893, in Las Vegas, New Mexico, a mob hanged a Mexican outlaw leader for the murder of a ranch hand. According to the *Las Vegas Daily Optic,* the "mob was said to number 1000 with 900 being Hispanic."[11]

What contribution did Anglo-American settlers make, then, to the tradition of mob violence that already existed among Spanish speakers in the American West? Like others throughout the world, Spanish speakers both in Mexico and in the United States adopted the word *lynching* from their Anglo-American neighbors. Initially the literal "ley de lynch" was common, but quickly the words *linchar* (to lynch), *linchado* (lynched), and *linchamiento* (lynching) developed in the Spanish-language press. The term entered the Spanish language at least as early as the 1850s and was so commonplace by the 1890s that it could appear alone in a newspaper's column heading with no need for explanation. Editors and others used these new Spanish words to describe certain acts of mob violence no matter whether the mob was composed of English or Spanish speakers. Yet, at the same time, there also seemed to be a connotation that Americans were more prone to commit "linchamientos" than other groups and that when they did, they were more likely to target ethnic Mexicans. For example, the California editor Francisco P. Ramirez creatively coined the term "linchocracia" (lynchocracy) to condemn and describe Anglo-orchestrated anti-Mexican mob violence in the 1850s.[12] Throughout the late nineteenth and early twentieth centuries, numerous individuals echoed Ramirez's protests of the targeting of Mexicans and Mexican Americans by Anglo mobs. Such protests had failed to end such mob violence, but this essay argues that the "linchamiento" of Rafael Benavides proved a turning point. Emphasis is placed on three particular factors: the growth of institutionalized legal systems, a change in the climate of public opinion, and the renewed power of the new Mexican government to protect its citizens both within its own borders and on American soil.

Given the long history of mob violence against Spanish speakers both by other Spanish speakers and by Anglo mobs, the execution of Rafael Benavides could not have been surprising to the residents of the small and relatively remote community of Farmington. Benavides himself, like most victims of lynching, remains largely unknown to historians. Little is known of his life. He was born into an apparently impoverished family in Salazar, New Mexico, in 1889. His birth in an American territory made him an American citizen, though many Anglos continued to perceive all persons of Mexican descent as "Mexican" outsiders, no matter their nativity.[13]

Regardless of his citizenship, with no formal education, Benavides was unable to read or write and therefore restricted to the life of a manual laborer. Although both a husband and father, he appears to have been separated from his family, who were living across the border in Mancos, Colorado, at the time of his death. The probable reason for the separation was Benavides's earlier conviction for a criminal offense, details of which will be revealed later. This would certainly explain the response of his wife when asked whether she wanted his body returned for committal. Her only words were "Bury him."[14]

The circumstances surrounding the lynching were established in some detail by contemporary newspaper reports. On the night of Wednesday, November 14, 1928, a drunken Benavides broke into the home of a Spanish-speaking family in the nearby town of Aztec and attempted to assault a young girl, only to be scared off by the screams of her sister. Benavides then became involved in a brawl when he attempted to force entry into another house. Eventually he made his way to the ranch of a prominent Anglo farmer, George Lewis. Although Lewis was away on a hunting trip, his wife was asleep at home. Awoken by Benavides, Mrs. Lewis attempted to defend herself with a shotgun, only to discover it was empty. Benavides physically assaulted the farmer's wife and then carried her to a remote hillside, where he left her naked and unconscious. The sixty-year-old woman sustained injuries to her face and chest, including boot marks where she had been furiously kicked. When she regained consciousness some hours later, she staggered to the nearest house, where an alarm was raised. Sheriff George Blancett assembled a posse, which pursued Benavides to the loft of an abandoned house near the Colorado border. When Benavides refused an order to surrender, the posse fired a series of shots into the house, one of which struck the fugitive in the abdomen. Benavides was then arrested and returned to Farmington.[15]

Informed that Benavides would not recover from his wound, Blancett withdrew an armed guard on the hospital. The masked men who abducted Benavides therefore faced no resistance. According to one rumor, Benavides himself struggled forcefully, "striking and biting his kidnappers." In his fearful rage he is reputed to have pushed one of his assailants out of the truck as it sped toward the abandoned farm. This story may account for the bruise above one of Benavides's eyes where the butt of a revolver struck him. At the same time, it seems improbable that a dying man who had been administered a powerful sedative should have summoned up such reserves of physical energy.[16] There is certainly no intimation of superhuman strength in the haunting image of Benavides captured by a local photographer. In the picture, the dead man hangs suspended from a tree limb, his head bowed to his chest, his hands tied behind his back.[17]

Before assessing the political repercussions of the Benavides lynching, it is important to place the case within the broader historical context of mob violence in New Mexico.[18] Between 1848 and 1928, our research suggests that at least fifty-four persons of Mexican descent in New Mexico met their deaths at the hands of lynch mobs. During the same time period, we calculate that at least 597 persons of Mexican origin or descent were lynched in all of the southwestern states.[19]

Identifying and counting victims of lynch mobs is an inexact science at best. We readily admit that our list of lynching victims is imperfect. There are undoubtedly victims of mob violence who do not appear in our data. Some whom we do include may not merit inclusion in the eyes of others. We claim only that we have been consistent according to our own understanding of lynching. In compiling the data, we have followed the lead of most scholars of mob violence and adopted the definition of *lynching* established by the National Association for the Advancement of Colored People (NAACP): a retributive act of murder for which those responsible claim to act in the interests of justice, tradition, or community order.

It should be noted that this definition was not universally agreed upon by lynching activists when it was proposed in 1940. Such a definition certainly did not govern the use of the word *lynching* by Anglos or Mexicans prior to 1940. The definition of the word varied according to the race, ethnicity, and class of the speaker. All of this is to underline the difficulties of using the word *lynching,* an American word that maintains an American connotation even when translated into other languages, for anyone interested in studying acts of extralegal violence, acts that history reveals are not limited to American mobs.[20]

In any event, numbers of ethnic Mexicans killed by mobs provide only a part of the story. Mob violence in New Mexico can be truly understood only in the broader context of racial and ethnic relations in the state and, in particular, in the process of cultural and political accommodation between the state's Anglo and Nuevomexicano elites. Anglos initially settled New Mexico in small numbers. As late as 1900, there were only 50,000 Anglos in the territory, compared with 125,000 Nuevomexicanos. As a result, many early pioneers intermarried with the Nuevomexicano population. By 1870, this situation was true of 90 percent of the married Anglo men in Las Cruces; in Mesilla, 83 percent; and in Doña Ana, 78 percent. This cultural interaction muted racial and ethnic tensions between the two peoples. The overwhelming size of the Nuevomexicano population also constrained Anglos from assuming hegemonic control of the political system. In many areas of the southwestern states during the nineteenth and early twentieth centuries, Mexican Americans were effectively disfranchised. By contrast, the Nuevomexicano elite in New Mexico wielded political power on a scale unparalleled in any other part of the American Southwest. Although Anglos attained control of the territorial legislature in 1886, Nuevomexicanos continued to hold elected office at all levels of government. As late as 1909, eleven of the twenty-one representatives in the New Mexico House of Representatives were Nuevomexicanos. Four Nuevomexicanos also served as governor in the years prior to Benavides's murder: Donaciano Vigil (1847–48), Miguel Otero (1897–1906), Ezequiel Cabeza de Baca (1918), and Octaviano Larrazolo (1918–19). A similar arrangement of racial power sharing operated within the criminal justice system. While Anglos monopolized the most eminent positions within the legal hierarchy, Nuevomexicanos controlled important elected offices such as sheriff. The active participation of Nuevomexicanos in the political and legal systems protected against the unrestrained power of Anglos and promoted racial and ethnic cooperation over conflict. As Charles Montgomery affirms, Anglos and Nuevomexicanos were "locked in a precarious balance of power, a sometimes cooperative though always suspicious relationship that redounded to all levels of New Mexico society."[21]

The ties between the Anglo and Nuevomexicano elites were also secured by the campaign to attain statehood for New Mexico. New Mexico remained a territory under federal jurisdiction until 1912. Congressional opposition to statehood rested on the racist assumption that only a white majority population could be entrusted with the responsibility of self-government. One pamphlet distributed in Santa Fe argued that the "Territory should not be admitted as a State because the majority of its inhabitants" were "catholic" and a "mixture of peons and Indians" and therefore "a people unworthy to live in the great American Republic."[22] The Nuevomexicano elite attempted to establish their claim to a white racial identity and the political privileges this bestowed by calling themselves "Spanish Americans," a name which invoked their common European heritage with Anglos. The Anglo elite supported Nuevomexicanos in their assertion of whiteness, since it represented the best strategy of securing statehood. In this and other respects, the elites shared common class and political interests that transcended ethnic antagonism.[23]

The cultural, political, and economic interaction between Anglo and Nuevomexicano elites affected the pattern of mob violence in New Mexico. In the southern states, the primary motivation of mob violence against African Americans was racial prejudice. Southern whites used terror and intimidation as a means of consolidating their control of the region. By contrast, lynching in New Mexico cut across racial and ethnic lines. Lynching protected the economic interests of the propertied classes, both Anglo and Nuevomexicano. The Nuevomexicano elite consciously distinguished itself from the majority Mexican population and was prepared to orchestrate acts of mob violence in defense of its socially and economically privileged status. In 1893, for instance, Cecilio Lucero, a member of a notorious gang, was arrested in Las Vegas for the murder of a ranch hand who had caught him stealing sheep. Members of the community seized Lucero from his prison cell and hanged him.[24] Although Mexican mobs lynched Mexicans in other parts of the Southwest, such intra-ethnic violence was far more common in New Mexico.[25]

There were nonetheless clear constraints to the extralegal force commanded by the Nuevomexicano elite. The power-sharing relationship between Anglos and Nuevomexicanos was not evenly replicated throughout New Mexico. In certain areas, English-speaking and Spanish-speaking elites joined forces to eliminate horse and cattle thieves regardless of their race or ethnicity. In other areas, competition over grazing rights often broke into ethnic conflict between Nuevomexicano sheepherders and Anglo cattlemen. These patterns were further complicated by the relative size of the two populations. In those areas of the territory where Anglos were a minority, it was essential that they reach some level of accommodation with the Nuevomexicano population. This acculturationist impulse had far less force in those regions where Anglo settlers assumed a majority status.

One region of intense Anglo-Mexican conflict was southeastern New Mexico, a region commonly known as "Little Texas" because of the large influx of Anglo settlers from that state in the post–Civil War era. Competition for economic resources created bitter ethnic rivalry in these newer areas of Anglo colonization. Texas cattlemen ruthlessly forced Nuevomexicano sheepherders from the land. Nuevomexicano retaliation fueled further Anglo aggression, creating a vicious cycle of violent retribution. In areas such as Little Texas where ethnic hostility was pronounced, vigilantism could easily transform into indiscriminate racial warfare. This is most clearly illustrated by the Horrell War. The Horrells were ranchers who had recently settled in New Mexico after fleeing Texas, where they had killed four officers of the pro-Republican state police. They wasted little time in getting into trouble in New Mexico. Driven by the desire to avenge the murder of one of their family members, the Horrells took arbitrary action against the entire Nuevomexicano community. On December 20, 1873, the Horrells murdered four Nuevomexicanos at a dance in Lincoln; later that month, they lynched five Nuevomexicano freighters fifteen miles west of Roswell. The Horrells also intercepted and killed Severanio Apodaca while he was transporting a load of grain to a local mill. In all of these cases, the ethnic identity of the victim appears to have been the only reason they were killed.[26]

Mob violence against Nuevomexicanos reached its pinnacle during the range wars of the 1870s and 1880s. The indiscriminate violence of the Horrells combined with more traditional acts of vigilantism against alleged horse and cattle thieves. In August 1884, the *Raton Comet* reported that a band of Mexican horse thieves was active in the local area. "Immediate flight is their only chance for safety, as their speedy extermination has been decided upon by a set of resolute, determined men, who have suffered by their depredations," the *Comet* reported.[27] Although the fate of these particular horse thieves is uncertain, the "speedy extermination" of Mexicans became common practice. In July 1889, for instance, a deputy sheriff in Socorro County was shot dead as he attempted to arrest Mexican cattle thieves. The suspects were apprehended and imprisoned in an empty house. On the night of July 21, a band of cattlemen stormed the house and then shot and hanged the inmates.[28] The conflict over grazing rights between Anglos and Nuevomexicanos and the more general impulse to punish criminals created an era of violence. During the 1870s and 1880s, mobs lynched at least forty-three Nuevomexicanos.

The area of New Mexico where Rafael Benavides lived lay outside the influence of Anglo and Nuevomexicano interaction. The demographic balance had clearly swung in favor of Anglos by the 1920s. Benavides lived in a community where Nuevomexicanos were socially, economically, and politically marginalized. A system of de facto segregation curtailed social interaction among Anglos and Nuevomexicanos. Physical separation in turn created a psychological distance between the two peoples. In the absence of any power-sharing relationship, Anglos therefore came to regard Nuevomexicanos as a distinct and inferior racial other. Oral tradition suggests that several Nuevomexicanos were lynched in northwestern New Mexico in the late nineteenth and early twentieth centuries, but research into the surviving written records has only been able to verify one case, the 1882 hanging of Guadalupe Archuleta at Bloomfield, a settlement located just a few miles from Farmington.

Archuleta, according to his defenders, was in the midst of performing his duties as justice of the peace when he shot and killed an Anglo. The shooting and subsequent lynching of Archuleta further divided the town into a Nuevomexicano and an Anglo camp. Archuleta's killing no doubt provoked such division because of ongoing ethnic conflict between the two groups over grazing rights. The lynching occurred at a pivotal moment in this conflict. According to the historian Frances Leon Swadesh, Archuleta's lynching "effectively silenced all Hispano challenge to Anglo strong-arm tactics along the San Juan."[29] Memories of these early conflicts did not fade quickly, and ethnic tension between the two groups persisted well into the twentieth century. For instance, only four years before the Benavides lynching, the *Farmington Times Hustler* printed the call of one local citizen for the "organization of the whole state into active divisions of the KKK."[30]

It is difficult to imagine a situation any less dangerous than the one in which Rafael Benavides found himself.[31] Benavides's position as an illiterate laborer of the mestizo, or mixed-race, class afforded him little social protection from the violent prejudice of Anglos. In contrast to the Nuevomexicano elite, who claimed a pure European ancestry, lower-class Mexicans were perceived as a degenerate mongrel race who had assumed the worst characteristics of their Indian and Spanish ancestors. Anglos feared what they perceived as the moral depravity of the mestizo class and sought to protect themselves through the brutal enforcement of racial boundaries. The murder of an Anglo woman in particular incited the vengeance of the lynch mob. On May 5, 1893, a mob of seventy men stormed the jail in Las Lunas and seized three Nuevomexicanos arrested for the murder of two Anglo women. The three suspects—Victorio Aragon, Antonio Garcia, and Antonio Martinez—were all hanged.[32]

Benavides was a member of the despised mestizo class who committed the one offense most liable to arouse the violent retribution of Anglos. Although he did not murder Mrs. Lewis, his lynching must be attributed to the impulse of Anglo men to protect their wives and daughters from physical assault by what they believed to be morally degenerate Mexicans. Although Anglos perceived any assault upon a white woman as an implicit rape, there is no actual evidence that Benavides attempted to sexually assault Mrs. Lewis. Had there been the intimation that such an offense had occurred, it would almost certainly have been reported by the press. Newspaper accounts of lynchings often contained salacious details of the sexual crime committed by the victim. There is no evidence of this "folk pornography"[33] in press reports of the Benavides case, even after Farmington came under intense attack for permitting the mob violence. Nonetheless, the lynching contained an important element of ritual. The photograph of Benavides's corpse shows that the lynchers tied his bedgown above his waist so as to expose his genitals. Evidently, the mob was not content to murder Benavides but committed a deliberate act of public humiliation intended as a symbolic reassertion of Anglo male supremacy.

Despite the dramatic outburst of ethnic violence in Farmington, Rafael Benavides was the last Nuevomexicano to be lynched in New Mexico. This section and the ones that follow explore why Benavides's murder was such a turning point. A satisfactory answer will not be found solely by sifting through the details of the Farmington lynching. Public figures and forces condemning lynching were at work long before 1928 in New Mexico. And Benavides's lynching did not convince everyone in the state that lynching was wrong and should be abandoned. What Benavides's lynching did do was decisively tip the balance of public opinion toward those in New Mexico who favored due process solutions to problems of social order and away from those who favored informal methods of control such as vigilantism and mob violence. The result was that would-be lynchers after 1928 would no longer have the support of the majority of their fellow citizens. This mattered. Potential lynchers could no longer count on escaping arrest by the authorities. They would have to be careful with their identities and with the location of their planned murder. Ethnic and racial violence was clearly still possible after the lynching of Rafael Benavides, but potential lynchers who had previously been protected by a widespread belief in "rough justice" now found themselves dangerously isolated from majority opinion.[34]

During the late nineteenth and early twentieth centuries the New Mexico press shared a consensus of opinion in support of mob violence against Nuevomexicanos. Newspapers commonly restricted their reports of lynching to a factual recounting of events, and the absence of editorial opinion can be interpreted as an implicit endorsement of mob action. On occasion, the press also expressed more outspoken support. In 1881, the *Santa Fe Democrat* argued that the failures of the legal system justified mob violence. The editorial ran under the title "Let There Be More Hanging, and Less Sniveling."[35] In 1889, the *Socorro Chieftan* commented on a lynching in Kelly, New Mexico: "Horse thieves will be found scarce around Kelly and Magdalena after this. That juniper tree of justice out there is a court that grants no appeals." The newspaper gave no information about who committed the killings but instead speculated that the two Mexicans "came to their death by pulling their necks too hard against a rope."[36] In January 1890, a mob in the mining community of Georgetown seized a Mexican "desperado" from sheriff's officers and hanged him. The *Silver City Sentinel* published an editorial that openly encouraged such acts of retribution. According to the paper, the courts had failed to protect innocent citizens from the incursions of Mexican outlaws. The lynching was therefore a legitimate act of self-defense intended to discourage further criminal outrages. The editorial asserted, "It is high time that the citizens should awake to the importance of putting a stop to this promiscuous shooting. Let a few judicial hangings occur, and the shooter will give this county the go-by."[37]

Occasional muted condemnations of lynching can be found in New Mexico dating back to the nineteenth century. Even these editorials, so guarded in their criticism, make it clear that public support for vigilantism and lynching was widespread throughout the state. For example, in 1876, after reporting that "Judge Lynch had evidently been around last night," the *Albu-*

querque Review commented: "We cannot but deprecate this action, yet taking all things into consideration, the parties concerned were not so much to blame."[38] Similar logic was displayed in the *Santa Fe New Mexican* in 1881. In January, authorities in Albuquerque arrested three Nuevomexicanos accused of the murder of Colonel Charles Potter. On the night of January 31, a mob estimated at two hundred in number seized the suspects from the county jail and hanged them. The editor of the *New Mexican* began by stating that "lynching in general is to be condemned" but then went on to defend the actions of local vigilantes. He believed that "in cases such as the cowardly and dastardly murder of Colonel Potter it is very doubtful whether justice can be too swiftly meted out." The editor went even further, encouraging similar action to purge the community of other dangerous criminals: "the sooner such a fate does overtake them the better will it be."[39]

Press support of vigilantism reflected and reinforced a broader community approval of the actions of lynch mobs. The Socorro Committee of Safety, which executed at least two Nuevomexicanos in the 1880s had, according to one observer, "the tacit endorsement of the highest territorial officials," being "composed of the reputable Americans of the town including in its membership, bankers, clergymen, merchants, ranchmen, miners, lawyers, doctors, and all others interested in the enforcement of law and order."[40] As a witness to the lynching of a Nuevomexicano in Las Vegas observed, there were many in the town "who viewed the actions of the Vigilantes as meet and proper."[41] In order to deter official inquiry, local citizens often enforced a conspiracy of silence. In 1953, Marietta Wetherill recalled her attempt forty years earlier to report the hanging bodies of two Nuevomexicanos that she had encountered on the road to Cuba, New Mexico. Wetherill was told that if she were smart, she would not report the lynching and that "she shouldn't know anything about it either." When she returned to the spot of the hanging four hours later, the bodies were gone. Wetherill concluded that "hanging wasn't a hard matter to do apparently at all."[42]

The silence surrounding this lynching and others like it effectively stymied investigation. Local authorities, even when in possession of specific information, usually made only the most cursory attempts to secure the arrest and imprisonment of mob leaders. Only once was anyone prosecuted for the mob murder of a Nuevomexicano. In August 1877, O. P. McMains stood trial for the lynching of Cruz Vega in Colfax County. The case was eventually thrown out for lack of evidence.[43]

The lynching of Rafael Benavides received considerable sanction from the

New Mexico press. Some individuals and newspapers emphatically endorsed the actions of the mob. According to a letter published in the *Farmington Times Hustler,* the men who abducted and murdered Benavides performed a "noble and patriotic service" because they protected the community from further criminal incursions. The *Durango Herald-Democrat* was more blunt, stating that "the degenerate Mexican got exactly what was coming to him."[44] Newspapers such as the *Herald-Democrat* made much of the fact that Benavides was a convicted felon. On September 5, 1914, Benavides was sentenced to a term of five to seven years in the New Mexico State Penitentiary for the rape of a ten-year-old Nuevomexicano girl.[45] Prison had apparently failed to reform him. In a blatant act of recidivism he had drunkenly assaulted an innocent woman and left her for dead. The failure of the penal system therefore forced the people of Farmington to take preventive action against any further criminal outrages Benavides might perpetrate. As the *Rio Grande Farmer* concluded, "He will commit no more crimes." The lynching of Benavides, it was believed, would also serve as a salutary lesson to other potential offenders. In the words of the *Mancos Times-Tribune,* "a more pronounced means of instilling fear into the hearts of the criminal class, was never resorted to."[46]

There was nothing surprising about such editorials. Newspapers throughout the southern and western states had for decades attempted to exonerate the actions of lynch mobs by emphasizing the supposed failure of the courts to protect innocent people from dangerously violent criminals. What is remarkable is that many newspapers, despite their acceptance of Benavides's guilt, denounced his lynching as unjustified even under these circumstances. A thorough analysis of press reaction to the Benavides lynching reveals that the public consensus in support of lynching had collapsed by 1928. The *Santa Fe New Mexican* is a potent illustration of this sea change in popular opinion. As noted above, decades earlier the paper enthusiastically endorsed the lynching of three Nuevomexicanos accused of murder. Yet in 1928, it led press reaction in an impassioned denunciation of mob violence. In a widely reprinted editorial, the paper condemned lynching as "a dangerous experiment" because it claimed innocent victims, and demanded a "thorough and searching investigation" of the incident. The *New Mexican* articulated the influence of Progressive politics on public discourse about law and order. Its publisher, Bronson M. Cutting, had moved to Santa Fe from Long Island, New York, in 1910. As a former chairman of the board of commissioners of the New Mexico State Penitentiary, Cutting had a clear interest in the promotion of the criminal justice system over the lawless behavior of the lynch mob. In 1927 Cutting had also been appointed as a Republican to the U.S. Senate following the death of the incumbent, Andrieus A. Jones. A year later, he won election in his own right. As the holder of such high political office, Cutting had to protect the reputation of his adopted state. However, he also had a reputation for actively promoting the political rights of Nuevomexicanos. These concerns informed the denunciation of the Benavides lynching in the pages of the *New Mexican*.[47]

How is this adverse press reaction to be explained? A number of interrelated social and political forces had by the late 1920s contributed to a decline in popular acceptance of mob violence. It is important to consider the impact of reformist impulses at state, national, and international levels.

In other southwestern states, protest against the lynching and murder of Mexicans assumed a confrontational character. In Texas and California, where mob violence was more endemic, Mexicans rose up in violent retaliation against their Anglo oppressors. The men who embodied this spirit of armed resistance have become folkloric heroes: Joaquín Murrieta, Juan Cortina, and Tiburcio Vásquez. Anglos refused to distinguish between general lawlessness and legitimate acts of resistance, indiscriminately labeling any challenge to their legal and political power as "banditry." Although some of these outlaws did engage in indiscriminate acts of robbery and violence, others pursued an explicitly political agenda. Scholars therefore commonly describe these Mexican outlaws as "social bandits."[48] The Texas outlaw Juan Cortina best illustrates the distinction between banditry and political resistance. Between 1859 and 1873, Cortina led a small army of outlaws against the U.S. military. Anglos considered Cortina a dangerously violent criminal. Cortina, by contrast, proclaimed that his purpose was to punish Anglos who murdered Mexicans and escaped prosecution because of the racism of the southwestern legal system. "There are to be found criminals covered with frightful crimes," roared Cortina. "To these monsters indulgence is shown, because they are not of our race, which is unworthy, as they say, to belong to the human species."[49]

New Mexico, like Texas and other parts of the borderlands, had a history of resistance and self-defense. In New Mexico, however, such resistance was not often directed at Anglo mobs. The most dramatic illustration of armed opposition to Anglo oppression in the state is Las Gorras Blancas, or the White Caps. By the late 1880s Nuevomexicano farmers in San Miguel County faced financial ruin as a result of the fenced enclosure of formerly communal lands. Las Gorras Blancas were a band of masked night riders who resisted confiscation of the pasture lands, tearing down fences, burning barns and haystacks, and destroying livestock. A handbill distributed by the riders in March 1890 declared: "Our purpose is to protect the rights and interests of the people in general and especially of the helpless classes."[50] However, Nuevomexicanos do not appear to have utilized similar tactics in the struggle against ethnic violence. Daring acts of physical resistance were confined to the issue of land enclosure, not the lynch mob. It should also be emphasized that Las Gorras Blancas was a class as well as an ethnic movement, since its raids were directed against both Anglo and Nuevomexicano property owners.[51]

Nuevomexicanos did mobilize in collective protest against ethnic prejudice. According to Phillip Gonzales, between the late 1880s and early 1930s Nuevomexicanos organized "mass meetings of indignation" on twenty-six separate occasions. Yet not one of these demonstrations was directed against lynching.[52]

The contrast between New Mexico and other southwestern states emphasizes distinct regional variation in the pattern of response to mob violence against Mexicans. In New Mexico, at least, neither vigorous protest by the Nuevomexicano elite nor acts of armed resistance can account for the demise of lynch law.

The institutionalization of a formal legal system had a more important impact on public opinion than did public protests by Nuevomexicanos. The Benavides incident appeared to belie the transition of the southwestern states from a remote frontier society to a more stable social order. During the early decades of western settlement, many observers believed that vigilantism fulfilled a vital function of the frontier. In the absence of a fully functional legal system, the preservation of public order became the responsibility of community-minded citizens. Although not sanctioned by law, these vigilance committees acted impartially and in the interest of the common good. As Ray Abrahams observes, contemporary accounts portrayed lynch law "in positive terms as fundamentally the cool-headed response of public-spirited citizens to an emergency in which life and property had become dangerously insecure."[53]

The historical record does not support this uncritical acceptance of vigilante committees. Far from acting in the interests of law and order, Anglo vigilantes lynched Nuevomexicanos in deliberate defiance of the authorities.

This was especially the case in those areas where Anglos did not control the legal system. The actions of the Socorro Committee of Safety offer a telling example. In March 1881, three members of a wealthy Nuevomexicano family murdered an Anglo who had insulted them. Skeptical that the Nuevomexicano sheriff would arrest prominent members of his own community, Anglos independently organized a Committee of Safety. The committee seized one of the suspects, Onofrio Baca, from an arresting officer and hanged him. Some months later, the committee lynched another Nuevomexicano, this time for rape. The following day, further evidence was uncovered that established his innocence.[54] An assessment of New Mexico vigilantism by Montague Stevens reveals the dangers of mob violence: "Well, these cattlemen got together and made an association of Vigilantes. That part was all right but the trouble was that most of the Vigilantes were the worst thieves of the lot."[55]

Whether or not frontier justice had ever served a legitimate purpose, what was important was the perception that New Mexico no longer had need of vigilantes. By the late 1920s the establishment of an institutionalized legal system throughout the southwestern states undermined the legitimacy of frontier justice. An analysis of San Juan County court records between 1887 and 1928 demonstrates that the authorities commonly secured the indictment and conviction of serious criminal offenders.[56] The sentencing policy of the court appears to have been in part determined by the ethnic identity of the convicted felon, evidenced by the fact they handed down particularly harsh prison terms upon Nuevomexicanos. The minimum sentence for a Nuevomexicano convicted of rape was two to three years; the maximum sentence was life.[57] By contrast, the only Anglo convicted of the offense received a one-year sentence.[58] Lengthy prison terms were also imposed on Nuevomexicanos convicted of murder. Donaciano Aguilar was incarcerated for ninety-nine years in 1909 and Edumenio Meastas for fifty to sixty years in 1927.[59] Arturo Rosales also affirms that after 1910 the use of the death penalty in New Mexico assumed a more explicitly racial dimension. The disproportionate number of Nuevomexicanos executed during these years demonstrates that state authorities had to a certain extent supplanted the role of the lynch mob.[60]

Since there appeared to be indisputable evidence that Rafael Benavides committed an assault on Mrs. Lewis, the Anglo citizens of Farmington should have been confident of his conviction by a court of law. On November

27, the *Santa Fe New Mexican* affirmed that the actions of the mob therefore served no legitimate purpose. "In raw frontier communities where law was not yet established, Vigilantes were sometimes necessary. It is a question for San Juan county to decide as to whether she holds herself as a raw, lawless, frontier district," the paper observed. Although most newspapers accepted that Benavides was guilty of having committed a serious criminal offense, this did not in their opinion sanction the actions of the lynch mob. In the words of the *Alamogordo News*, Benavides was a "miserable wretch" who had committed an almost unspeakable crime. However, he had already been arrested and would no doubt have been convicted by a court of law had he lived. Other newspapers expressed a similar sentiment that the barbarity of Benavides's crime did not in itself justify the actions of the mob. According to the *Farmington Times Hustler*, Benavides was a "beast man," the "perpetrator of the most revolting crime ever committed in the county." But he was also entitled to be tried according to the due process of law. Lynch mobs, "however well-intentioned, are dangerous means for dispensing justice and when less well-intentioned are a most dangerous menace to life, liberty and property."[61]

The increased power of the state and the growing stability of the legal system also acted as a deterrent to potential vigilantes. The state was now more capable of protecting prisoners threatened by lynch mobs. Vigilantes also had reasons to be cautious about the newly strengthened legal system. If judges and juries determined to eradicate lynching, the courts would have been much more effective in doing so than in New Mexico's territorial period.

Given the strength of the legal system and the expanded power of the state, why had a band of outlaws resorted to vigilante violence? The lynching of Rafael Benavides seemed to be an aberration, an unwelcome reversion to an era when citizens ignored due process conventions for informal, community justice. The press acknowledged that racism had been the principal determining factor. Every one of the Nuevomexicanos convicted of a capital offense in San Juan County committed his crime on members of their own ethnic community. So long as this was the case, Anglos appear to have respected the due process of law. However, when a Nuevomexicano committed a criminal outrage against an Anglo, it inflamed a violent ethnic prejudice. The *Santa Fe New Mexican* astutely recognized this double standard. Had he survived his bullet wound, Benavides would have been tried and convicted by the authorities. Those men who dispensed frontier justice could claim to have upheld the law; the mob that murdered Benavides undermined it.[62]

Many New Mexicans would have been uncomfortable with the racism in the execution of Benavides in any event, but the shifting national perception of lynching in the interwar era made the episode even more troubling. The phenomenon of mob violence was in irreversible decline throughout the United States by the 1920s. According to the Tuskegee Institute, the peak lynching decade of the 1890s claimed the lives of 1,333 people. By the 1920s, the figure had fallen to 321. While still disturbing, and a sign of the continued tolerance of mob law in the United States, this amounts to a decline of 400 percent within a single generation.[63] The interaction of a number of forces shaped a new political climate less tolerant of the violent lawlessness of the mob. News reports of European atrocities in World War I caused a reconsideration of racial violence at home. The Red Summer of 1919 also intensified fears that mobs threatened the United States' own democratic order.[64] These events gave added political impetus to the antilynching campaigns of civil rights organizations. The NAACP launched an unrelenting political offensive against lynching in 1910. Less than a decade later, in 1919, the Commission on Interracial Cooperation mounted a regional campaign to mobilize southern liberal opposition to mob violence. The increasing political outcry encouraged Missouri representative Leonidas C. Dyer to introduce a federal antilynching bill to Congress in 1921. Although a southern filibuster in the Senate resulted in the defeat of the bill, the surrounding publicity stirred further popular outrage against lynch mobs. The federal government responded by assuming a more activist role in the arrest and prosecution of mob members.[65]

The Benavides lynching therefore threatened to place New Mexico outside the pale of national opinion. Newspapers across the country reported the incident. This unwelcome publicity tarnished the reputation of New Mexico and threatened its association in the popular imagination with the violent racial intolerance of the southern states.[66] Newspapers across the state branded the lynching an act of barbarism that disgraced the people of New Mexico before the rest of the nation. According to the *State Tribune,* "The good name not only of the county but of New Mexico is at issue."[67]

Political pressures not only within the United States but without also explain the critical reaction to the case. The ink of the signatories to the Treaty of Guadalupe Hidalgo had barely dried before the Mexican government received reports of the violent mistreatment of its citizens within the United States. The diplomatic protests of the Mexican government had a powerful cumulative effect upon the course of mob violence. Federal authorities initially insisted that they had no jurisdiction to intervene in the internal affairs of individual states. By the last decade of the nineteenth century, however, Mexican demands proved too persistent to ignore. In unrelated incidents during the fall of 1895, Anglo mobs lynched two Mexican citizens, Luis Moreno and Florentine Suaste. Confronted by furious Mexican protests, the United States government sanctioned the payment of a two-thousand-dollar indemnity to the families of both victims.[68]

Mexican authorities continued during the interwar era to place unrelenting pressure on the U.S. State Department. Three episodes that occurred in the decade before the lynching of Rafael Benavides illustrate how the forceful diplomacy of the Mexican government fostered official intolerance of mob violence.

On September 13, 1919, a mob in Pueblo, Colorado, lynched two men for the murder of a local police officer. The victims, Salvador Ortez and José Gonzales, were both Mexican citizens.[69] The Mexican embassy in Washington immediately instructed the local consul, A. J. Ortiz, to launch an investigation. Although Ortiz did not discover the identities of the mob leaders, he did establish that the dead men were entirely innocent.[70]

While the Mexican government routinely investigated the murder of Mexican nationals in the United States, the degree of Mexican protest often fluctuated according to the political situation within Mexico and its international relationship with the United States. In 1919, Mexico's interest was energized by recent diplomatic tensions with the United States. Mexico understood that attention to the Pueblo lynching case would cause the American government acute embarrassment. In recent months the State Department had imposed increasing pressure on the Carranza administration for the protection of American citizens in Mexico. The failure to defend Mexicans from American mobs implied a blatant double standard. The *Houston Post* concurred with Mexican officials when they observed that the United States was in no position to claim the moral high ground in its diplomatic disputes with Mexico: "After the stern warnings our government has sent to Mexico against further outrages on our citizens, it is going to be humiliating in the extreme for our government to receive similar complaints from the Mexican government making charges against our people who have claimed to be so much higher in the scale of civilization."[71]

Mexican diplomatic protest therefore pressured the federal government to take remedial action against lynch mobs in an attempt to more purposefully fulfill the ideals of American democracy. On November 11, 1922, a mob in Weslaco, Texas, lynched a suspected murderer named Elias Zarate. Racial tension spread rapidly through the local region. Within hours, an armed mob marched through the streets of Breckenridge in an attempt to scare Mexicans out of town. Ambassador Manuel Téllez issued the State Department a demand for their protection. At the recommendation of Secretary of State Charles Evans Hughes, the governor of Texas sent a detachment of Rangers to safeguard against any further violence. The crisis soon passed.[72]

In 1926, Mexican diplomatic protest culminated in the arrest and conviction of Sheriff Raymond Teller. Teller and his fellow law officers had been implicated in the lynching of four Mexicans in Raymondville, Texas. According to the sheriff, the Mexicans had been arrested for the murder of two of his officers. Teller was taking the suspects from jail out into the countryside in search of their cache of arms when he was ambushed. The prisoners were killed in the resultant gunfight. Yet according to other testimony, Teller and his officers had themselves tortured and then shot the Mexicans. For decades the State Department had invariably taken the reports of local law officers at face value in its investigations of the murder of Mexicans. These reports repeatedly failed to identify those responsible for the lynchings, instead concluding vaguely that the victims had met their deaths at the hands of persons unknown. This case demonstrated a new determination to avoid diplomatic tensions with Mexico over the lynching of its citizens on American soil. Not only did the State Department reject the conclusions of the sheriff's report, but federal pressure upon state authorities was critical in ensuring that Teller and his fellow officers were tried, convicted, and sentenced to prison.[73]

New Mexican newspapermen and community leaders paid attention to the events in Texas and Colorado. They were no doubt unsurprised when Mexican authorities made similar remonstrations to secure the arrest and prosecution of those responsible for the lynching of Rafael Benavides. When Ambassador Téllez undertook an investigation into the incident, Assistant District Attorney George Bruington immediately announced his intention to determine the nationality of the dead man. Bruington informed the press that the nurse who treated Benavides claimed he told her his father was an African American. The story received a strong emphasis in several newspapers, which described Benavides as "a Negro Mexican half-breed."[74] Although pure speculation on the part of the assistant district attorney, this appears to have been an attempt to attribute the criminal misconduct of Benavides by implication to his "blackness." The insinuation of a racial hierarchy that elevated Mexicans above African Americans may also have been a means of defusing diplomatic protest. Ambassador Téllez was in any event obliged to abandon his investigation. Although the racial identity of Benavides's father could not be determined, the district attorney conclusively established that he was a citizen not of Mexico but the United States. The publicity in part generated by Mexican protest did, however, adversely affect state authorities. An editorial in the *Farmington Times Hustler* reflected the determination not to allow any further outbreaks of mob violence. "It will take San Juan County a long time to live down the bad name received by this lawless act," observed the paper. "The outside world will long remember the lynching but will forget the terrible crime that caused it."[75]

Protest of the lynching of Rafael Benavides by the Mexican government and condemnation of the episode by local and state newspapers and community leaders were important developments in the evolution of New Mexican attitudes toward vigilantism and extralegal violence. But the newspapermen and diplomats who criticized Benavides's lynching did not change attitudes toward lynching in New Mexico by themselves. Rather, these critics of lynching succeeded in preventing future lynchings because the values they upheld were now more widely internalized among the people of New Mexico. Residents of New Mexico, like citizens of the United States in general, underwent a slow, gradual transformation in their attitudes toward lynching. In the nineteenth century, most New Mexicans had supported lynching as a necessary evil because of the frontier condition of the territory and the weakness of its courts. As those courts improved, however, attitudes toward lynching evolved. By the twentieth century, more and more New Mexicans had come to believe that justice should be meted out not by vigilantes but through the legal system in a deliberate and formal manner that emphasized due process rights and procedures. The lynching of Rafael Benavides did not reinvigorate the older tradition in New Mexico. Instead, it forced New Mexicans to evaluate what they thought about lynching and vigilantism. The arguments and criticisms put forward about the Benavides lynching, both within New Mexico and without, helped New Mexicans understand why they were now so uncomfortable with extralegal violence. In the end, the lynching of Rafael Benavides confirmed and accelerated a change in attitude that had been taking place in the previous quarter century. The murder of Benavides tipped the balance of public opinion in favor of those opposing mob violence and thus became the last lynching of its kind.

NOTES

Originally published in the *New Mexico Historical Review* 80, no. 3 (summer 2005): 265–292. © 2005 by the University of New Mexico Board of Regents. All rights reserved. Reprinted by permission.

1. *Farmington Times Hustler,* November 23, 1928.

2. *Farmington Times Hustler,* December 7, 1928; *Santa Fe New Mexican,* December 5 and 6, 1928.

3. Robert J. Tórrez, "New Mexico's Last Lynching," *'Round the Roundhouse* (November 11–December 9, 2003): 6.

4. F. Arturo Rosales, correspondence with authors, August 5, 2002.

5. Although Benavides was the last identifiable Mexican to be murdered in such a public manner by a mob, Mexicans certainly continued to suffer other forms of group violence. The Los Angeles Zoot Suit Riot of August 1943 is a stark illustration of continued conflict between Anglos and Mexicans. Although anti-Mexican violence continued after 1928, Benavides's lynching coincided with a subtle but decisive shift in Anglo attitudes. According to our research, in the years that followed, would-be mob members were discouraged by the threat of public condemnation and prosecution by the courts after 1928. *Los Angeles Times,* October 11, 1933; *New York Times,* October 11, 1933; Mauricio Mazón, *The Zoot-Suit Riots: The Psychology of Symbolic Annihilation* (Austin: University of Texas Press, 1984); Carey McWilliams, "The Los Angeles Riot of 1943," in *Violence in America: A Historical and Contemporary Reader,* ed. Thomas Rose (New York: Random House, 1969), 168–80.

6. On resentment of the term *Mexicans,* see Brian Michael Jenkins, "The Border War: A Study of the United States–Mexico Relations during the Mexican Revolution, 1910–1920," (master's thesis, University of California, Los Angeles, 1965), 8.

7. Miriam Taylor, "San Juan County: Farmington," unpublished paper, Farmington Public Library; Hartsill Lloyd Clark, "A History of San Juan County, New Mexico" (master's thesis, University of Tulsa, 1963), 69–80, 91–98; Bureau of the Census, *Abstract of the Fifteenth Census of the United States* (Washington, DC: Government Printing Office, 1933).

8. Mrs. Fremont Older, *California Missions and Their Romances* (New York: Van Rees, 1938), 67–68; Frank Shay, *Judge Lynch: His First Hundred Years* (New York: Ives, 1938), 64–65.

9. *Los Angeles Star,* August 7, 1852; *Sacramento Daily Union,* July 28, 1852; *Nevada Journal,* August 7, 1852; Hubert Howe Bancroft, "Popular Tribunals—Volume I," in *The Works of Hubert Howe Bancroft* (San Francisco: History Company, 1887), 36:477; Ken Gonzales-Day, *Lynching in the West,* 1850-1935 (Durham, NC: Duke University Press, 2006), 210.

10. *Albuquerque Republican Review,* April 15, 1871; *Santa Fe Weekly New Mexican,* September 25, 1871.

11. *El Nuevo Mexicano*, June 3, 1893; *Las Vegas Daily Optic*, May 31, 1893, 2; *El Boletin Popular*, June 1, 1893; Carlos C. de Baca, *Vicente Silva: The Terror of Las Vegas* (Truchas, NM: Tate Gallery, 1968), 38–39; Mitchell C. Sena, "Third-Rate Henchman of a First-Rate Terror," *True West* (February 1979): 28–29, 40–44.

12. For Ramirez's editorials and reports, see *El Clamor Publico*, April 25, 1857; November 14, 1857; January 23and June 19, 1858; January 29 June 5, 11, and 18, and September 17 and 24, 1859. "Linchamiento," "linchar," and "linchado" were used in a wide number of Spanish-language newspapers from the 1850s (Los Angeles's *El Clamor Publico* and San Francisco's *El Eco del Pacífico*) to the 1890s and beyond (Santa Fe's *El Boletin Popular* and *El Nuevo Mexicano*). See, for example, *El Nuevo Mexicano*, February 11 and June 3, 1893. For an indispensible discussion of Ramirez and his criticism of American democracy and lynching, see Coya Paz Brownrigg, "Linchocracia: Performing 'America' in El Clamor Publico," *California History* 84, no. 2 (Winter 2006): 40–53.

13. Ironically, Roger Taney's infamous *Dred Scott* decision guaranteed Benavides's citizenship rights. Although Taney did not mean for these rights to apply to nonwhites, his interpretation that constitutional rights followed the flag into the territories still prevails. See *Scott v. Sandford*, 60 U.S. 393 (1857).

14. Department of Corrections, Penitentiary of New Mexico, Record Book of Convicts, #3384, New Mexico State Archives, Santa Fe; *El Paso Times*, November 18, 1928.

15. The events surrounding the shooting and arrest of Rafael Benavides were widely reported in the press: *Farmington Times Hustler*, November 16 and 23, 1928; *Albuquerque Journal*, November 16, 1928; *Aztec Independent*, November 16, 1928; *Roswell Morning Dispatch*, November 16, 1928; *Roswell Daily Record*, November 16, 1928; *El Paso Times*, November 17, 1928; *La Prensa* (San Antonio), November 17, 1928; *Las Vegas Daily Optic*, November 17, 1928; *Santa Fe New Mexican*, November 17, 1928; *Raton Daily Range*, November 17 and 20 1928; *Alamogordo News*, November 22, 1928; *Santa Rosa News*, November 23, 1928; *Roy Record*, November 24, 1928.

16. *El Paso Times*, November 17, 1928; *Farmington Daily Times*, October 13, 1928; *Raton Daily Range*, November 17, 1928.

17. Vertical file, Salmon Ruins Museum, Bloomfield, New Mexico.

18. Most of the scholarship on lynching and mob violence in New Mexico focuses on specific localities. One recent overview for the territorial period is Nancy Gonzalez, "Untold Stories of Murder and Lynching in Territorial New Mexico" (master's thesis, University of New Mexico, 2003).

19. This essay arises from a larger study of the lynching of persons of Mexican origin or descent throughout the United States. For a fuller discussion of the statistics presented here, see William D. Carrigan and Clive Webb, "The Lynching of Persons of Mexican Origin or Descent in the United States, 1848–1928," *Journal of Social History* 37 (2003): 411–38.

20. Some of these lynching victims were naturalized American citizens, while others were Mexican nationals resident in the United States. It is not always possible to determine the citizenship of a particular individual. In the interest of linguistic

simplicity, when referring to the broader southwestern states, we use the word *Mexican* to describe all persons of Mexican origin or descent. The Mexican community of New Mexico is also known by a number of terms, including *Spanish American, Nuevomexicano,* and *Hispano.* We use the term *Nuevomexicano* when referring expressly to the Mexican population of New Mexico. This term has been chosen over the other alternatives for its parallel with state-specific terms for Mexicans in other states such as Texas ("Tejanos").

The definition of lynching is open to interpretation, so it is important to explain the criteria used to calculate our statistics. In describing and analyzing mob violence, historians use words such as *lynching, vigilantism,* and *rioting.* It is often difficult to distinguish between these different forms of violence, both in the writing of historians and in the historical record itself. The key characteristics that distinguish one type of mob violence from another are the level of community approval and the degree to which premeditation and deliberation preceded the killing. On the one hand, historians see vigilantes as organized and controlled. Vigilantes choose their victims carefully, usually for some alleged crime or specific violation of the moral order. They also enjoy significant, if not universal, community approval and support. On the other hand, and at the opposite extreme, historians place rioters, whose acts of violence are generally not approved by the community and whose victims are likely to be chosen indiscriminately. The use of the word *lynching* has changed over time. Early in the twentieth century, *lynching* and *vigilantism* were nearly synonymous. Neither word was to be applied to a mob killing unless it exhibited both widespread community support and a certain level of discrimination on the part of the mob. During the twentieth century, however, the definition of lynching slowly changed to embrace almost any conceivable form of mob violence. Those who calculated lynching statistics were no longer bound to prove community approval, and they also began to include certain cases in which individuals were killed indiscriminately by riotous mobs. The NAACP formalized this new, expanded definition of lynching in 1940, and in the last half century, most historians of lynching, including the authors, have used this definition. For further insight on the shifting classification of lynching, see Christopher Waldrep, "War of Words: The Controversy over the Definition of Lynching, 1899–1940," *Journal of Southern History* 66 (2000): 75–100; and Waldrep, *The Many Faces of Judge Lynch: Extralegal Violence and Punishment in America* (New York: Palgrave Macmillan, 2002).

21. Charles Montgomery, "The Trap of Race and Memory: The Language of Spanish Civility on the Upper Rio Grande," *American Quarterly* 52 (2000): 488–89; Darlis A. Miller, "Cross-Cultural Marriages in the Southwest: The New Mexico Experience, 1846–1900," *New Mexico Historical Review* 57 (1982): 341; Juan Gómez-Quiñones, *Roots of Chicano Politics, 1600-1940* (Albuquerque: University of New Mexico Press, 1994), 329–30, 354; Laura E. Gómez, "Race, Colonialism, and Criminal Law: Mexicans and the American Criminal Justice System in Territorial New Mexico," *Law & Society Review* 34 (2000): 1129–1202; Charles Montgomery, "Becoming 'Spanish-American': Race and Rhetoric in New Mexico Politics, 1880–1928," *Journal of American Ethnic History* 20 (2001): 60.

22. *Republican Review,* March 11, 1876, quoted in Gonzalez, "Untold Stories," 8.

23. John Nieto-Phillips, "Spanish American Ethnic Identity and New Mexico's Statehood Struggle," in *The Contested Homeland: A Chicano History of New Mexico,* ed. Erlinda Gonzales-Berry and Daniel R. Maciel (Albuquerque: University of New Mexico Press, 2000), 97–142; Montgomery, "Trap of Race and Memory," 480.

24. *El Nuevo Mexicano,* June 3, 1893; *Las Vegas Daily Optic,* May 31, 1893; *El Boletin Popular,* June 1, 1893; de Baca, *Vicente Silva,* 38–39; Sena, "Third-Rate Henchman."

25. In February 1885, Jose Trujillo Gallegos was lynched in San Miguel County by a mob of men led by Cresensio Lucero. Gallegos, it was alleged, had murdered his family. In 1893, a mob of Nuevomexicanos hanged Ireneo Gonzalez for attempted murder. *Santa Fe New Mexican Review,* February 23, 1889; *El Nuevo Mexicano,* February 11, 1893; *Albuquerque Democrat,* February 7, 1893; *Santa Fe New Mexican,* February 7, 1893.

26. *Santa Fe New Mexican,* January 2, 1874; Maurice G. Fulton, *History of the Lincoln County War,* ed. Robert N. Mullin (Tucson: University of Arizona Press, 1968), 21–24; Robert N. Mullin, *A Chronology of the Lincoln County War* (Santa Fe, NM: Press of the Territorian, 1966), 11; P. J. Rasch, "The Horrell War," *New Mexico Historical Review* 31 (1956): 228; Ann Buffington, Lincoln County Historical Society, and New Mexico Federal Writers' Project, *Old Lincoln County Pioneer Stories: Interviews from the WPA Writer's Project* (Lincoln, NM: Lincoln County Historical Society, 1994), 1–3.

27. *Raton Comet,* August 10, 1884.

28. *Santa Fe New Mexican,* July 25, 1889. See also Fulton, *History of the Lincoln County War,* 29, 66; and Mullin, *Chronology of the Lincoln County War,* 12–13.

29. Frances Leon Swadesh, *Los Primeros Pobladores: Hispanic Americans of the Ute Frontier* (Notre Dame, IN: University of Notre Dame Press, 1974), 94–95; *Santa Fe Daily New Mexican,* November 1, 1882; Philip Rasch, "Feuding at Farmington," *New Mexico Historical Review* 40 (1965): 229.

30. *Farmington Times Hustler,* February 13 and 20, 1924, quoted in Robert W. Duke, *San Juan County Roars in the '20s* (Flora Vista, NM: San Juan County Historical Society, 2000).

31. Benavides may or may not have known about the lynching of Guadalupe Archuleta. Those Nuevomexicanos in the area who did remember might have warned Benavides that the man Guadalupe Archuleta killed was named John Blancett. One of the leaders of the lynch mob that killed Archuleta was also a Blancett. On the eve of Benavides's crime, the sheriff of San Juan County was George Blancett.

32. *Santa Fe New Mexican,* May 6, 1893; *El Boletin Poplar,* May 11, 1893.

33. Jacquelyn Dowd Hall, *Revolt against Chivalry: Jesse Daniel Ames and the Women's Campaign against Lynching* (New York: Columbia University Press, 1979), 150.

34. For a convincing discussion of the cultural struggle between those who favored "rough justice" and those who favored due process throughout the United States, see Michael Pfeifer, *Rough Justice: Lynching and American Society, 1874-1947* (Urbana: University of Illinois Press, 2004).

35. *Santa Fe Democrat,* January 3, 1881, quoted in Gonzalez, "Untold Stories," 8–9.

36. *Socorro Chieftan,* July 27, 1889.

37. *Silver City Sentinel,* quoted in *Santa Fe New Mexican,* January 9, 1890.

38. *Albuquerque Review,* June 24, 1876, quoted in Gonzalez, "Untold Stories," 19.

39. *Santa Fe New Mexican,* February4, 1881. The three men lynched by the mob were identified as Miguel Barrera, Escolastico Perea, and California Joe.

40. Charles Potter, "Reminiscences of the Socorro Vigilantes," ed. Paige W. Christiansen, *New Mexico Historical Review* 40 (January 1965): 25.

41. Miguel Antonio Otero, *My Life on the Frontier, 1864-1882* (New York: Press of the Pioneers, 1935), 192–93. Otero referred to the lynching of Manuel Barela. Although it was reported in a number of sources, there is some uncertainty as to the precise date of the lynching, which occurred either in 1879 or 1880. See Milton W. Callon, *Las Vegas, New Mexico: The Town That Wouldn't Gamble* (Las Vegas, NM: Las Vegas Daily Optic, 1962), 71, 94; and F. Stanley, *The Las Vegas Story* (Denver: World, 1951), 163–64.

42. Marietta Wetherill Oral Interview, MSS 123 BC, Pioneers Foundation Oral History Collection, Center for Southwest Studies, University of New Mexico, Albuquerque.

43. Colfax County District Court Records: Criminal Cases #351–70, New Mexico State Archives; Lawrence R. Murphy, *Philmont: A History of New Mexico's Cimarron County* (Albuquerque: University of New Mexico Press, 1972), 119–22; Morris F. Taylor, *O. P. McMains and the Maxwell Land Grant Conflict* (Tucson: University of Arizona Press, 1979), 39–55.

44. *Farmington Times Hustler,* November 30, 1928; editorial, *Durango Herald-Democrat,* republished in *Santa Fe New Mexican,* November 26, 1928; and *Farmington Times Hustler,* December 7, 1928.

45. Department of Corrections, Penitentiary of New Mexico, Record Book of Convicts, #3384.

46. Editorial, *Rio Grande Farmer,* republished in *Santa Fe New Mexican,* November 27, 1928; editorial, *Mancos Times-Tribune,* republished in *Farmington Times Hustler,* November 30, 1928.

47. *Santa Fe New Mexican,* November 17, 1928. For more information on Cutting, see Richard Lowitt, *Bronson M. Cutting: Progressive Politician* (Albuquerque: University of New Mexico Press, 1992).

48. This influential concept was initially conceived by Eric Hobsbawm in his book *Bandits* (London: Weidenfeld and Nicolson, 1969).

49. For further information on the life and career of Juan Cortina, see Charles W. Goldfinch and José T. Canales, *Juan N. Cortina: Two Interpretations* (New York: Arno, 1974); and Jerry D. Thompson, ed., *Juan Cortina and the Texas-Mexico Frontier, 1859-1877* (El Paso: Texas Western Press, 1994).

50. Howard Bryan, *Wildest of the Wild West: True Tails of a Frontier Town on the Santa Fe Trail* (Santa Fe, NM: Clear Light, 1988), 211. The story of Las Gorras Blancas is told in Andrew Bancroft Schlesinger, "Las Gorras Blancas, 1889–1891," *Journal of Mexican American History* 1 (Spring 1971): 87–143; Robert W. Larson, "The White Caps of New Mexico: A Study of Ethnic Militancy in the Southwest," *Pacific Historical Review* 44 (May 1975): 171–85; and Robert J. Rosenbaum, *Mexicano Resistance in the*

Southwest (Austin: University of Texas Press, 1981; reprint, Dallas: Southern Methodist University Press, 1998), 99–124.

51. Fabiola Cabeza de Baca, *We Fed Them Cactus,* 2nd ed. (Albuquerque: University of New Mexico Press, 1994), 89–90.

52. Phillip B. Gonzales, "La Junta de Indignación: Hispano Repertoire of Collective Protest in New Mexico, 1884–1933," *Western Historical Quarterly* 31 (2000): 161–86.

53. Ray Abrahams, *Vigilant Citizens: Vigilantism and the State* (Cambridge: Polity, 1998), 53–54.

54. Manuel Maria de Zamacona to James G. Blaine, April 19, 1881, Notes from the Mexican Legation in the United States to the Department of State, 1821–1906, National Archives, College Park, MD; Erna Ferguson, *Murder and Mystery in New Mexico* (Albuquerque: Merle Armitage Editions, 1948), 21–27; James B. Gillett, *Six Years with the Texas Rangers,* 1875-1881 (1921; reprint, Lincoln: University of Nebraska Press, 1976); *El Paso Times,* April 8, 1881.

55. Montague Stevens, Pioneers Foundation Oral History Collection, tape 351, reel 5, Center for Southwestern Studies, University of New Mexico.

56. The observations that follow are based upon a systematic study of the county civil and criminal record books for the years 1887 to 1928: San Juan County District Court Criminal Docket no. 1, New Mexico State Archives; San Juan County District Court Criminal Docket no. 2, San Juan County Courthouse, Aztec, NM.

57. Criminal Docket no. 1, case 379: *State of New Mexico v. Teodoro Martinez* (1914); Criminal Docket no. 2, case 150: *Territory of New Mexico v. Prudencio Trujillo* (1904).

58. Criminal Docket no. 1, case 177: *Territory of New Mexico v. Joseph Palen* (1902).

59. Criminal Docket no. 1, case 299: *Territory of New Mexico v. Donaciano Aguilar* (1909); Criminal Docket no. 2, case 516: *State of New Mexico v. Edumenio Maestas* (1924). Our conclusions about the institutional bias of the legal system against Nuevomexicano defendants are commensurate with a broader territorial study by Donna Crail-Rugotzke, "A Matter of Guilt: The Treatment of Hispanic Inmates by New Mexico Courts and the New Mexico Territorial Prison, 1890–1912," *New Mexico Historical Review* 74 (1999): 295–314.

60. F. Arturo Rosales, *¡Pobre Raza! Violence, Justice, and Mobilization among México Lindo Immigrants,* 1900-1936 (Austin: University of Texas Press, 1999), 141. Robert Tórrez notes that Spanish speakers were not executed in disproportionate numbers during the territorial period. He does note, however, that Mexican nationals were more likely to be put to death than Anglos or Spanish-speaking citizens of the United States in this period. Robert Tórrez to William D. Carrigan and Clive Webb, December 31, 2002, correspondence in possession of authors.

61. *Alamogordo News,* November 22, 1928; *Farmington Times Hustler,* November 16, 1923; November 23, 1928.

62. *Santa Fe New Mexican,* November 27, 1928.

63. "Lynchings: By Year and Race," http://www.law.umkc.edu/faculty/projects/ftrials/shipp/lynchingyear.html.

64. Philip Dray, *At the Hands of Persons Unknown: The Lynching of Black America* (New York: Random House, 2002), 235, 254, 256–57, 258.

65. W. Fitzhugh Brundage, *Lynching in the New South: Georgia and Virginia*, 1880-1930 (Urbana: University of Illinois Press, 1993), 248–49, 251. See also Robert L. Zangrando, *The NAACP Crusade against Lynching*, 1909-1950 (Philadelphia: Temple University Press, 1980).

66. Newspapers outside of New Mexico that reported the lynching included the *Montgomery Advertiser*, November 17, 1928; *New York Evening Post*, November 17, 1928; *Atlanta Constitution*, November 18, 1928; and *Norfolk Journal and Guide*, November 24, 1928.

67. *New Mexico State Tribune*, quoted in *Farmington Times Hustler*, November 30, 1928.

68. U.S. House of Representatives, document no. 237, 55th Cong., 2nd sess. (3679), 1–3; U.S. Senate, report no. 1832, 56th Cong., 2nd sess. (4064), 28–30.

69. *Des Moines Capital*, September 14, 1919; *Delaware Herald*, September 15, 1919; *New York Call*, September 15, 1919; *New York Sun*, September 15, 1919.

70. *New York Times*, September 16, 1919; *Denver Post*, September 20, 1919.

71. *Houston Post*, September 18, 1919. An editorial in the *New York Globe* of September 16, 1919, also noted the apparent hypocrisy of U.S. diplomatic protests: "When two Americans are killed in Mexico, even though it be in a section of the country remote from any city and notoriously infested with bandits, a roar for intervention goes up throughout this country. When two Mexicans are killed in a civilized American city by a mob it is regrettable, to be sure; but, after all, they look somewhat like Negroes, and everyone knows what we do with the latter."

72. *El Heraldo de Mexico* (Los Angeles), November 17 and 18, 1922.

73. Undated newspaper clipping, January 10, 1927, Oliver Douglas Weeks Collection, Rare Books and Manuscript Unit, Nettie Lee Benson Latin American Collection, University of Texas at Austin; undated newspaper clippings, George Coalson Collection, South Texas Archives, Texas A&M, Kingsville; *Houston Chronicle*, January 11–13, 1927; *La Prensa*, January 26, 1927; *El Cronista del Valle* (Brownsville, TX), September 9–11, 15, and 18, 1926; January 16, 22, and 27, 1927.

74. *Santa Fe New Mexican*, November 22, 1928; *Roswell Morning Dispatch*, November 16, 1928.

75. *Farmington Times Hustler*, November 23, 1928.

The Specter of Lynching in France

Familiar Word, Unfamiliar Reality

JOËL MICHEL

YNCHING IS A GENUINELY AMERICAN WORD that most languages have adopted with a loose meaning. In France, for instance, since the press created a lynching mood around the murder of several children in the 1970s,[1] public figures under attack from the press tend to present themselves as victims of media lynching—as Clarence Thomas did in the 1990s when he complained of "high-tech lynching." This trend has produced modern formulations that would have baffled the first American users of the word, including "predicted lynching," "permanent lynching," and, with the Internet gaining ground on the traditional press, "digital lynching."

In France, the word *lynchage* lacks the historical and emotional significance that it has in the United States. In French dictionaries, literal and metaphorical meanings share equal space. The verb *lyncher* is given the following definition: "to execute someone considered guilty in an expeditious manner and without trial" or "to mistreat seriously."[2] To the French, lynching is a remote concept that does not evoke the actual suffering of thousands of black people who were shot, hanged, or burned. In the mind of many French people, the history of African Americans comes down to two things: first, slavery and its abolition and, second, the civil rights movement. An entire century of segregation and lynching has been forgotten.

Even if extralegal violence is not unknown, the word *lynching* is rarely used in French history. Two cases of what many today would label lynching have been described by French historians: on June 26, 1791, farmers set the castle of Poleymieux on fire and dismembered the body of their lord, Guillin de Montet, and on August 16, 1870, in a Dordogne village, hundreds of people tortured the owner of the castle, Alain de Moneys, before burning him alive. In both cases, authors analyze the horrific nature of these crimes by referring not to lynching but to cannibalism—perceived as the worst of all crimes that can be committed against another human being. Events of such brutality seem so unusual, so disturbing, that anthropologists rather than historians have attempted to shed some light on them.[3] As this paucity of known cases demonstrates, lynching-like violence is so rare in France that it is exotic.

The American practice of lynching was reported quite early to the French public. In June 1837, the *Revue Britannique* published a translation from English of an article entitled "Les femmes américaines et la loi de Lynch." This "loi de Lynch" remained the preferred term until the end of the nineteenth century. In 1862, Victor Hugo used it in *Les Misérables* in the chapter titled "Disorder a Partisan of Order."[4] Nevertheless, it was only after the Civil War that inquisitive travelers, pioneer sociologists making field trips in America, particularly some of Frédéric Le Play's disciples, started telling their well-read audience about American lynching violence. They often did so in outstanding and reputable periodicals, but the mainstream press often gave stories about lynching violence no more space than a brief article here and there about the bloodiest stories.

One would expect that accounts of racially motivated violence would produce indignation in France, perceived by its citizens to be the "country of human rights." Surprisingly, most of these accounts are cautiously noncommittal and sometimes even supportive. Toward the end of the nineteenth century, the major encyclopedic dictionaries describe lynching as a specific type of punishment, albeit expeditious, for moral misconduct, "particularly by negroes."[5] The founder of criminology, Cesare Lombroso, considered lynching a "savage" yet "efficient" defense technique in cases where "extreme legality gets to the point where crime remains unpunished."[6] In his *Réflexions sur la violence*, George Sorel, who drew his information from one of Le Play's most influent disciples, Paul de Rousiers, admired the American man, a "man of order who, unlike French men, never wavers" and who has enough energy "to eliminate, in the name of higher interest, the criminals who compromise the nation's future."[7] One case, however, caused a scandal in Europe: the lynching of Italians in New Orleans in 1891. Some heavily criticized the violence. Others like Paul de Rousiers strongly endorsed the "New Orleans vigilantes committee that hanged mobsters, much to the delight of all honest men."[8]

French authors almost always agreed with American preconceptions on the "Black issue" because they shared similar attitudes toward Africans. However, one might wonder why they agreed so candidly with the concept that lynchings were a matter of "self-defense" for whites. One of Le Play's disciples, while touring the United States, wrote in 1876 about the chaos following the Civil War: "The KKK no longer existed, but unfortunately, in many Southern States, vigilantes committees and summary lynchings remained the only way Whites could protect their property and their lives."[9] Another one of Le Play's disciples suggested that Americans based their society "on the idea of race," feeling that the federal government should compromise some of its principles and "tolerate a method of lynching against Negroes that it would not tolerate against Whites."[10] In 1901, the *Revue politique et parlementaire*, a scholarly periodical, deemed lynching "unworthy of a great Republic," only to publish a dozen years later an article that would have fit well in a southern newspaper: "Through political action (amendments to the Constitution) and natural action (lynchings), the Southern states of the American Republic are bravely paving their way towards a resolution of the negro problem, to their own profit and according to their particular views."[11] The idea of solving the "Black issue" by sending African Americans back to Africa was popular not only among southern whites; the organizing committee of the 1900 Universal Exposition in Paris cynically approved of it and suggested that, since African Americans were enduring hard times as a result of repeated lynchings, they should be encouraged to emigrate to French West Africa, a colony lacking local leadership.[12]

During the interwar years, the French press gave scant attention to lynching. Beginning in 1932, the International Red Aid organization attempted to gather global public support for the so-called Scottsboro boys, as it had done successfully in the 1920s against the condemnation of the anarchists Nicola Sacco and Bartolomeo Vanzetti. The impetus likely came from the American Communist Party, which had already engaged fully in that struggle. Echoes of this campaign even reached French colonies as remote as Madagascar. However, because it combined ideology and manipulation to allegedly save "sons of workers and farmers" who were to be murdered by "American imperialists," it had few supporters in France, even among Communists, and was barely heard of in other circles. The European left was then too busy advocating domestic causes to pay attention to America.

During and after World War II, the reality of American racism became more apparent with the presence of Allied troops. Some French were appalled at how American authorities treated their black soldiers.[13] After the war ended, black artists who settled in Paris befriended prominent leftists and became influential. Criticism of lynching remained a popular rhetorical strategy for anti-Americanists, who won over large swathes of the public during the Cold War period. During the decade that followed the liberation, the French far left made lynching a symbol of capitalist exploitation before the focus turned to support for the growing civil rights movement. In 1947, at its national convention, the French Communist Party called the United States "the country where Negroes are being lynched," thus echoing Soviet propaganda.[14] The word *lynching* was used in a variety of contexts. Sartre denounced the execution of the Rosenbergs as a "legal lynching that covers an entire people in blood."[15] And yet, even in the early 1960s, some intellectuals on the right showed enough complacency toward the United States to minimize the gravity of lynching. Raymond Cartier, a reporter who represented the point of view of southern whites to the French public, refused to declare whether lynching "was indeed efficient."[16] For most well-informed French, to discuss lynching largely meant expressing political views on the United States.

ENEMIES WITHIN AND OUTSIDE

Lynching is sometimes considered a form of American exceptionalism. But if such acts of violence were unknown in old Europe, the underlying spirit of lynching was not. The history of collective violence against individuals in Europe reveals some not unexpected similarities with American lynching.

The history of the defeated South made it unique: here was a society that believed it was still at war with, or at least under siege by, a foreign enemy and later with an enemy within. Refusing to surrender, it spent all its energy trying to rebuild, which meant restoring white supremacy. During the Civil War, southern mobs killed carpetbaggers, scalawags, and Republicans, sometimes in greater numbers than blacks. In Reconstruction, southern whites brought blacks, the enemy within, to heel, although they still felt besieged as Congress passed civil rights laws that threatened to expand national authority.

Such a violent reaction to peril has been observed in many societies that perceived they were under the threat of an enemy. Western European nations usually have no enemy within—although some central and eastern European nations managed to find one: the Jew. However, the threat of an outside enemy did make lynching possible in France, as those suspected of collaborating with the enemy were met by the people's summary justice. After Verdun's fall, for instance, in September 1792, when the enemy was thought to be everywhere, a "national emotion" of this kind led to the slaughter of the "nation's enemies" in Parisian jails.[17] At the start of the 1870 war between France and Prussia, the farmers of Hautefayt, a village in the Dordogne region, lynched a young nobleman and then bragged that they had just roasted a Prussian spy.[18] During World War I, the culture of war infused the civilian world to the point that the enemy was portrayed as the devil in the name of an irreconcilable antagonism between civilization and humanism on one hand, barbarity and German atrocities on the other. The "rear" hunted down everything that looked or sounded "Boche," or "Kraut"—names, shops, potential spies.[19] These people found themselves universally suspected and ill treated, sometimes even lynched. In 1944, the *Epuration* meant that those who had collaborated with the Germans or dealt with them in one way or another were punished. It was a time when lynching traitors seemed no less legitimate than lynching a German paratrooper who had landed behind the lines. Such an event was reported by the Nobel Prize laureate André Gide, who, in 1951 described "the horrific lynching of a very young German paratrooper at the beginning of the war" and specified that angry farmers had beaten the soldier "to death with their fists, rakes and shovels."[20]

Yet the threat of an outside enemy is only occasional. In the United States, once the North had withdrawn and washed its hands of what happened in the South, white southerners turned to the enemy within. The post-Reconstruction era marked the beginning of the racialization of lynching, the near exclusive targeting of African Americans. But racism was not limited to the United States. Racially motivated lynchings reflected the way whites viewed blacks throughout the Western world. In western Europe, society did not respond defensively in the face of this enemy as the American South did. Sometimes Europeans saw blacks as they might see a circus animal, more a source for amusement than a threat.[21] The United States is the only country where large numbers of former slaves lived with their former rulers. If the American South can be enlighteningly compared with South Africa, it must also—as Mark Twain sensed—be paralleled with European colonies in Africa, where summary justice was widespread.[22] In this respect, American exceptionalism proceeded from the fact that "contrary to the rule . . . the colonized have migrated, not the colonizers," writes Raymond Cartier.[23]

The vast corpus of literature on African colonies leaves no doubt about the fact that the relationship between the victors and the vanquished is just the same as the one between master and slave. A superior humanity must educate and contain beings who are frightening enough to require constant supervision and, in some cases, the use of terror. A fear identical to that provoked by the African American hobo in the rural U.S. South haunted the white colonizer in Africa. Acts of violence perpetrated against Moroccan farmers echoed those on old plantations of the South. Fear of the natives rising up in mass against the colonizers fueled deep anxiety. The colonizers perceived that the majority of natives could not be assimilated and that the use of force was inevitable. True lynching was rare, as the police often took the place of the lynch mob, and whites relied upon the colonial law-enforcement agents to bring individuals to heel. But when great collective fears arose, European colonizers turned to pogrom, as in Algeria in 1945. On May 9, in Sétif, nationalist demonstrators were brutally repressed. This provoked riots in which 110 Europeans lost their lives and numerous rapes were committed. Reprisals followed, and European militias helped forty thousand soldiers, with support from the air force, to kill thousands of Algerians.[24]

The situation was even worse in sub-Saharan Africa, especially in Central Africa. In the Belgian Congo and in the Portuguese colonies, "Negroes" were just barely granted recognition as being human. The more Europeans felt like superior agents of civilization, the more inhumane treatments they inflicted upon the "savages," as André Gide observed in the 1920s.[25] Colonizers may not have described their actions as lynching, but they mutilated, tortured, and summarily executed Africans.

Cruelty often proceeds from denying others their humanity and categorically refusing to identify with them. That is how one can destroy others and still claim to be civilized. On rare occasions, this type of behavior found its way to metropolitan France.[26] Racism was commonplace, but acts of extralegal violence against the immigrant workforce in France developed only during the Algerian war of independence when *ratonnades* (racist manhunts) targeted Algerians. One such infamous episode was the October 17, 1961, massacre in Paris, when French police officers threw Algerian protesters into the Seine.

Times of economic crisis often trigger a resurgence of acts of violence more similar to lynching against those who are less likely to be assimilated, even if they make up a tiny community. Attacks against Roma people in Marseilles or in Rome are signs of such violence. Recently, riots and lynchings of black farm workers have taken place in southern Italy.[27] When the majority sees immigrants competing for local jobs, lynching can appear spontaneously.

To conclude this comparison, in the United States, the desire to exert white supremacy was a primary motivation in the majority of lynching cases. However, European whites also lynched colored people, albeit far from home. Their victims were natives who were denied even the basic civil rights African Americans enjoyed and who had no chance of seeking justice from a European court. They may not have used the word *lynching*, and their acts of violence may not have been carried out in the same manner that southern mobs executed their victims, but one could say that there were collective equivalents in the form of pogroms, acts of military and police repression, disappearances, and flat-out murders, all of which were very frequent in the history of colonization.

POPULAR JUSTICE VERSUS LEGAL VIOLENCE IN MODERN FRANCE

Though lynching may be considered rooted in a distinctive southern culture, it has its counterpart in the American West, dating back to the California gold rush and the time when cattle owners fought against farmers. Having almost disappeared in the twentieth century, this popular violence is far less unique than its legend suggests, as frontier situations permit or encourage violence everywhere in the world. This type of violence, carried out to control crime in areas where legal authorities are weak, kills less often than violence perpetrated by outright racists—although, at the same time, lynchings to control crime disproportionately target blacks and ethnic minorities. Surely America is not the only country to seek justice outside of law, as shown by the resistance against the monopoly of legitimate violence as well as the gap between formal justice and popular expectations elsewhere in the Western world.

In his well-known theory of the modernization process, Norbert Elias contended that as states mature, they enforce their claim to a monopoly over violence. In most countries where a vigorous central state develops, the state increasingly limits the possibility of private violence. Elias's theory applied to early modern Europe, and it is not our purpose to discuss its relevance regarding the American experience.[28]

However, Pieter Spierenburg makes a convincing argument in explaining that the high homicide rate in the United States is caused by America's robust and early democratic tradition, which represented an obstacle to the state's capacity to establish a monopoly on force and weaponry that European rulers managed to impose long before democracy took hold.[29]

Michael Pfeifer's smaller-scale analysis of "rough justice" in America runs along the same lines. He finds that popular sovereignty was in conflict with judicial formalism and argues that legal reforms did not proceed from the central state but from the eastern urban middle class, and then he identifies a "cultural conflict over criminal justice" and over the right to punish by legal or extralegal violence.[30] Lynching is the extreme form of such extralegal violence. The monopoly of violence and the formalism of law enforcement on the one hand and the vitality of popular justice on the other always stand in direct relationship, but the scale of possibilities greatly varies according to national historical experience. However, one can better understand the use of private violence in each country, or each region of a country such as the United States, by analyzing how legal violence is accepted rather than by using opaque categories such as "exceptionalism."

The tendency to seek violent justice exists beyond the borders of the United States. The frequency of the act and the number of victims in the Unites States may be exceptional, but this fact must not conceal the existence of a potential lynching spirit and mob violence in Europe as well, persistent well into the twentieth century. In this respect, to study France, a country where the criminal justice system emerged early, may prove challenging. France and the United States are at opposite extremes, the former exemplifying centralized and respected violence and the latter characterized by diffuse violence by citizens.

Obviously, as the French nation-state arose, the taming of violence triggered abundant resistance to law-enforcement officers and legal officials. Since the publication of Eugen Weber's *Peasants into Frenchmen* in 1976, this trend has been widely noted by historians of rural France.[31] Addressing endemic violence in rural communities, scholars have shown that this resistance was not passive or archaic but a new kind of active resistance that bore at least two forms: On the one hand, when riots erupted, the mob would anticipate action taken by authorities and take responsibility in place of the authorities for defending the community and its rights.[32] On the other hand, a network of institutions and a set of parajudicial methods for conflict resolution made punishment possible without resorting to law or interpersonal violence.[33]

For the most part, violence aimed at authority or at individuals disappeared from the French countryside around 1860. In the second half of the nineteenth century, the relationship between rural communities and the judiciary changed thoroughly.[34] In this context, the well-known case of Alain de Moneys, who was lynched in 1870 by farmers in Hautefayt, Dordogne, seems anachronistic.[35] However, those peasants who thought they were acting for the greater good learned at their own expense how strong the state had become. The authorities condemned the actions of the mob as monstrous, and this judgment was approved by the social body that supported the state. Even in the United States, lynching a white man after having tortured and burned him was hardly a common practice. Whites reserved that kind of treatment for blacks. Indeed, in the case of Alain de Moneys's lynching, the judiciary clearly thought the guilty peasants had put themselves outside civilization. That they would take responsibility for seeking justice themselves had become completely unacceptable to the authorities.

The Third Republic began in 1870 and would prove to be the most stable government in French history, falling only to the invasion of France during World War II. This era ushered in more effective government and more popular confidence in authorities. Mob violence, now limited to the cities, came under control. When a mob intended to take vengeance on a criminal offender, national law-enforcement agents made sure that it did not. These police officers were the instrument of the national state, unlike in the United States, where police derive their authority from the local community. French law-enforcement officers were feared and respected, and this made it very unlikely that a mob would have treated them the same way southern mobs treated sheriffs and their deputies, overpowering them and taking from them their prison keys. In France, mobs would shout outside of a courtroom, but actually taking action against symbols of public authority almost never occurred. Retaliatory lynchings were extremely rare. Still, members of the lynch mob that killed several Italian workers in the salt fields near Marseilles in August 1893 were exculpated by the court.[36] Most people in France still considered immigrants barbarians, and that made them somewhat vulnerable to mob violence.

Throughout the course of French history, the state failed to exercise it authority to police and punish crime only under exceptional circumstances. When state power failed, ordinary people would resort to violence, claiming the authority to act as a sovereign right. This happened most notoriously in the French Revolution. The 1792 threat of foreign invasion prompted lynchings known as the "September massacres" in Paris. But the interpretation of this event remains contentious. Some, like François Furet, see it as a pretotalitarian warning before the full-scale "Terror" took hold; others blame it on the weakness of the revolutionary government, on the internal strife between government organs that left an institutional void that popular violence inevitably filled.[37] In this respect, the Terror was a period when power was centralized to the point that any attempt at an anarchic and popular form of justice—whether it be lynchings or any other miscarriage of justice—was held off. Terror courts curbed legitimate popular violence by institutionalizing revenge.[38] At the local level, Donald Sutherland describes the importance of a "redistributive culture of justice" in Aubagne, one that flourished in a relative institutional void.[39] Yet the Terror did not condemn the September 1792 violence, only the form it took; the mob and its leaders shared the same political views. They only disagreed about who should bring justice. The "people" still saw violence as a sovereign right—hence the rituals of justice that often preceded massacres, when mob leaders assumed the trappings of the state, establishing a tribunal with a president, judges, and jurors. Some of these makeshift tribunals even cleared accused persons of all charges. Likewise, some lynchings in the United States were preceded by a mock trial. However, in the mind of political leaders, sovereignty cannot be fragmented, and no fraction of the "sovereign" people could exercise it directly. Organized terror by the state makes spontaneous violence recede, and the state can effectively label as "counterrevolutionary" those who resort to it.[40] Centralized monopoly of violence became the main remedy for summary justice. Throughout the nineteenth century, *Septembriseurs* (literally "September breakers") remained a particularly negative model in French political history.

The events that unfolded in France in 1944 seemed closer to a form of popular justice arising as a result of the collapse of all authorities except local ones. In the spring of 1944, as the fighting that led up to the *Libération* erupted everywhere, so did a wave of purges, both legal and (at least during the first year) extralegal, known as the *Épuration*.[41] Many summary executions took place as the fighting against the Germans continued in a climate of civil war and with various *Résistance* groups seizing local power. In many cases, executions took the form of hanging on the village square, with the entire populace cheering, sometimes after a trial had been led by a "court" made up of *Résistants*. Still, neither the victims nor the perpetrators used the word *lynching*. They saw the violence as comprising acts of war—a French-on-French war that was an inevitable consequence of wartime collaboration by some. Most of the extralegal purge took place in the fall of 1944, particularly in southern France, where local resistance movements prevailed quickly and more completely than elsewhere. Then, in May and June 1945, when survivors of German concentration camps returned, vengeance accelerated as the population exploded in anger. Most French people concluded that the law was too slow, overly compassionate, and deficient. No one called these killings lynchings, but lynching-like acts occurred during those few weeks, sometimes right on the platform at the railway station.

The most spectacular episode of the purge, and the most widespread, was the head-shaving of women accused of "horizontal collaboration."[42] Head shaving was theatrical: it was done in a public area, sometimes in front of the city hall or by the city fountain, and was often preceded by a carnivalesque parade in which the accused women were beaten and humiliated. They were not put to death, but once shaved, most were sentenced to prison terms. These women, unmasked by the vox populi, had sold or given themselves to German soldiers, and by doing so, many believed, they had betrayed their husbands and their country. They had soiled the nation by soiling their own bodies.[43] The mob was calmed only when punishment was prompt and performed in public, not when it was decreed after a long trial behind closed doors. By assuming control of the executions, villages or neighborhoods could vouch for the purge. Clearly, a situation where authorities were nonexistent and later complacent facilitated an explosion of anger mixed with a determination to seek justice—and probably prevented more serious acts of violence by quenching an immense thirst for revenge. Similarly, women were being shaved in Italy in the chaos that followed Mussolini's demise.[44] The same temptation to shave the "Krauts' girls" arose in northern France and Belgium at the time of the 1914 invasion. But unlike in 1944, authorities restored order immediately and sent the accused women to three different camps. The army then took over and restored formal legal procedures.[45]

THE LATE FADING OF THE LYNCHING SPIRIT

From the mob's perspective, to administer immediate punishment on the very spot where a crime was committed, in front of an audience willing to participate, is far better than to learn the guilty will be sentenced to a long prison term. The same is true in many situations: disappointment at how modern justice works feeds a persistent desire for direct popular justice. In this respect, there is no American exceptionalism; rather, a lynching spirit that no longer finds a stage to exhibit itself in public as it once did in the

United States, but whose occasional manifestations in France and elsewhere in Europe leave no doubt of the moral legitimacy, in the end, of a form of popular violence that is now only a historical memory.

Since the end of the eighteenth century, formal criminal justice carried out by the state has become progressively more lenient. Reformers have successfully banished torture and other inhumane treatments. Instead, new execution methods are supposed to reduce suffering. Sentences have adapted to modern sensibility. Such a process, however, is only fueled by the will of public authorities and the governing elite. In large sectors of the population, the courts' indulgence is not held blameworthy so much as their incapacity to satisfy a desire for justice (which is in fact likely a desire for revenge). What people want is to be involved in carrying out the sentence, but the judiciary keeps the public away from even witnessing the punishment and claims to exercise its authority in the name of a higher purpose than the punishment of any given crime. Moreover, issuing lenient sentences does not serve the interest of those who want to see the convict endure as much suffering as he has caused. For many, the *lex talionis,* or eye-for-an-eye justice, remains a truer and more effective form of justice than any kind of crime control bureaucratically administered.

Bearing this in mind, David Garland explains how mobs of southern whites tortured and burned their victims after 1890, decades after authorities had renounced cruel treatments, not because they were primitive, but because they embodied values that modern and egalitarian America had given up.[46] Such lynchings, Garland writes, are not abnormal or archaic but self-conscious and reactionary acts. Lynching is a form of criminal justice—however minor or restricted in time and space—that feeds on a resolute hostility toward the evolution of criminal punishment. Michael Pfeifer also elaborates on this theme of dissatisfaction in the face of a legalistic and formalistic abstraction.[47] In France, similar thoughts are sketched around the concept of vengeance. According to the historian Raymond Verdier, the state has taken exclusive ownership of the possibility of revenge by making it an attribute of political authority and a method of government.[48] Judge and prosecutor replace the victim in the role of the offended. The relationship between the criminal and his victim is downgraded. This is not always well received, even if the state remains respected because it provides safety. A disembodied justice does not satisfy the victim's desire for reparation; it only maintains social order. Still, the crowd continues to confuse justice with revenge; it wants revenge for the victim, not for society.

Instead of attempting to describe (even sketchily) the various evolutions of sensibility according to times or places, let us focus on the most visible example: capital punishment—the last chance for the crowd to confront, even in an increasingly indirect way, the man facing death. It brings about nostalgic memories of direct justice and fuels a surviving lynching spirit. In France, public executions evolved, as they have elsewhere: accessory punishments such as branding, stocks, and public exposition were abandoned in the first half of the nineteenth century.[49] Authorities gradually moved executions to early morning and closer to the prison rather than in the city center. Officials removed the scaffold so that the guillotine would not be seen from afar. But in France, executions were not performed away from the public eye as early as they were in many U.S. states. Until World War II, they remained public, and according to the press, they were accompanied by what some journalists labeled a "procession of indecency." Indeed, the celebratory disorder accompanying Eugène Weidmann's execution in Versailles elicited the decree of June 24, 1939, prohibiting public executions.

Until that decree, capital punishment remained a public show in France— and the public attended until the very end. The taste for blood and the rejoicing around the scaffold were not unlike the satisfaction of a picnicking mob after a well-publicized lynching in the American South. In this respect, French and American experiences are not so far apart: in America, "lynching reached most consumers as a spectacle," and most people experienced lynching "second hand."[50] However, while the American press specialized in morbid accounts, the French press, feeling more uncomfortable, did refer to offensive conduct and filthy language in the mob but hardly ever gave a full picture of it—although French journalists were never reluctant to give grisly details about local crime. When reporting on executions, they focused on the executioner and the preparation, providing few details about the lynching spirit that was present.

Some cases have become famous, such as Jean-Baptiste Troppman's 1870 execution in Paris, narrated by the Russian novelist Ivan Turgenev. The prefect of police decided the execution should take place earlier than planned in order to avoid reprisals from the populace, who wanted the corpse. In the words of Flaubert, the mob, which he compared to the one that "soiled Rome on circus days," behaved in a way that "anticipated the Paris Commune."[51] Two men managed to break through the line of soldiers, crawl under the scaffold, and dip their handkerchiefs in the blood dripping through the cracks. Similarly, at an unruly 1897 execution in Hazebrouck, in northern France, women dipped their handkerchiefs in the bloodstained basket containing the remains that were being taken away for dissection. As late as 1939, the mob overwhelmed law-enforcement agents to dip their handkerchiefs in the blood of the man who had just been executed. On January 11, 1908, in northern France, four members of the "Pollet's gang" were executed in Béthune in front of a crowd outraged by the barbarian nature of their crimes. The ten-man gang had terrorized local farmers for a decade, burning their feet so they would reveal where they held their money—much like the infamous "chauffeurs" who roamed the area shortly before 1800. The execution attracted tourists from Belgium and Germany, much like those who flocked to American lynchings on specially chartered trains. Insults were screamed under cell windows, and songs were written for the occasion—the mob chanted them uninterruptedly for hours before the execution after having waited all night in neighboring cabarets. Applause, cheers, and obscenities saluted the arrival of the convicts and the fall of their heads in sawdust—scenes that were considered "indescribable," repugnant, and disgusting by the authorities. And yet the same show was put on in Lille in 1910, when, after the execution, the corpse was escorted to the cemetery by twenty thousand workers who heaped insults upon the condemned man into his grave. Filmmakers such as Pathé disregarded the law and filmed the 1908 quadruple execution. That was enough to persuade authorities that they had to censor films in France, and it triggered a vast campaign for the abolition of capital punishment. As a comparison, the public in New York would certainly not have watched the horrific Paris, Texas, lynching of 1893, but eagerly viewed pictures of it. Likewise, Paris, France, had a taste for blood and sensationalism, and from 1901, the movie company Pathé satisfied this macabre inclination by screening short films of executions in various countries until the police prefect put an end their filming.[52]

Once authorities moved executions behind prison walls, mobs screamed their hatred and demanded that the offender be turned over to them when convicts came out of the court. In the twenty-first century, such vehement manifestations have largely receded. The media have partly diverted the public from the feeling of revenge by convincing it that victims and families need to mourn to find peace. This new trend, in which references to psychology are ubiquitous, has helped the lynching spirit recede even in the most traditional layers of society.[53] Yet it sometimes reappears against outside elements, especially migrants, in barbaric ways that echo the lynching of African Americans.

USE AND LIMITATIONS OF THE COMPARISON

France and the United States are apparently very different when it comes to extralegal popular violence. Still, the comparison that has been sketched here leads us to qualify the idea of American exceptionalism for two reasons.

First, in the American South, the form of lynching that survived the latest as a brutal means of social, racial, and economic control of black farmhands, playing the same role as segregation in towns, seems to make the United States exceptional compared to other Western societies. But is this comparison accurate when one takes into account the fact that European nations did not import black slaves but instead sent colonists to exploit blacks in Africa? Southern racial violence is nothing exceptional if the South is set in a structurally justified comparison with colonial rule: white American southerners and French settlers (as well as Belgian, German, Portuguese and others—not to mention South Africans) have much in common. My initial remarks on the complacent way the French, even intellectuals, tended to react when confronted with cases of lynching in America, which they always linked with the "savage" and often "inferior" nature of the blacks, shows that the ideology of white supremacy pervaded Western society as a whole, at least until World War II.

Second, lynching considered as popular justice, mainly in the nineteenth century, makes the United States perhaps less exceptional than one might think, because the "lynching spirit" of the crowd remained very strong in parts of western Europe as well, in contrast with the too "civilized" evolution of the punitive system. All the same, this "spirit" led French mobs to threaten or to enjoy official executions; it led American mobs to lynch. The possibility or incapacity to act is explained in part by the different status of law-enforcement forces. The real difference between the United States and Europe lies, on a more general level, in the way violence prevails in U.S. society, while other Western societies are more tame. This is a broader frame in which American exceptionalism has been and has to be tackled—be it about "monopoly of violence" against democratic individualism, homicide rates, or industrial relations and class warfare.

The comparison, however, has its limitations. It bears the risk of constraining the demonstration in a kind of formalism: executing a black person randomly picked or taken away from the judiciary or executing a Nazi collaborator with the same summary methods and the same popular approbation can both be considered a form of lynching. Who would claim that the moral and human implications of both acts are the same? Comparing the acts does not make it possible to compare their authors. Besides, is it possible to reduce lynching to an ordinary form of violence? The ferocity of scenes that took place in Texas or Mississippi in 1930 would be unacceptable for a European public in a time of peace, whatever could be said of its well-preserved lynching spirit. The violence that lurks in societies and the preservation of a spirit of vengeance are one thing; increasing intolerance of open cruelty is another. We have only touched upon the history of sensibility, and its national nuances, probably considerable, are yet to be explored.

NOTES

1. Christian Delporte, "De l'affaire Philippe Bertrand à l'affaire Patrick Henry, un fait divers dans l'engrenage médiatique," *Vingtième Siècle,* October–December 1998.

2. *Trésor de la langue française,* Centre national de ressources textuelles et lexicales, http://www.cnrtl.fr/definition.

3. Paolo Viola, "The Rites of Cannibalism and the French Revolution," *Quaderni online,* Quaderno III, People and Power: Rights, Citizenship and Violence, http://www.library.vanderbilt.edu/quaderno/Quaderno3/quaderno3.html; Viola, "Violence révolutionnaire ou violence du peuple en révolution," in *Recherches sur la Révolution,* ed. Michel Vovelle and Antoine de Baecque (Paris: La Découverte, 1991), 95–102. The nobleman used the bones found in the village cemetery as fertilizer. Just hours after his lynching, two young men carried his right hand and his heart to a neighboring village, where residents ate and chewed the flesh. For the 1870 case, see Alain Corbin, *Le village des cannibales* (Paris: Aubier collection historique, 1990).

4. He refers to summary executions committed by the national guard and writes about the 1832 riots in Paris: "People were for order in combination with lack of discipline. . . . The first comer took it upon himself to save society. . . . Fierce Lynch law, with which no one party had any right to reproach the rest, for it has been applied by the Republic in America, as well as by the monarchy in Europe. This Lynch law was complicated by mistakes. On one day of rioting, a young poet, named Paul-Aimé Garnier, was pursed in the Place Royale, with a bayonet at his loins, and only escaped after taking refuge at the porte-cochère of No. 6." Victor Hugo, *Les Misérables,* (Paris, 1862), 2:101–2.

5. *La grande encyclopédie,* 31 vols., ed. H. Lamirault, coord. Camille Dreyfus (Paris, 1885–1902); the *Littré* dictionary, 1889 ed. On March 24, 1922, *Le Figaro* wrote of a culprit caught in the act that he "endured a small lynching" before being questioned.

6. Cesare Lombroso, *Le crime, cause et remèdes* (Paris: Schleicher frères, 1899), 540.

7. Georges Sorel, *Réflexions sur la violence* (Paris, 1908), chapter 6, "La moralité de la violence," 140–41.

8. Paul de Rousiers, *La vie américaine* (Paris: Firmin-Didot, 1892), 218. The 698

pages of this work are the result of a "reasoned investigation" made in the United States in 1890; the book was very successful and prized by the Académie française. The opposite view can be found in Jules Angot des Rotours, "Chronique du mouvement social: Angleterre, Etats-Unis," *La réforme sociale*, January 16, 1900, 185–90.

9. Claudio Jannet, *Les États-Unis contemporains: les moeurs, les institutions et les idées depuis la guerre de Sécession* (Paris, 1876), 87.

10. Henry Joly, *Problèmes de science* (Paris: Hachette 1910).

11. R Sheperd, *Revue politique et parlementaire* 27 (1901): 435. From an even more racist standpoint, Raoul de la Grasserie wrote: "The white man rarely marries a negro woman. On the contrary, the inferior race looks for whites and that is the main cause for lynching in the United States." *Psychologie et sociologie de l'eunuchisme et du célibat* (Paris, 1914), 173.

12. "Exposition universelle de Paris," in *Les colonies françaises, Sénégal-Soudan, agriculture, industrie, commerce* (Paris: Chattanel, 1900), 103–4.

13. Alice Kaplan, *The Interpreter* (London: Free Press, 2005); Louis Guilloux, *Ok, Joe!*, trans. Alice Kaplan (Chicago: University of Chicago Press, 2003).

14. The USSR exploited this theme as Japan had done before the war and knew where to find its inspiration: when the 1903 Kichinev pogrom provoked outrage in the American public, the Russian press responded by denouncing lynching.

15. *Libération*, July 19, 1953.

16. Raymond Cartier, *Les Cinquante Amériques* (Paris: Plon, 1961), 305.

17. Mona Ozouf, "Massacres de septembre: qui est responsable?" *L'Histoire*, no. 342 (May 2009): 52–57.

18. Alain Corbin, *Le village des cannibales* (Paris: Aubier, 1990).

19. Christophe Prochasson and Anne Rasmussen, *Vrai et faux dans la grande guerre* (Paris: La Découverte 2004).

20. André Gide, *Ainsi soit-il* (Paris, 1951), 1177.

21. European zoos hosted "ethnological expositions" until World War II. The Paris zoo hosted thirty such events between 1877 and 1912. The massive participation of troops from the French colonies in World War II had an impact. But African villages were still put on show at the 1931 Colonial Exposition.

22. George M. Fredrickson, *White Supremacy: A Comparative Study of American and South African History* (New York: Oxford University Press, 1981); Ivan Evans, *Cultures of Violence: Racial Violence and the Origins of Segregation in South Africa and the American South* (Manchester: Manchester University Press, 2009); Mark Twain, *King Leopold's Soliloquy: A Defense of His Congo Rule*, in *"Following the Equator" and Anti-Imperialist Essays* (New York: Oxford University Press, 1996).

23. Cartier, *Les Cinquante Amériques*, 302.

24. Benjamin Stora, *Histoire de l'Algérie coloniale, 1830–1954* (Paris: La Découverte, 1991); Jean-Louis Planche, *Sétif 1945: Histoire d'un massacre annoncé* (Paris: Perrin, 2006); Marcel Reggui, *Les massacres de Guelma, Algérie, mai 1945: une enquête inédite sur la furie des milices coloniales* (Paris: La Découverte, 2006).

25. André Gide, *Voyage au Congo* (Paris: Gallimard, 1927); Gide, *Retour du Tchad* (Paris: Gallimard, 1928).

26. David A. Shafer, *The Paris Commune: French Politics, Culture, and Society at the Crossroads of the Revolutionary Tradition and Revolutionary Socialism* (New York: Palgrave Macmillan, 2005).

27. The situation seems particularly serious in that country, where the large population of Romanian immigrants faced discrimination. The press reports cases of lynching and violence, sometimes after rapes were committed. Hatred is also directed at Gypsies, who are subject to frequent attacks in Hungary.

28. Norbert Elias, *The Civilizing Process: The History of Manners* (Oxford: Blackwell, 1969); Elias, *The Civilizing Process: State Formation and Civilization* (Oxford: Blackwell, 1982).

29. Pieter Spierenburg, "Democracy Came Too Early: A Tentative Explanation for the Problem of American Homicide," *American Historical Review* 111, no. 1 (2006): 104–14; Spierenburg, "Violence and the Civilizing Process: Does It Work?" *Crime, Histoire et Sociétés* 5, no. 2 (2001): 87–105.

30. Michael Pfeifer, *Rough Justice: Lynching and American Society, 1874–1947* (Urbana: University of Illinois Press, 2004), 96.

31. Eugen Weber, *Peasants into Frenchmen: The Modernization of Rural France, 1870–1914* (London: Chatto and Windus, 1979). The first chapter is entitled "A Country of Savages." Alain Corbin "L'histoire de la violence dans les campagnes françaises au 19ème siècle: Esquisse d'un bilan," in "Violence, brutalité, barbarie," special issue, *Ethnologie française* 21 (July–September 1991): 224–36.

32. Nicolas Bourguinat, *Les grains du désordre: L'État face aux menaces frumentaires dans la première moitié du XIXe siècle* (Paris: Éditions de l'École des Hautes études en sciences sociales, 2002).

33. Raymond Verdier, "Le système vindicatoire, esquisse théorique," in *La vengeance: Études d'ethnologie, d'histoire et de philosophie,* (Paris: Éditions Cujas, 1980). Verdier describes the vindicatory system as regulating social order, which guarantees crimes will not go unpunished but also brings appeasement and reconciliation; modern criminal justice systems destroy it and consider vengeance an "occult, regressive and subversive" act. See also François Ploux, *Guerres paysannes en Quercy: Violences, conciliation et répression pénale dans les campagnes du Lot (1810–1860)* (Paris: Éditions de la boutique de l'histoire, 2002).

34. Frédéric Chauvaud, *De Pierre Rivière à Landru: La violence apprivoisée au 19ème siècle* (Paris: Brepols 1991).

35. Corbin, "L'histoire de la violence."

36. Gérard Noiriel, *Le massacre des Italiens : Aigues-Mortes, 17 août 1893* (Paris: Fayard, 2010).

37. Jean-Clément Martin, *Violence et Révolution: Essai sur la naissance d'un mythe national* (Paris: Seuil, 2006).

38. Sophie Wahnisch, "De l'économie émotive de la terreur," *Annales ESC* 57, no. 4 (July–August 2002): 889–913.

39. Donald Sutherland, *Murder in Aubagne: Lynching, Law, and Justice during the French Revolution* (Cambridge: Cambridge University Press, 2009).

40. Philippe Goujard, "La violence et la Terreur," in *Recherches sur la Révolution,* ed. Michel Vovelle and Antoine de Baecque (Paris: La Découverte, 1991), 87–94.

41. The expression "épuration sauvage" (wild purge) is used by those (victims and journalists rather than historians) who denounce the injustice it represented as well as a "Communist conspiracy." To this day, it has remained a sensitive topic, so I will not go into a useless discussion of numbers. Henri Rousso explained the situation in "L'épuration en France, une histoire inachevée" *Vingtième Siècle* 33 (January–March 1992): 78–105.

42. Fabrice Virgili, "Les tontes de la Libération en France," *Cahiers de l'Institut d'histoire du temps présent* 31 (1995): 53–65.

43. A number of people claiming that the potential mix of French and German blood harms the unity of the French nation echo the fear of miscegenation felt by some white supremacists. Conversely, in this particular case, the scapegoat theory could apply.

44. It seems that during the Spanish Civil War, in areas controlled by Franco's troops, women in Republican families were head-shaved.

45. Jean-Yves Le Naour, "Femmes tondues et répression des 'femmes à boches' en 1918," *Revue d'histoire moderne et contemporaine* 47, no. 1 (January–March 2000): 148–58.

46. David Garland, "Penal Excess and Surplus Meaning: Public Torture Lynchings in Twentieth-Century America," *Law & Society Review* 39, no. 4 (December 2005): 793–833.

47. Pfeifer, *Rough Justice.*

48. Raymond Verdier, *Vengeance,* (Paris: Éditions Autrement 2004).

49. Renée Martinage, *Punir le crime: La répression judiciaire depuis le code pénal* (Paris: CNRS, l'espace juridique, 1989).

50. Christopher Waldrep, ed., *Lynching in America: A History in Documents* (New York: New York University Press, 2006), 3.

51. Alexandre Zviguilsky and Jacques Léauté, *Actes du colloque sur la peine de mort dans la pensée philosophique et littéraire: autour de "L'exécution de Troppmann" d'Ivan Tourguéniev* (Paris: Association des Amis d'Ivan Tourguéniev, 1980). For quotations, see Michelle Perrot, "Huit morts à Pantin en décembre 1869," *L'Histoire* 30 (January 1981): 28–37.

52. Albert Montagne, "Crimes, faits divers, cinématographie et premiers interdits français en 1899 et en 1909," *Criminocoprus,* http://criminocorpus.revues.org/207, 2009.

53. Obviously, it would be even more crucial to discuss the insensitivity to others' pain because the sight of violence has been generalized through television.

Informal Justice in Northern Ireland

RACHEL MONAGHAN

A 19-year-old Westrock man had two legs broken in a so-called punishment attack at his home on Sunday evening. The incident happened shortly after 6.30pm when up to eight masked men forced their way into his home and beat and jumped on his legs.
—"Westrock Man Attacked," *Andersonstown News,* January 18, 1997

A man has been taken to hospital with gunshot wounds to the leg . . . the shooting happened shortly before 10.30 pm on Tuesday when a number of masked men forced their way into a house. The victim was taken into a yard to be shot.
—"Man Shot in Leg," *News Letter,* October 12, 2000

THE EPIGRAPHS TO THIS CHAPTER are illustrative of the informal justice that is meted out in Northern Ireland by both loyalist and republican paramilitary groups. Such activities are frequently referred to in the literature and the media as informal justice, popular justice, rough justice, vigilantism, paramilitary "punishments," and the black criminal justice system.[1] According to police statistics from the period between 1973 and the end of March 2010, 3,200 people had received what they term paramilitary-style shootings, and a further 2,562 people had become victims of paramilitary-style assaults between 1982 and the end of March 2010.[2] Like most crime statistics, these figures signify only those recorded by the police and represent only the tip of the iceberg.[3] This essay introduces the reader to the history and development of the informal justice system in working-class areas of Northern Ireland and offers an explanation of the rationale for paramilitary "punishments."

The Origins of Informal Justice

Historically, the origins of informal justice in Northern Ireland can be traced back to precolonial Ireland. In the period prior to colonization by the English in the sixteenth century,[4] the Brehon laws—a set of customs, customary laws, and institutions advocating a predominately restorative justice approach—were to be found among the indigenous Irish population. These laws functioned as both a legal and a social code ensuring the harmony of the tribal communities of Ireland at this time. As Michael Davitt, the founder of the Irish National Land League explains, "The Brehons were the judges, next in importance to the chiefs, and their persons were sacred."[5] Central to the legitimacy and authority of the Brehon laws was their acceptance by the community, and this was dependent upon community cohesiveness. The hierarchical nature of the tribal communities meant that the status of both the victim and the offender was considered when sentences were handed down. Additionally, mitigating factors including the existence of provocation and the extent of the damage caused could also be considered. As Laurence Ginnell notes, "There were no prisons . . . and there were hardly any public servants who could correctly be called police or detectives. The people were their own police."[6] The most common punishment was a fine, with expulsion from the community reserved for perpetrators of "vile" crimes and habitual criminals.[7] The Brehon laws sought to restore harmony within the community by reintegrating the offender and placating the victim or his or her immediate relatives with the payment of compensation. With the advent of colonization, the Brehon laws were suppressed and eventually disappeared around the early part of the seventeenth century, following the extension of English law to Ireland.

In the subsequent two centuries, secret organizations and revolutionary agrarian societies developed alternative systems of justice in opposition to those of the British. According to Peter Alter, "The earliest important example of an agrarian secret society, which in many ways served as a model for all those that followed, was that of the Whiteboys, founded around 1760."[8] The Whiteboys, or Levellers, as they were often known, emerged in county Tipperary and then spread to other parts of southwest Ireland. They were concerned primarily with the plight of local tenants, farmworkers, and smallholders but would also oppose the payment of dues they considered "illegal," such as tithes for the Protestant Church. They would often appear in times of economic hardship and disappear once conditions improved. Then, when times were hard again, they would reappear under the same name or a new one. For example, in 1785 a society called the Rightboys was to be found in operation in southwest Ireland, with aims akin to those of the Whiteboys, and in 1826 the Ribbon Society, or Ribbonmen, was established.[9]

The activism of such organizations involved a mix of intimidation, physical force, and violence. To counter measures designed to enclose common land and impound trespassing livestock, ditches were filled in and hedges and fences pulled down. In instances where new tenants had been introduced or where stewards or agents were put in place by landlords, houses were burned or destroyed, livestock killed, and the landlords, tenants, stewards, or agents assaulted. Institutions of the state, including police stations, were also subject to attack, and individuals suspected of providing information to the authorities about the secret organizations were liable to have part of their lips or tongues cut off.[10] Sinister warnings were given to the rural population not to oppose the secret organizations; the Whiteboys, for example, "erected gallows, made coffins, and dug graves in the public roads, all obviously intended as portents of the fate awaiting those who refused to obey their mandates."[11] The various secret organizations enjoyed considerable support from the rural populations among whom they operated; they were the "champions of the oppressed," and the "the Boys" became an affectionate and exonerating turn of phrase.[12]

Revolutionary agrarian societies associated with the Irish national movement emerged in the nineteenth century. These societies operated openly and had clear political objectives centered on agrarian reform and the national question. The most prominent association of this type was the Irish National Land League, founded in 1879. The Land League engaged in a number of activities, including resisting bailiffs, organizing rent strikes, and establishing its own courts. These courts provided alternative arbitration, and in rural areas the Land League became recognized as "the source rather than the breaker of the law."[13] The Land League's law could see rents withheld, farms of evicted tenants kept empty, new rents unilaterally fixed, and landlords boycotted by the community.[14] Individuals found guilty of breaking this "moral law" were liable to punishment. Punishments included the firing of warning shots into homes, physical injuries such as ear clipping or gunshot wounds to the legs, and ultimately, death.[15] Such organizations relied like their secret counterparts on retaining community support and legitimacy, and to this end they had to remain aware of the sensitivities of their support base. Johnny Connolly suggests that the punishment of "carding," whereby those guilty of infringing the "moral law" would have a piece of wood with nails driven through it raked along their backs, was discarded in response to community abhorrence.[16] The Land League was eventually outlawed in 1881 and martial law imposed; however, revolutionary agrarian violence continued throughout the 1880s.

In addition to the development of revolutionary agrarian societies, the Irish Republican Brotherhood (IRB) was founded in 1858. Its objective was to secure the removal of British rule and the establishment of an Irish republic. The IRB formed provisional governments during its unsuccessful rebellion of 1867 and the Dublin Easter Rising of 1916. They claimed political authority in Ireland and decreed their enactments the law of the Irish republic, thereby refusing to recognize the legitimacy of the British justice system. As a secret society, members of the IRB were obliged to swear an oath of allegiance and adhere to the society's code of conduct. Violations were met with violence, and traitors could expect to be executed.[17]

Throughout the nineteenth and early twentieth century, increased agitation by Irish nationalists continued. This culminated with Sinn Féin winning 73 of the 105 Irish seats in the 1918 general election and declaring itself the provisional government of Ireland, Dáil Éireann. Mary Kotsonouris notes that Sinn Féin's initial attempt to create "National Arbitration Courts" in the summer of 1919 "amounted to little more than an aspiration."[18] However, the following year it issued a decree establishing "Courts of Justice and Equity," and Dáil courts were in operation between 1920 and 1922. These were hierarchical courts that operated at the parish, district, and supreme court levels and dealt with a range of offenses including theft, property damage, violation of licensing laws, and robberies. Judges were able to demand the return of stolen goods, impose fines, order beatings, and banish offenders from the area or order their removal to an island for the duration of their sentence (Dáil Éireann had no prison facilities).[19] At the parish level, judges were elected from among the local people, and the courts were intended to offer cheap and immediate access to justice. They tended to operate on the principle of attempting to reconcile parties in dispute; this can be seen in the punishment options available to the judges and reflects the need for legitimacy and support for the courts themselves. Subsequently, they received public support, and when required, Irish Republican Army (IRA) volunteers imposed the sentences of the court. With the establishment of the Free State government in 1922, the British court system in Ireland passed to Saorsta

Éireann. In 1923, the Dáil courts were brought to an end, and their judgments were no longer enforceable.

From the discussion above, informal justice in Ireland can be seen to have
involved both restorative and retributive styles of punishment. The Brehons
laws stressed the restoring of harmony to the community and thus relied on
a restorative justice approach, imposing fines for the majority of offenses. Expulsion from the community, the most severe of punishments, was reserved
for habitual criminals and those found guilty of "vile" crimes. In contrast,
retributive justice was predominantly utilized by secret organizations such as
the Whiteboys, revolutionary agrarian societies, and the IRB, with the harsh-
est penalties reserved for informers or traitors. The Dáil courts in operation
between 1920 and 1922 employed a mix of retributive and restorative justice
approaches. What is common to all of these informal justice mechanisms
is the desire of the organization involved to solicit and maintain popular
community support for their actions; this is in part reflected in the types of
punishments deemed acceptable. Given these past experiences of informal
justice systems operating in parallel to the formal state system, it is not surprising that similar mechanisms have emerged in Northern Ireland during
the "Troubles," and it is to this that I now turn.

THE BEGINNINGS OF INFORMAL JUSTICE IN NORTHERN IRELAND

Since the onset of the Troubles in the late 1960s, informal justice mechanisms and policing arrangements have developed in the working-class areas of Northern Ireland. Within Catholic areas citizen defense committees
(CDCs) were established with the aim of protecting Catholic enclaves from
attacks by loyalists. At this time sectarian clashes and riots were frequent,
the violence culminating in the summer of 1969 when Catholic houses on
Bombay Street in the Lower Falls (Belfast) were set alight by a loyalist mob.
Sources suggest that some 1,505 Catholic families in Belfast alone were
burned out of their homes between July and September 1969, with more
than 200 houses either razed to the ground or completely gutted.[20] The burn-
ings led the CDCs to undertake foot and car patrols and to erect and super-
vise barricades in and around Catholic areas. These are the earliest example
of organized activities with a central committee based in Belfast coordinat-
ing policy and liaising with some 95 delegates representing 75,000 persons
living in nationalist areas.[21]

In August 1971, the government reintroduced the policy of internment without trial, whereby individuals could be arrested and held indefinitely. During the four years the policy was in effect, a total of 1,981 people were detained; 95 percent of those interned were from the Catholic community.[22] Subsequently, the activities of the CDCs were taken over by the newly established Catholic Ex-Servicemen's Association (CESA) formed in protest at internment. Although unarmed, CESA members had previous military training and at the association's peak, it claimed more than eight thousand members.

Outside of Belfast, similar organizations were also formed, in nationalist areas of Derry, Northern Ireland's second city, for example; there a local defense association established its own "police force" to deal with petty crime. The Free Derry Police, led by a former international soccer player, operated independently of republican paramilitaries for a brief period in the early 1970s.[23] "Punishments" were usually in the form of verbal reprimands stressing the need for community solidarity.

With the reemergence of the (Provisional) IRA in January 1970 following a split within the republican movement, the IRA quickly created a special unit tasked with policing republican areas. With the establishment of "no-go" areas in both Belfast and Derry, the IRA became the "sole arbiter of order behind the barricades."[24]

Comparable developments can also be found in Protestant working-class areas with the formation of vigilante/defense associations. The Ulster Defence Association (UDA) was formed following the amalgamation of such organizations in 1971. As one member explains, their activities were "vigilante stuff, balaclavas, pick handles, all that."[25] The UDA engaged in mounting roadblocks, patrolling the streets, and gathering evidence against petty criminals. Likewise, the Ulster Volunteer Force (UVF) adopted a similar policing role in the areas in which it operated. Patrols by the UDA and UVF were not designed to usurp the police but to assist them. Unlike their republican counterparts, loyalist paramilitaries were not necessarily illegal organizations. Although originally banned by the government in 1966, the UVF was made legal in April 1974 but then banned again in October 1975. The UDA, on the other hand, was not banned until 1992, and violent acts carried out by UDA members were claimed by the Ulster Freedom Fighters (UFF) from 1972 onward. The UFF, however, was proscribed shortly after its violent campaign started.

"Crimes" Liable for "Punishment"

Much of the informal justice carried out by paramilitaries in Northern Ireland is in part a response to demands from the community in which they operate to "do something" about crime and antisocial behavior. The purge by the reenergized IRA in the fall of 1970 in the Ballymurphy area of west Belfast is illustrative of this. Those targeted included alleged local criminals, illegal drug users, teenage girls suspected of fraternizing with British soldiers, and anyone believed to be connected to, or to have sympathy with, the state.[26] For example, housewives who persisted in giving cups of tea to soldiers had their homes daubed with slogans, and teenage girls who went out with soldiers had their heads shorn and were tied to lampposts with a placard round their necks with details of their "crime."[27] As Kevin J. Kelley notes,

> Car thefts, muggings, break-ins and vandalism were now prevalent in communities. . . . The social fabric was being slowly ripped apart in Catholic neighbourhoods as the police vanished and as rioting replaced Gaelic football as the most popular activity among teenage boys. Some organization clearly had to exert some kind of authority if criminal anarchy were not to become the norm. . . . The IRA . . . had both the wherewithal and the desire to protect its base from inner-directed lawlessness.[28]

The IRA's decision to assume a policing role was also based on the need to ensure its own security and survival "so that operations could not be sabotaged by informers."[29] Similarly, within Protestant working-class areas loyalist paramilitaries began to respond to teenage crime and vandalism. Local "hoods" were warned, and claims of responsibility for kneecappings (bullet wounds to the knees) of criminal elements began to appear in the local press.[30] As a company commander of the UVF explains,

> We want to see the end of punishment attacks [but] in the same breath there is a community out there who is reliant on the UVF to mete out punishment, because in many cases the [police] aren't responding, and in other cases they are directing people to us knowing they will get more satisfaction. There is a need for our community to deal with habitual offenders. You can only do so much to help someone on the straight and narrow, but when you see pensioners getting mugged or robbed and stuff like that happening in your own area, there is a cry

for help from the community and the [police] are abdicating their responsibility, then there is a duty for the UVF to look after their own people.[31]

Activities liable for "punishment" by both republican and loyalist paramilitaries can be differentiated into "normal" and "political" crime. "Normal" crime encompasses those activities that would be considered illegal in the formal justice system such as vandalism, car theft, muggings, the selling of alcohol to minors, and rape as well as activities deemed "antisocial behavior" by the community and paramilitary groups. Behavior considered "antisocial" is wide ranging and can include fighting with paramilitary group members, annoying the local community by gathering at street corners, playing music too loudly, verbal abuse of elderly residents, and inappropriate disposal of trash. Punishments can also be meted out to those criminals who are considered to have been treated too leniently by the formal criminal justice system. For example, the UVF gave a punishment beating to a former Presbyterian minister who had received only a warning from the police for possession of an illegal homosexual pornographic video.[32] In contrast, "political" crimes include informing, or "touting," as it is locally known; misusing a paramilitary group's name; collaborating or fraternizing with the "enemy"; or bringing the police into the area. For example, an individual involved in a robbery received a punishment shooting as a result of the subsequent police chase, which brought officers into a Catholic neighborhood.[33]

Paramilitary punishments are not confined to alleged criminals but are also meted out to group members for breaching internal codes or disobeying orders. IRA volunteers are governed by the "Green Book," which sets out what is expected of them and the consequences of any misdemeanors. An internal police force known as the "Nutting Squad" was established to ensure the discipline of its members. As a former volunteer explains, they are the ones who put a hood over the heads of informers prior to shooting them in the head ("nutting") and leaving their bodies on the border between Northern Ireland and the Republic of Ireland.[34] It has been suggested that many of the loyalist punishments result from disputes over money, with members being accused of swindling, skimming funds from the group, the payment of misappropriate "cuts," or committing robberies for personal gain.[35] According to a member of the Red Hand Commando (RHC) brigade staff, "Most of it [punishments] would be internal. A lot of it would be [in response to] antisocial [or] drug-related [behavior] or discipline [issues] with the paramilitary ranks. . . . If it is a misdemeanor it could be a slap round the head; if it's something serious he could get one [bullet] in the leg; the very extreme is being shot in the head, which is very unusual."[36] Within both republican and loyalist paramilitary organizations, members suspected of informing were usually executed. For example, the IRA volunteer Brian McNally was shot in July 1984, and the UFF killed Arthur Bettice, a UDA member, at his home on the Shankill in November 1981. Furthermore, paramilitary groups take action against rival groups operating in their respective communities. In the 1970s, the Provisional IRA launched a purge against the Official IRA in some parts of Belfast and in October 1992 targeted the Irish People's Liberation Organisation (IPLO) following the gang rape of a woman in the Divis flats complex and their involvement in the growing drug trade. One IPLO member was executed and another ten members shot with assault rifles; the group disbanded shortly thereafter.[37] Similarly, loyalist paramilitary groups have throughout the course of the Troubles engaged in feuds with each other. In 1975, a violent feud erupted in Belfast between the UDA and UVF; members' homes were bombed, but there was no loss of life. The feud of 2000 between the UDA/UFF and the UVF, which lasted from July to December, resulted in seven men being killed and an eleven-year-old girl being shot in the back, and more than 281 households in the Shankill area of west Belfast sought rehousing after being forced from their homes or deciding to leave in fear of intimidation.[38] The most recent feud, in 2005, between the UVF and Loyalist Volunteer Force (LVF) lasted some six weeks, in which time the UVF murdered four men it alleged had LVF connections and attempted to murder another fifteen. When the two organizations agreed to a truce, the LVF announced its decision to disband.[39]

Thus paramilitary groups punish not only alleged criminals and individuals engaged in "antisocial behavior" in the areas in which they operate but also members of their own and rival organizations.

The Punishment Process

Both republican and loyalist paramilitaries insist that their involvement in informal justice and policing of their respective communities is a response to community pressure. Incidents or issues of concern can be brought directly to the paramilitary organization, or the group may become aware of an incident themselves. Paramilitaries contend that punishments are only undertaken once an investigation is carried out, although this is disputed.

For example, a victim of punishment beating stated: "They don't go and investigate nothing like. If they hear something or if they just don't like you, they'll do you anyway."[40]

Prior to the mid–1970s the IRA was responsible for informal justice in nationalist areas, with a special unit tasked with dealing with crime and the republican youth movement Na Fianna Éireann undertaking early policing activities.[41] With the establishment of "incident centers" in republican areas staffed by Sinn Féin members to monitor the IRA's truce of 1975, informal justice was transferred from the IRA to Sinn Féin, with the "incident centers" evolving into "advice centers." These were known locally as "Provo police stations." A Sinn Féin local government politician explained that following the reporting of a "crime" or incident of "antisocial behavior" an investigation would be undertaken by the civil administration officers (CAOs) assigned to deal with the case. Once all the details were collected, the information would be verified and a decision made as to the next step. If the culprits were not known, then a warning would be placed in local newsletters, the republican press, and sometimes through a leaflet drop in the area. For example, in August 1981 the IRA in Belfast placed a warning in the local republican press to those engaged in the hijacking of vehicles and looting of small businesses: "The IRA condemns such activities and warns those responsible that such behavior will not be tolerated."[42] If, on the other hand, the culprits were known, they would be brought before the CAOs and given the opportunity to defend themselves; however, this was not always the case. A further decision would then be taken as to whether a warning would be issued or the case should be passed to the IRA to mete out punishment.[43] IRA volunteers suspected of "crimes" would be brought before a jury of their peers and if found guilty, sentenced accordingly. The republican press would often carry IRA statements regarding executions: "The Belfast Brigade of the IRA claims responsibility for the execution of Patrick Murray. . . . As an IRA volunteer, [he] was fully aware of his right to be tried by a jury made up of his peers who could not pass a sentence of execution unless the evidence . . . against him was substantiated and proven. . . . Murray admitted his role as an informer."[44] Within the loyalist paramilitary groups, special teams or persons were assigned to an investigatory and punishment role. As an RHC commanding officer explains, individuals known as "provosts" are responsible for punishment attacks, and before a member of the community is punished, an investigation is carried out and the accusation proven.[45] Similarly, the UVF contends that an investigation is carried out, and in cases of a minor nature the local group is best placed to deal with the matter, but in more serious cases a unit attached to the leadership of the organization is brought in.[46] Those members of the UDA suspected of informing were investigated by the UFF's Special Assignment Section. For example, the UFF admitted responsibility for the killing of Edward "Ned" McCreery, a former UDA commander, following an investigation into his activities. In a statement from the group, they contended that their investigation had shown he "had colluded with both the Special Branch [of the police] and the 'enemies' of Ulster."[47]

Throughout the course of the Troubles a system of graduated tariffs commensurate with the seriousness of the "crime" under consideration developed. The scale of sanctions includes warnings, threats, curfew, fines or restitution, placarding, tarring and feathering, beatings, shootings, exiling, and ultimately death. Placarding and tarring and feathering were very public spectacles, with the individuals being paraded in front of the community and punished. Examples include the tarring and feathering of four young men one Sunday morning in January 1971 in front of Mass goers on the Falls Road of west Belfast; in the Shankill in 2008 two men were forced to walk the road with placards saying "I'm a thief and a burglar."[48]

Similarly, alleged informers' bodies are left in public places for the community to see and thus provide a warning to others. According to a senior member of the IRA, such incidents lead other informers to come forward: "Usually when a body is left on the street two or three people come forward and give themselves up . . . That's two or three less to do us damage and two or three less to be executed."[49]

In contrast, the bodies of most of the so-called disappeared, those fourteen individuals abducted by republican paramilitaries at the height of the Troubles, have not be found. In 1999, the IRA admitted that it had murdered nine of the disappeared, including Jean McConville, a mother of ten who was taken from her Divis home by IRA members after being accused of being an informer. Her family strongly deny that she was an informer, and an investigation by the police ombudsman in 2006 found no evidence that Mrs. McConville had passed information to the security services. Her body was found in 2003. To date eight bodies have been retrieved.[50]

As in the formal criminal justice system, in theory the punishment ordered would be influenced by mitigating factors such as age, gender, past criminal history, and family background. In cases involving children, often the parents would be approached and told to exercise greater parental control, and in some instances the parents were punished. For example, a father was shot after "repeatedly ignoring IRA warnings to discipline two of his sons who had been involved in persistent acts of anti-social behaviour."[51] In the postceasefire period (from 1994 onward) examples of young people under the age of sixteen receiving physical punishment from the paramilitaries can be found. In March 1999, a thirteen-year-old was beaten by a loyalist gang of men armed with baseball bats and told to leave Northern Ireland, and republican paramilitaries beat a fifteen-year-old with hammers and baseballs bats in July 1999. Media reports of young people being shot have also become more frequent. In January 2004, the Irish National Liberation Army kidnapped a fourteen-year-old and shot him in the leg, and loyalist paramilitaries shot a fifteen-year-old boy in both legs in Newtownards in April 2003.

Similarly, although there appears to have been reluctance especially during the 1970s by both republican and loyalist paramilitary groups to punish females severely, this has also changed over time. In the early days of the Troubles, Catholic women accused of informing within republican areas were tarred and feathered. It has been suggested that the community would not "accept wounding as a legitimate form of punishment for female offenders."[52] Since the mid–1980s, republican groups have on occasion subjected women to punishment beatings and executed female informers. In September 1985, Catherine Mahon and her husband were shot in west Belfast by the IRA. Police figures also suggest that loyalist groups do on occasion mete out punishment beatings and shootings to females, but this is not the norm. This is confirmed by a victim of a punishment beating who explained that in his housing complex the UDA "don't beat girls. . . . If you're a girl you're all right."[53]

Individuals subject to punishments can be abducted off the street or from a pub or attacked in their own homes or at the homes of friends and families. In some cases, individuals to be punished are told to turn up at a certain time and place in order to receive their punishment. Failure to do so often results in a harsher punishment. As a victim of a punishment beating explains, "I got the message that I had to meet them round at the bar. . . . So I went to the bar . . . and they said to me, 'When a white car pulls up you just jump into it and we'll take you away.' So a white car came. . . . I done all this because I didn't want anybody to come to my home, kicking the door in and doing it, so that's why I went with them."[54] There have been a number of instances of mistaken identity where the paramilitaries have punished the wrong person. For example, John Brown, a seventy-nine-year-old man, was incorrectly identified as a pedophile and subsequently shot in both knees and ankles.

The severity of a punishment beating or shooting may also be dependent upon mitigating factors. Beatings can be inflicted by the paramilitary members' own fists and feet or may involve the use of implements such as baseball bats (with or without nails in them), iron bars, sledgehammers, pickaxe handles, and hurley sticks. Victims may be tied upright to fence railings, rendering them unable to shield themselves. Some individuals have also had cinder blocks dropped on their limbs. Punishment shootings can also vary in terms of where an individual is shot, the number of times, and the caliber of the weapon used. Most shootings are to the legs—hence the term *kneecapping*—but victims can also be shot in the ankles, wrists, and elbows. Shootings involving six bullets to a combination of the knees, elbows, wrists, and ankles are locally known as "six-packs." With the exception of executions, paramilitary punishments are not meant to result in death, and some victims of such attacks have ambulances called for them by the paramilitaries. When deaths do result as a consequence of a beating or shooting, they are considered to have "gone wrong." Examples include the UDA's beating of Charles McConnell-Strain in 1998, who died as a result of his injuries, and Edward Taggart, aged nineteen, who was trying to flee an IRA punishment when he was shot in the back in the Divis Flats in 1985.[55]

Paramilitaries can also order individuals out of a local neighborhood, city, town, Northern Ireland, or the island of Ireland. Those told to leave are normally given twenty-four or forty-eight hours to do so. The length of time of the expulsion order can be indefinite or for a fixed period, such as six months or a year. Exiling is an attractive option to paramilitaries, as it removes undesirable elements from the community and is a less brutal form of punishment. Thus females and young people under sixteen have been ordered out and in some cases, whole families. The exact number of people who have been exiled by the paramilitaries is unknown.

Informal justice has a substantial history in Ireland, and its roots can be traced to precolonial days. The development of informal justice mechanisms in Northern Ireland is linked to the Troubles. Community demands for paramilitaries to do something about crime in their areas were initially due to a combination of reasons including a policing vacuum, particularly in republican areas, where the police were seen as an instrument of the British state and not considered legitimate. In loyalist areas, though the police were considered legitimate, they were perceived as inadequate. In addition, levels of petty crime and "antisocial behavior" were increasing in working-class areas;

the community called for a prompt, visible, and effective response, and there was also a perceived failure of the formal criminal justice system to deal adequately with offenders.[56]

Punishments are not confined to alleged criminals but also meted out to paramilitary organization members and rival groups. Both republican and loyalist paramilitaries operate a graduated tariff of sanctions, which in theory can be influenced by mitigating circumstances. Despite the Northern Ireland peace process, which has culminated in the decommissioning of the main paramilitary group weapons and the acceptance of the Police Service of Northern Ireland by Sinn Féin and the nationalist community, paramilitary punishments still occur, albeit with a greatly reduced frequency of two to four per week. The Independent Monitoring Commission reported that the Provisional IRA has not engaged in any punishment attacks since February 2006.[57] Punishments in republican areas are now carried out by dissident republicans (those groups who oppose the peace process) such as the Real IRA and the Continuity IRA. Punishments still also occur in loyalist areas as well. Thus the history of informal justice in Northern Ireland and the reasons for its development suggest that punishments will continue.

NOTES

I would like to thank Dawn Purvis for her assistance with aspects of the fieldwork.

1. "Informal justice": Rachel Monaghan, "The Return of 'Captain Moonlight': Informal Justice in Northern Ireland," *Studies in Conflict and Terrorism* 25, no. 1 (2002): 41–56; "popular justice": Paddy Hillyard, "Popular Justice in Northern Ireland: Continuities and Change," *Research in Law, Deviance and Social Control* 7 (1985): 247–67; "rough justice": "Rough Justice as UVF Renegade Shot," *Sunday Life*, August 29, 1999, 14; "vigilantism": "Vigilantes Got the Wrong Man," *Andersonstown News*, April 4, 1998, 4; Andrew Silke, "The Impact of Paramilitary Vigilantism on Victims and Communities in Northern Ireland," *International Journal of Human Rights* 4, no. 1 (2000): 1–24; "paramilitary punishments": Colin Knox, "The 'Deserving' Victims of Political Violence: 'Punishment' Attacks in Northern Ireland," *Criminal Justice* 1, no. 2 (2001): 181–99; Brian Rowan, "Punishment Attack in Belfast Linked to UDA," *Belfast Telegraph*, January 24, 2008, 12; "black criminal justice system": Michael Morrissey and Ken Pease, "The Black Criminal Justice System in West Belfast," *Howard Journal* 21 (1982): 159–66.

2. Police Service of Northern Ireland, "Casualties as a Result of Paramilitary-Style Attacks 1973–31 Mar 2010," http://www.psni.police.uk/ps_attacks_cy.pdf. Figures for paramilitary-style assaults other than shootings have only been available since 1982.

3. For a more detailed discussion of the problems associated with crime statistics,

see John Muncie, "The Construction and Deconstruction of Crime," in *The Problem of Crime*, ed. John Muncie and Eugene McLaughlin (London: Sage, 2001), 7–70.

4. Despite the English first invading Ireland in 1172, their control and authority of the island was contested and incomplete. It was not until the reign of Henry VIII that the monarch's authority was cemented with Henry becoming king of Ireland in 1541. Subsequently, Henry embarked upon a policy of conciliation and fusion of the Irish and English populations in Ireland and extended English law to the entire island.

5. Quoted in D. B. Cashman, *The Life of Michael Davitt* (London: Cameron and Ferguson, 1885), 194.

6. Laurence Ginnell, *The Brehon Laws* (London: T. Fisher Unwin, 1894), 186.

7. Ibid. What constitutes a "vile" crime remains unclear, as Ginnell fails to offer a definition.

8. Peter Alter, "Traditions of Violence in the Irish National Movement," in *Social Protest, Violence and Terror in Nineteenth- and Twentieth-Century Europe*, ed. Wolfgang J. Mommsen and Gerhard Hirschfeld (London: Macmillan, 1982), 140. The Whiteboys name refers to the white shirts or garments worn by members as a means of identification.

9. Ibid.

10. Ibid.; James S. Donnelly, "The Whiteboy Movement, 1761–5," *Irish Historical Studies* 21 (1978): 20–54; Christine Bell, "Alternative Justice in Ireland," in *One Hundred and Fifty Years of Irish Law*, ed. Norma Dawson, Desmond Greer, and Peter Ingram (Belfast: SLS Legal, 1996), 145–67.

11. Donnelly, "The Whiteboy Movement," 29.

12. Ibid.; R. F. Foster, *Modern Ireland, 1600–1972* (London: Penguin, 1989), 224.

13. Johnny Connolly, *Beyond the Politics of "Law & Order": Towards Community Policing in Ireland* (Belfast: Centre for Research and Documentation, 1997), 19.

14. Bell, "Alternative Justice in Ireland"; Alter, "Traditions of Violence."

15. Foster, *Modern Ireland*.

16. Connolly, *Beyond the Politics*.

17. Léon Ó Broin, *Revolutionary Underground: The Story of the Irish Republican Brotherhood, 1858–1924* (Dublin: Gill and Macmillan, 1976).

18. Mary Kotsonouris, "Revolutionary Justice—the Dáil Éireann Courts," *History Ireland* (Autumn 1994): 32.

19. Ibid; Connolly, *Beyond the Politics*; Dorothy Macardle, *The Irish Republic* (1938; reprint, New York: Farrar, Straus and Giroux, 1965).

20. Kevin J. Kelley, *The Longest War: Northern Ireland and the IRA* (London: Zed Books, 1988); Peadar Whelan, "Remembering the Past: Bombay Street, 1969," *An Phoblacht*, August 13, 2009, http://www.anphoblacht.com/news/detail/38678, accessed July 31, 2010.

21. Connolly, *Beyond the Politics*.

22. Martin Melaugh, "Internment: Summary of Events," Conflict Archive on the Internet, http://cain.ulst.ac.uk/events/intern/sum.htm, accessed August 31, 2010.

23. Eamonn McCann, *War and an Irish Town* (London: Pluto, 1980).

24. Connolly, *Beyond the Politics*, 22.

25. John White, quoted in Ian S. Wood, *Crimes of Loyalty: A History of the UDA* (Edinburgh: Edinburgh University Press, 2006), 6. White went on to murder Senator Paddy Wilson of the Social Democratic and Labour Party and his assistant Irene Andrews in 1973. White confessed to the murders in 1978 and was sentenced to life imprisonment.

26. Jim Cusack and Henry McDonald, *UVF: The Endgame* (Dublin: Poolbeg, 1997).

27. Patrick Bishop and Eamonn Mallie, *The Provisional IRA* (London: Corgi, 1997).

28. Kelley, *The Longest War*, 148–49.

29. Ibid., 149.

30. "Knee-Cap Job," *Combat* 1, no. 34 (1974); "Sparks from the Anvil," *The Ulster* 1 (May 1976).

31. Interview by fieldworker, November 2005.

32. David McKittrick et al., *Lost Lives: The Stories of the Men, Women, and Children Who Died as a Result of the Northern Ireland Troubles* (Edinburgh: Mainstream, 2001), 1405–6.

33. Interview by the author, November 1999.

34. Eamon Collins, *Killing Rage* (London: Granta, 1998). Ironically, Collins suffered a similar fate and was found brutally murdered near his home in January 1999. For more information, see David McKittrick, "Trimble Accuses IRA of Murder," *Independent*, January 29, 1999, http://www.independent.co.uk/news/trimble-accuses-ira -of-murder-1076840.html.

35. Andrew Silke, "Ragged Justice: Loyalist Vigilantism in Northern Ireland," *Terrorism and Political Violence* 11, no. 3 (1999): 1–31; Richard Sullivan, "UVF Disciplines Hoods Who Helped Themselves," *Sunday World*, January 10, 1999, 22.

36. Interview by fieldworker, November 2005. The Red Hand Commando is a small loyalist paramilitary group closely associated with the UVF.

37. "Drug Rings Smashed," *An Phoblacht/Republican News*, November 5, 1992; McKittrick et al., *Lost Lives*, 1300.

38. Springfield Intercommunity Development Project, *The Feud and the Fury* (Belfast: SICDP, 2001).

39. Angelique Chrisafis, "LVF Disbands after Loyalists Declare Truce," *Guardian*, October 31, 2005, http://www.guardian.co.uk/uk/2005/oct/31/northernireland .angeliquechrisafis, accessed July 31, 2010.

40. Interview by the author, September 1999.

41. Hillyard, "Popular Justice"; Ronnie Munck, "The Lads and the Hoods: Alternative Justice in the Irish Context," in *Whose Law and Order?*, ed. Mike Tomlinson et al. (Belfast: Sociological Association of Ireland, 1988), 41–53.

42. "Warnings," *An Phoblacht/Republican News*, August 15, 1981.

43. Human Rights Watch/Helsinki, *Children in Northern Ireland* (New York: Human Rights Watch, 1992). Sinn Féin's Gerry Kelly denied the existence of civil administrators tasked with informal justice on a Channel 4 News broadcast, May 21, 2000.

44. "Informer Executed," *An Phoblacht/Republican News*, August 21, 1986.

45. Interview by fieldworker, November 2005.

46. Interview with company commander by fieldworker, November 2005.

47. "War Commentary," *New Ulster Defender* 1/2 (July 1992).

48. Bishop and Mallie, *Provisional IRA;* Allison Morris, "PUP Denies UVF Had Part in 'Walk of Shame' on Shankill," *Irish Newsletter*, January 14, 2008.

49. Bishop and Mallie, *Provisional IRA*, 404.

50. Three bodies were found in 2010, including that of Charlie Armstrong, who went missing on his way to Mass in 1981.

51. "Punishment Shooting," *An Phoblacht/Republican News*, March 25, 1982.

52. Morrissey and Pease, "Black Criminal Justice System," 164.

53. Interview by the author, January 2000.

54. Interview by the author, October 1999.

55. Kieran McDaid, "'Punishment Victim' Dead for Two Days," *Belfast Telegraph*, October 2, 2003; McKittrick et al., *Lost Lives*, 1026.

56. Colin Knox and Rachel Monaghan, *Informal Justice in Divided Societies: Northern Ireland and South Africa* (Basingstoke: Palgrave Macmillan, 2002).

57. Independent Monitoring Commission, *Twenty-Third Report* (London: Stationery Office, 2010).

PART 2

American Lynching and International Meanings

How the British, Japanese, Russians, and Slovaks
Gave Meaning to American Lynching

M OB VIOLENCE HAS A DRAMATIC HISTORY stretching far beyond the boundaries of the United States, as the essays in part 1 have documented. The word *lynching* has its own history as well, one well worth studying, as the word had and has enormous political power. Labeling a violent event a *lynching* is hardly a neutral act. The rhetorical history of lynching has America at its center. While it seems very unlikely that America exported the notion of mob violence, as other people in other places hardly needed the help of outsiders to form mobs, the word itself is an American export. Robert Zecker examines the ways emigrants to the United States made sense of the violence they encountered. He finds that Slavic newspaper editors reprinted numerous stories of American lynchings, generally endorsing the violence. Zecker argues that immigrant newspapers reported American lynchings sympathetically as part of a program to socialize the new arrivals into American culture.

Not only did foreigners grapple with the meaning of *lynching* when they came to America, Americans journeyed to foreign countries, weaving the word *lynching* into their criticisms of American mob violence. Sarah Silkey finds in the British leg of Ida B. Well's traveling antilynching campaign the beginnings of an American exceptionalism on the question of racial violence. In the mid-nineteenth century the British press regularly reported "lynchings" in the United Kingdom. After Wells raised the issue, leading British politicians and journalists began accepting American claims that peculiarities in the American condition made the Americans especially prone to mob violence. This became part of the British national identity: people in Britain did not lynch.

Two of the essays that follow show how the American word *lynching* allowed the enemies of the United States a propaganda advantage in World War II and in the Cold War. Fumiko Sakashita finds that after 1919 Japanese journalists and politicians began denouncing American lynching to promote their own country's ambitions to lead nonwhite peoples against Western imperialism and racial prejudice. In World War II the Japanese directed anti-imperialist propaganda at African Americans. Most American blacks rejected the propaganda, but it did influence their thinking. Many African Americans agreed with Japanese charges of American racial hypocrisy. Japanese rhetoric criticizing Western imperialism and white supremacy contributed to African

Americans' "Double V" campaign, arguing for a patriotic fight against the Axis but, at the same time, calling for a fight against American racial prejudice as well.

Meredith Roman finds that between 1928 and 1933 the Soviet Union identified lynching as a defining feature of Western capitalism. The Soviets defined lynching in such a way as to make it impossible in the USSR. At the center of this moment came the Scottsboro Boys controversy. When the U.S. Supreme Court returned a decision favorable to the African American defendants in that case, the Soviets began to lose interest in American lynching. In 1956 when white Mississippians shot and killed Emmett Till, the Russian press hardly took notice.

The essays that follow highlight a new approach to the study of "lynching," namely the study of the word itself and its rhetorical history. While the behavior and actions of lynch mobs will always be of great interest to historians, we hope that these essays demonstrate that there is much to be gained from studying the history of this word. It has a demonstrated rhetorical power, jumping across oceans, and the study of the word can open windows on the minds and attitudes of peoples not just in the United States but across the globe. Ironically, such rhetorical studies of lynching demonstrate simultaneously the international reach of the United States in the nineteenth and especially the twentieth century while also highlighting the limitations of American cultural hegemony as Americans have in no way been able to control the meaning of the word once it enters the language and culture of other nations. Americans invented the word, and growing American influence helped spread it, but Americans could not control its meaning or the use foreigners made of it.

"Let Each Reader Judge"

Lynching, Race, and Immigrant Newspapers

ROBERT ZECKER

T HE HEYDAY OF EASTERN and southern European emigration from roughly 1880 to 1914 brought around fifteen million people to the United States, with more than 225,000 identified as Slovak. Slovaks primarily were fleeing the poverty of their hilly region of Upper Hungary, but many also resented the official Magyarization policy that relegated them to third-class status in their homeland. Slovaks were familiar with oppression, most notably in the form of laws barring the use of Slovak (and other non-Magyar) languages in public. They also endured occasional official violence, such as soldiers' 1907 murder in Černova of people protesting the imprisonment of Father Andrej Hlinka. Slovak immigrants were familiar with the violence of pogroms against Jews and Romanies (gypsies) prevalent throughout east central Europe. And Slavic immigrants toiling in industrial jobs in the United States had experienced the brutality of the "Cossacks," state militias who beat or murdered strikers, as in the infamous 1897 Latimer massacre of Slavic miners. Slovak immigrants, then, knew all too well the scorn and violence rulers often visited on minority groups.[1]

What seems to have been new to such immigrants, though, was the atrocity of lynching, in which hundreds if not thousands of citizens publicly hung, shot, burned, or otherwise tortured primarily black victims. Slavs' emigration to America coincided with an upsurge of acts of mob law against blacks, and such matters did not go unnoticed by immigrant newspapers. While historians have recently debated the precise nature of collective, extralegal violence, Slovak and Rusyn newspapers referred to such public mob killings as *lynčovania*. These extralegal killings of mostly black—and less frequently, Mexican, Italian, and Jewish—victims as reported in Slavic papers and identified as "lynchings" are the focus of this essay. Almost weekly, fatal acts of mob law were publicized in newspaper accounts of these rituals of white supremacy.[2] That Slavic newspapers saw fit to reprint such accounts alongside old-country news, church socials, and picnics may at first seem surprising. Why did this concern immigrants, or at least immigrant newspapers' editors? What message did immigrant editors hope to convey to their foreign-language readers by continually placing these horrific stories on the front page?

By the first decade of the twentieth century, Slovak and Rusyn newspapers such as *Slovák v Amerike* (Slovak in America), *Jednota* (Union), and *Amerikansky russky viestnik* (American Rusyn messenger) had already published hundreds of accounts that were reported as lynchings. These accounts, together with frequent reports of urban race riots (*plemenný boj*), minstrel-show jokes, and slighting references to "savage," "cannibal" Africans and Asians established a tutorial for immigrants on who were the most vulnerable citizens in their new homeland. Into the 1920s papers continued to feature lynching accounts almost weekly. Many of these public mob murders occurred in places where few Slovak immigrants dwelled, but some notorious lynchings also occurred in places with which Slovaks were quite familiar.

Slovak lynching accounts often followed the lead of mainstream papers and foregrounded moral equivalencies between black criminality and white mob violence. While the assertion of vengeance might seem macabre, such accounts provided a narrative that justified such extraordinary assertions of "the people's justice" by the enormity of the black victim's crime against white women or children. The articles often summoned the mob's "authority" to act; mob actions were characterized not as disruption but rather restoration of the peace and social order. Collective public murders, no matter how horrific, for Slovaks as for other white Americans fit into a framework of sometimes necessary communal grassroots justice when lenient courts failed to "avenge a poor white girl."[3]

Race was not an entirely unfamiliar concept to many southeastern European immigrants, but newcomers did have to learn what Jim Crow laws meant in their new homeland. Indeed, almost from the moment they got off the boat, immigrants had been telling stories about their first bewildered encounters with the "Negro," if one can believe what immigrant newspapers report.[4] The first sighting of blacks by steerage passengers became a trope, representing newcomers' fear and amazement at America. Newspapers did more than report facts, however. From humor pages to lynching reports, immigrant publications phrased community experiences in increasingly racial terms.

These accounts were largely translations of English-language news sources. Nevertheless, the selection of these items tells us something of what Slovak editors thought their readers needed to know about America. We can never know for certain how these articles were received by immigrants or how readers interpreted this material (and of course, not all immigrants came to the same conclusions on their conception of black people or on anything else, for that matter). Still, immigrant newspapers were in fierce competition with each other, and editors presented material they thought their readership desired or needed.

Moreover, writers of letters to the editor often argued vociferously with papers' stances on labor, politics, Slovak nationalism, and other topics. Such backlash is absent on the matter of lynchings, race riots, and portrayals of blacks. Either no immigrant readers saw fit to write, or editors neglected to publish such letters. In either case, most stories of white mob violence were left to stand alone, with little editorial condemnation, as a commentary on the new country's racialized landscape. In Slovak immigrant newspapers, selective translations of English-language articles reflected and shaped discourse that defined racial identity as black or white. Reading frequent accounts of public collective violence and the "savage" non-Europeans under imperial rule helped Slovak readers to "naturalize" the black-white divide. These publications aided in putting in place boundaries defining appropriate Slovak social identity as being in the latter group.

What horror, pity, and thoughts of black vulnerability, though, raced through the mind of an immigrant fresh off the boat who picked up a copy of *Slovák v Amerike* on June 26, 1903? "Negro Lynched—People's Awful Justice Condemns Criminal," proclaimed the headline of a story reporting the torture of George White of Wilmington, Delaware. Subheads focused not on the mob's actions but on the fact that the "Negro robbed and murdered the daughter of Evangelical minister E. A. Bishop," a crime for which he "was summarily burned alive."

The author began his story not with the violence of the mob that seized White from his jail cell but with a lengthy description of the black man's "awful crime": "Horrible was that crime to which he alone confessed in the following words: 'My boss Woodward sent me to the field and when I went there, I saw the pastor's daughter. I sneaked up on her and grabbed her by the neck and demanded all her money.' . . . He made sure she couldn't cry out, and choked her to suppress her screams, choked her until she lost conscious-ness." The account neglected to mention that this "confession" was delivered while White had a noose around his neck and was threatened with being burned alive. "He would not have been lynched if he had been a white man," the reporter admitted. "It was said, though, that he was a beast in human form and in an instant he was handed over to the authority of the lynch mob."

The article went on to detail the process by which more than three hun-dred men broke into the jail and delivered White to mob justice, creating "terrible theater as the crowd of people emptied their revolvers into him." After detailing White's cries for mercy, the writer noted, "At the end of this horrible justice everyone made sure to cut off a piece of his body to take for themselves as a souvenir!" After the lynching, "The people partied in the morning and the peace of the grave reigned over the whole countryside. The people bloodily avenged the death of a poor girl!"[5]

English-language papers were full of graphic reports of lynchings, serv-ing to create as well as publicize the caste system and shore up the solidar-ity of the Caucasian race.[6] For immigrants sifting their way through a new land's racialized shibboleths, community was even more directly formulated around an imagined whiteness fostered, in large measure, through cultural productions such as the immigrant press. Indeed, the particularly brutal American mob violence was such a new phenomenon to Slavs that a new English loan word had to be introduced into Slovak and Rusyn. Many stories described the work of white mobs using *zničiť* (destroy), *zabiť* (slaughter), *vraždiť* (murder), or *strieľať* (shoot), but very quickly *lynčovať* (lynching) was invented. Although Slovaks knew of their own oppression of and vio-lence against Jews, lynchings were evidently something new, for not even "pogrom" sufficed.[7]

As in the account of White's lynching, the assumption of authority by whites to judge and execute offending blacks was often portrayed for Slavic immigrants as a restoration, not a disruption, of "the peace of the grave" that should reign over a white-dominated countryside. In its excruciatingly de-tailed description of White's crime, his torture, and the tropes of white citi-zens acting to restore racialized justice, this account was quite explicit.

Indeed, almost from their first years in America, Slavic immigrants had read of lynchings. As early as 1896, *Slovák v Amerike* spoke of "Judge Lynch the Destroyer" in describing a California case in which three men (two blacks and a Mexican) were hung from trees by a crowd of 250 people. In what would become a frequent refrain in years to come, Slovak readers were informed that the sheriff and his deputies had been holding the men as prisoners but were unable to restrain the crowd in its search for justice and that members of the crowd "shot them through and through, and then lynched them."[8] In 1906 *Slovák v Amerike* reported that in Chattanooga "more than 4,000 whites had attacked the municipal jail for more than three hours" to get at two black men jailed for "violating" white women. As in the California case, "the heroic efforts of municipal police and members of the state police" proved ineffectual in repulsing the mob.[9] In coming years, such accounts were so frequent that a standard headline—"Judge Lynch" (*Sudca lynč*)—was employed.

Often it was an alleged black crime or resistance to white authority figures that led to collective violence. On February 5, 1914, *Národné noviny* (National news) reported on "People's Justice." "Black man Ben Dickerson was on the 29th of January in Oklahoma City shot dead by a crowd of citizens," the paper matter-of-factly reported. "A few days before that Chaffin, the business manager of the Kellogg Corn Flake Company, had been robbed, and out of anger, over a matter of $4, the unfortunate man Dickerson was shot dead. The mob of citizens arrived at the jail, seized the Negro, and murdered him." This, in full, is the text of a story that by 1914 was a regular feature in the Slovak press. One effect of such routine reports was perhaps to normalize the reign of terror against African Americans, even for newcomers who were mostly living far from the scene of these crimes. But whether Dickerson had actually robbed the white manager or merely had an argument with him over back wages, which was often the black "crime" that led to a lynching, immigrants were learning what minimal rights were afforded blacks in their new country. In such instances blacks resisting third-class treatment by white authority figures were subject to evisceration by "a mob of citizens" that rejected courts as inadequate protectors of the racial status quo. The "people's justice" was a folkway immigrants had to learn.[10]

Not all reports were this cut and dried, but even more vivid depictions often offered little sense of outrage or shock on the part of the translators. In 1904 *Amerikansky russky viestnik* reported, "In Cartersville, Georgia, a Negro was burned alive after a mob of 200 grabbed him from the hands of the sheriff." He had been accused of committing violence against a white girl. The reporter added, "While he was burning alive in the evening, he was hit by more than 500 shots."[11] And *Národné noviny* reported on a 1914 case unusual only in that it was a black woman who had been lynched. "The crowd summoned from the city murdered her and then hung her from a tree" after her "confession" to killing a twelve-year-old girl. "The corpse hanging from the tree," said the paper, "was used as a rifle target by the crowd. At the scene of the lynching were some 30 blacks, who were, however, prevented from interfering with the enraged people's justice."[12] "The people," with their enraged sense of justice, were set in opposition to helpless black onlookers.

Hundreds of formulaic lynching accounts appeared week after week in Slovak papers. By the time of this "black lady's lynching," the reporting of ritualized violence against blacks, as well as suspect immigrants, had been an ongoing feature in immigrant papers for twenty years.[13] Accounts followed a predictable format: a few brief paragraphs on Negro crimes, white outrage, and mob justice. Between 1890 and 1930, thousands of cases of collective violence were faithfully reported issue after issue in the major immigrant weeklies and dailies; often several accounts appeared in the same edition. These acts of violence were classified by immigrant newspapers as lynchings (*lynčovania*), although in English-language sources usage of the term varied according to several factors, including racial or ethnic background, region, and time.[14]

In 1896, *Amerikansky russky viestnik* reported, "Not far from New Orleans, there were two murders, the burning at the stake of Irishman Patrick Morris and his Negro wife. The enraged local citizens quickly judged him to have grossly exceeded the law and carried out the dreadful sentence on the terrified Morris." Another account related the case of Charles Mallpast, a white man lynched with his black wife and mulatto children in Arkansas after he tried to defend his family from an enraged mob of citizens. While the headline referred to Mallpast as "an innocent old man," the article noted, as in the case of Morris, that a crowd of "citizens" had "competently and speedily" shot and strung Mallpast up to a tree; no further condemnation of Arkansas citizens was added. The moral transmitted by such reports may have consisted in learning the social component of whiteness, behaving in a manner that placed one on the correct end of the racial divide.[15]

As in many English-language accounts, the report of Mallpast's lynching in *Slovák v Amerike* stressed the calm and deliberate fashion with which the disciplined white people set about their business. In Slovak papers' lynching accounts, depictions abound of lynchers as "citizens" who "competently" and "speedily" or "determinedly" engaged in restoring racialized justice and then retired peacefully. Reports of lynchings highlighted the discipline of whites who supposedly behaved in an orderly fashion, even as they burned a man alive. Depictions of white self-control were balanced against assertions of black brutality, irrationality, and licentiousness. Unlike wild and animalistic nonwhites, lynchers were said to be orderly and self-possessed; a "good" lynching was one allegedly free of irrationality or unneeded exuberance. (These same accounts speaking of white self-control and determined and orderly action to supplant malfunctioning courts nevertheless often detailed the torture and dismemberment of the victim by souvenir seekers. Such activity did not disrupt the binary between civilized whites and savage blacks in newspaper readers' or reporters' eyes.)[16]

Most such accounts didn't even go into as much detail as the articles on Morris and Mallpast, noting with little skepticism that a lynching had followed some horrible black crime. In 1913, *Národné noviny* decided the important fact in the double lynching in Mississippi of two black brothers was not their hanging and shotgun execution but the alleged murderous rampage by the teens that left "Eight People Dead." After drinking alcohol, "The two youths, it was reported, were walking along the street with loaded revolvers, when they began firing on the people." A troop train was dispatched from Natchez to try to restore order, but before it could arrive, citizens had taken matters into their own hands.[17]

Ritualized dismemberment of offending black bodies was often an attempt to assert control over a new generation of blacks who were achieving a degree of economic success in spite of the odds and thus disrupting the racial order. Immigrants, too, were regarded by many "old stock" Americans as usurpers of the prerogatives of nonimmigrant white people. Reading of the five hundred rifle shots fired into the "Cartersville Negro," such liminal immigrants likely felt simultaneous horror at the crime, contempt for the victims, and sober awareness of their own tenuous place in America's racialized justice system.[18] These accounts invariably characterized black self-defense itself as illegitimate, as did accounts of northern cities in which *plemenný boj*—race riots—broke out when blacks objected to subjugation.

Perhaps even more sobering is that many lynching accounts were only a paragraph long and even omitted the name of the victim. The ritual evisceration of a black person's body had become so prosaic that, even for immigrant readers, the specific details of a victim's identity or the specific alleged crime were regarded as unworthy of being reported. Lynching participants were determined to erase blacks' identity as moral or political agents. In this respect, editors who omitted a victim's identity achieved what lynch mobs had set out to accomplish—the negation of black personhood.[19]

Most longer accounts noted with little skepticism that collective violence invariably followed a conviction of the black victim for some horrible crime that justified the subsequent atrocity. This was the case in 1906, when *Amerikansky russky viestnik* reported that a *"Lynčovanie Nigra"* had occurred in Gadsden, Alabama, after a Negro named Richardson was only given a life sentence for the murder of a white woman.[20]

In this instance as in many others, immigrant readers learned that it was supposed leniency of the courts that led to the actions of the mob.[21] When four thousand whites broke into Chattanooga's jail and seized two black suspects and lynched them, *Slovák v Amerike*'s readers learned, "The authorities at this place have declined to condemn several Negroes to death, so that the unrest has broken out again, with hostility against imprisoned Negroes being particularly extreme."[22] Lynching accounts in English-language papers often condoned a higher people's justice that picked up when courts proved too permissive to control black crime; immigrant newspapers disseminated this message to newcomers, too.[23]

Dispatches printed in Slovak newspapers were almost always rewrites from English-language sources. The metropolitan press of the late nineteenth and early twentieth centuries was instrumental in homogenizing and modernizing a polyglot and diverse urban population, instructing citizens of mass society in the proper behavior necessary for negotiating in an anonymous, complex society. On New World race relations, immigrant newspapers culled rewrites of this homogenizing "received wisdom" and played their part, too, in instructing readers in how to behave as responsible Americans.[24]

This fashioning of a self-conception as part of the Caucasian race was something of a collaboration between native-born actors and ethnic elite, or perhaps a three-way collaboration, as Slovak readers frequently provided letters to the editor that quickly reflected their own racialized sensibilities. A letter writer from the steel town of Munhall, Pennsylvania, argued in 1918 in *Jednota* that "Lincoln freed the slaves, but the Slovaks in their slavery have it worse!" Similarly, by 1915 some Slovaks complaining of oppression in Europe compared Slovak "slavery" to the ease with which pampered blacks in America lived. "Indeed if you really look at it, we have it worse than the Negroes," Andrej Bugoš of Los Angeles wrote to *Národné noviny*. "Indeed these days in California Negroes are enslaved to luxury, and you see what 'tents' they have!" Stereotypes of sybaritic blacks were already gestating. And when a letter writer to *New Yorský denník* (New York daily) denounced a hated McKeesport, Pennsylvania, priest, he could think of no greater slur than that

Father Liščinsky "is defending the blacks, who treacherously worked against the Slovak people," presumably as strike breakers.[25]

Among Slovak immigrants, creating an imagined community was first a matter of conceptualizing a common Slovak nationhood and, second, fitting Slovak identity within a Caucasian polity. Slovak papers melded together a national identity for immigrants who may have had at best only a regional conception of themselves as residents of Zemplín or Trenčín province, not as Slovaks, when they first emigrated. When Juraj Kracha comes to America in Thomas Bell's autobiographical novel *Out of This Furnace*, the first "outsider" he makes fun of is not a *Čierny* (black) but an immigrant from Zemplín, whom Kracha mocks for pronouncing his own language incorrectly, and he later uses *Čierny* to refer not to African Americans but to dark and "gypsy-like" characters. Such identity formation did not occur in a void, however, but in a society in which blackness remained the ultimate mark of the outsider. Slovak immigrants fashioned identities out of an admixture of "assignment" and self-proclaimed "identity" and made fun of those who didn't make the grade. Fast-forward forty years, and Slovaks in Braddock, Pennsylvania (the setting of *Out of This Furnace*), were using "nigger" to denounce blacks perceived as ruining their neighborhood.[26]

In the intervening decades new distinctions, which became the most salient in the context of Braddock, were picked up through items in the Slovak press. Should Kracha, or any other Slovak, have leafed through *Jednota* on October 15, 1902, he would have yet again read of a *"Lynčovala nigrov"*: "In the town of Newbern, Tennessee, it is reported that a mob of nearly 500 people hung two Negroes from a telephone pole. . . . The marauding rabble arrived at the jail and seized the struggling Negroes, pronouncing justice at once that very day, condemning them, tearing the Negroes from jail and lynching them." This paragraph-long account is thus far typical of rewrites found in the Slovak press. In this instance, however, the editors tacked on a concluding sentence: "We are incapable of doing justice to these rabble judgments by the most unadorned Americans." The condemnation is unusual, for most stories, no matter how graphic the detail provided on the victims' torture, omit even such a cursory editorial remark and often instead link mob actions to the achievement, not a miscarriage, of justice. These few atypical, isolated words of condemnation likely did not leave as lasting an impression on immigrants as the steady repetition of stories of black criminality and victimization. After reading hundreds of lynching accounts, year after year, differences between Zemplín and Trenčín became less important than the line between black and white.[27]

Often even the most implausible portrayals of black licentiousness passed with little or no skepticism. *Slovák v Amerike* in 1895 reported as a matter of fact that "80-year-old William Henderson was lynched by upstanding citizens of Jackson, Missouri, after he had been caught dallying with 14-year-old Minnie Rust, the daughter of a respectable white family." The paragraph-long account concluded, "It is likely that the lynching will go unpunished." As another lynching account noted, "The enraged people are many."[28]

As in the English-language press, so, too, Slovak immigrant papers accepted black criminality as a given, and the many lynching accounts that ran in immigrant papers foregrounded the crimes for which the victim suffered, often almost giving more details on the victim's misdeeds than the tortures inflicted on him by the white mob. Just as the story of White's slow roasting alive in Wilmington began with a long account of his crimes, establishing an equivalency between black crime and white reaction, the Jackson account juxtaposed "upstanding citizens" with black sexual predations. Perhaps it is not surprising that by the 1910s papers frequently ran short crime stories giving prominent play to black murderers and stickup men.[29]

The frequency of lynching accounts and other articles foregrounding race suggests that the status of racial outsiders was a matter of morbid curiosity to new immigrants. Coverage of race was fraught with conflicting layers of condescension, belittlement, and repugnance at the brutality delivered to transgressors against white supremacy. As in English-language newspapers, the immigrant press sometimes documented lynchings in vivid detail, and there is evidence that initially newcomers were horrified by these acts of mob law. The report from Wilmington noted, "At the end of this horrible process everyone made sure to cut off a piece of his body to take for themselves as a souvenir!"[30] A similar account in 1901 noted that before a hanging victim was doused with gasoline, "All the pieces of his body were cut off and distributed to the crowd. Before they were done he cried and begged for mercy."[31]

Gruesome headlines were sometimes matched by macabre comments suggesting that initially some Slovaks reacted with revulsion. "Determinedly use knife to rip out his tongue and tear off his skin and hide," a subhead to a West Virginia story announced. "In Bluefield, it is reported that there was a bestial lynching of a black," the story began. "Near Devon in Mingo County this disgraceful deed was staged." The report then went into gorier detail:

In a second moment, though, there began a penetrating roaring and with the authorities' wholehearted support, they cut into pieces the body of the living Negro, cut him into pieces and distributed the various pieces to the participants in the cruel lynching. With a glance at the girl, the unfortunate Negro's sinful soul departed his body. The enraged people then cut his tortured body and took out his heart. It wasn't enough for them yet, they had to have a souvenir! Then they poured gasoline on the deceased and set him on fire. Such terrible, vengeful methods are beyond even committed criminals! Whether or not the people's feelings of outrage were assuaged, let each reader judge.[32]

The victim's humanity is nevertheless denied. In this whole lengthy story, the lynching victim is never named; he is the subject of the mob's action, an anonymous burning, tortured body for Slovak readers. And while "the people's feeling of outage" takes a form that prompted the editor to affix at least some atypical critique of mob justice, the story begins by foregrounding his crime (not alleged in the story but taken for granted). The criminal's deviance leads the item, with the black rapist chaining his white female victim to a tree, thereby setting up a moral equivalency between black crime and the later, overawing decree of bloody justice by the mob.

Another story related a 1911 Kentucky lynching in which ringleaders erected a stage and charged three dollars to townspeople wanting to shoot at the victim. In this case, the story condemned the barbarity, saying that "an opera was performed that was brutally plotted and would have shamed even the strangest of cannibals." The story noted,

The "committee" immediately announced that those who had bought a ticket would have the right to shoot at the Negro. The opera in a short time came true as a crowd of citizens of that town avidly witnessed and guffawed at the murder of the anguished Negro. When a bell was rung, the curtain was raised. Boys and women then rose up, and began shooting with fury at the tied-up Negro. . . . No one in the town in any way prevented this performance.[33]

The savagery of American assaults on blacks was likely not lost on Slovaks, and in these few cases editors affixed some condemnation of brutalities.

Yet for every such elaborate torture account, there were dozens of one-sentence or one-paragraph items merely stating a lynching had occurred. The brevity of such lynching fillers suggests how little such victims' plight registered with readers. The repetitive accounts that ran week after week alongside prosaic news largely served to numb white Americans to the practice, with even the most lurid accounts merely another accepted part of America's landscape.[34]

Through their readings on *Negrov lynčovanie,* even working-class eastern Europeans (who might have raised southern horror of a "raceless society" almost as much as "Negro misrule") consumed these national folkways, too. It is no special condemnation of Slovaks to say that in this regard they were typical of other white Americans. As they adjusted to their new homes, Slovaks learned of the permanent pariah status of blacks in myriad ways, not least through the lynching accounts that dotted nearly every paper.

A level of analysis that presents working-class struggle as occurring merely between capitalists and exploited workers fails to address the central question of why many workers settled for being white. The economic and psychic benefits of whiteness could be redeemed by newcomers reconfirming (or discovering for the first time) their valuable racial privilege in large measure through reading these newspapers. Slavs knew of the dangerous working conditions they faced and subjugation at home under "Mongolian" Magyar rule. What they had to learn in order to acculturate to America was a white frame of reference. Slovak papers' voluminous coverage of quotidian mob violence provided a lesson on the degree to which blacks were a vulnerable people apart.[35]

Longer accounts sent messages of black illegitimacy. *Jednota* reported that "in the town of Berkley, Virginia . . . the black man George W. Blount . . . was released by the police and before their very eyes strung up from a lamppost and burned alive." Before this, though, "masked men had seized Blount and taken him to a field, where he was beaten and then shot into pieces." This occurred even though "Blount was said to be the political leader" of blacks in the region.[36] Whether editors explicitly intended it or not, immigrant readers may have drawn the conclusion that even successful blacks were vulnerable.

Rhetoric on black depravity and criminality aside, blacks who succeeded were often recognized by whites as the real threats and thus became frequent targets of mobs. Disparities between images of criminality and the respectability of many lynching victims such as Blount, however, are not elaborated on by Slavic immigrants—neither editors nor readers—at least insofar as we may judge by the absence of letters denouncing such public extralegal murders. As early as 1908, Ray Stannard Baker noted that white southerners admitted that blacks who fit the stereotypes of laziness and unintelligence were no threat to Jim Crow. Rather, in spite of the self-justifying arguments of lynchers that this punishment was only meted out to the most brutal of criminals, especially rapists, such crimes were only a minority of the proximate causes. Black businessmen or landowners, followers of Booker T. Washington's uplift message, were often most vulnerable, for black achievement was the impermissible threat to the racialized status quo. When blacks migrated north, they were quickly violently resisted as threats to immigrants' natural rights to industrial jobs. The template for blacks as illegitimate competitors in the marketplace was arguably laid in accounts of successful blacks' murders.[37]

Stories were not always straightforward reports of noose and flaming torch. *Amerikansky russky viestnik* twice in 1903 reported that "the President is against lynching" and added that the editors were, too.[38] Articles on the violent suppression of strikes appeared alongside accounts of even more violent evisceration of the bodies of distant southern black men. "In the states of Georgia, Alabama, and Louisiana there lately has actually been a noticeable uprising, a war of the white people against the blacks of those places," *Jednota* reported in August 1904. "Whites have hunted blacks down like rabbits, and even flogged them to death. The indignation of whites has been greatly roused against blacks in all regions of the southern states." Directly beneath this report was a short item from Statesboro, Georgia. Near there "the rabble seized two Negro men, Paul Reed and Will. Cato, tied them together with chains, poured gasoline on them and burned them alive. The Negroes were quickly baked. . . . Neither the American authorities nor the unfortunate Negroes have been able to stop these terrible deaths."[39]

Certainly in the era of yellow journalism, sensationalist accounts were par for the course. But the very lurid and salacious nature of these accounts may have desensitized readers. In Slavic papers, graphic accounts of lynchings often appeared in the same issues with minstrel-show jokes in "humor columns." News columns likewise spoke of "cannibal" or "barbarous" Africans and Filipinos in need of white guidance. Sensationalist foreign coverage was a staple of yellow journalism, but this in and of itself served to hierarchize the world into civilized Europeans and savage others. Slovak papers translated accounts of the *"l'udožrúti"* of Africa—literally "people chewers." Qualifiers such as "savage" in accounts of African or Asian resistance to colonization were not neutral descriptors but ideologically loaded words that suggested non-Europeans were not fully civilized.[40]

These telling juxtapositions indicate that even lynching accounts, over time, may have become for immigrants (as for other white Americans) merely a gruesome part of a naturalized landscape of racial hierarchies. No doubt some were repulsed to read that a victim's body was "chopped into souvenir pieces,"[41] but like English-language newspaper readers, immigrants read of black savagery nearly every week, so that blacks over time became alien to Slovaks' perception of full citizens deserving of respect.

Occasionally some horror at the brutality of mob violence broke through the "just the facts" reporting. *Amerikansky russky viestnik* noted, "In the United States, Negroes are murdered in every way possible, and even burned to death from time to time in a few cases on the slightest pretext." The paper reported that when a mob of three thousand in Evansville, Indiana, was prevented from breaking into a jail where a black suspect was housed, "the enraged white mob reversed direction in anger, and started attacking every black they could find walking in the area. They laid dynamite under the foundations of black people's houses and their parishes in town and in the outlying area." The editor concluded, "Those people were greatly incited against the blacks, who obviously need some strong defensive society."[42] After three white Texas farmers were lynched, the editor of *Slovák v Amerike* commented, "[President] McKinley needs to look into this. He needs to introduce some culture here, and not in the Philippines."[43]

Jednota likewise saw fit to comment on the treatment of blacks in the South only when it wanted to critique America's imperialism in the Philippines, asking why the army was trying to "civilize" Asia when America had a war going on against its own black citizens in the South.[44] Perhaps it was the fact in Texas it had been whites who suffered at the hands of the people's justice or dissatisfaction with the country's imperial adventures that caused editors to critique the people's justice. The instability of race for new Americans and the perilous degree to which Nordic immigration restrictionists denounced southeastern Europeans as Asiatic or African may account for a report of an 1895 Denver case where Italians had been mistaken for blacks and lynched. It may be that Slovaks wanted to make sure they weren't so disastrously "misidentified."[45]

At home, though, collective violence against blacks more often passed without editorial outcry. To be sure, in 1897, *Slovák v Amerike* ended an account of an Arkansas lynching, "Nice granting of justice and acknowledgement of equality according to law!"[46] But after 1910 such denunciations grew increasingly rare. More frequent were prosaic accounts such as the 1920 lynching of Grant Smith. "After the lynching, the crowd peacefully departed," the brief item concludes. A similar item from 1911 in Purcell, Oklahoma, notes that three thousand citizens doused the victim, Peter Carter, with gasoline and burned him alive. The one-paragraph item concludes, "After the lynching, everything was peaceful."[47] *Slovák v Amerike* likewise noted regarding a Mississippi lynching, "When their work was done, the white people peacefully departed."[48]

When blacks sought to defend themselves from white mobs, Slovak papers screamed of *"plemenný boj"*—"race war." This was the term used in coverage of outbreaks in Chicago, East Saint Louis, and Tulsa during and immediately after World War I. In its coverage of the Chicago riots, *New Yorkský denník* nervously highlighted the military training and weapons stockpiling of black army veterans.[49]

Papers had been reporting since at least 1903 on whites cleansing cities of all blacks, establishing a binary for new immigrants of who was unacceptable on one's block.[50] The very act of black self-defense was recast as criminality; headlines asserting a "race war" established a moral equivalence between sides, with no hint that blacks were actually engaged in resistance to mobs. When blacks in Lawrenceville, Illinois, attempted to attend a carnival, they were set upon by a white mob and another "race war" erupted, reported *Slovák v Amerike*. Black use of public space was itself an outrage whites could be expected to resist.[51]

Immigrant papers, though, offered an escape from urban disorder. As early as 1903, papers featured real-estate ads selling Slovaks their idyllic "colony" away from the cities. Graphically illustrating the differing fates of blacks and white ethnics for decades to come, one such ad trumpets the beauties of Wallington, New Jersey—a "Slovak colony"—right alongside the account of the lynching of George White. While reading that the crowd hacked off souvenir body parts until White begged for mercy, immigrants also learned that Slovaks could gain the comforts of home ownership. Many readers were no doubt appalled by White's torturous death. The mobility available to some people and not others was probably apparent as well. The presentation of the routine torture of blacks alongside everyday realty ads for Slovaks already partially on the way to becoming "white" suggests that a race-tutoring project existed within the immigrant press. Nothing could spell out more gruesomely for newcomers just who was protected and who was perpetually vulnerable.[52]

There is even evidence that immigrants participated in one lynching. This lynching was related to Slovak newspapers by an eyewitness "reporter." In

1911 in Coatesville, Pennsylvania, a town with a 40 percent foreign-born population in which there were three National Slovak Society lodges,[53] a black man was arrested after trying to rob a Slavic immigrant and then shooting at police officers called to arrest him. Although the robber had been wounded during his arrest and was lying in a hospital bed, the crowd of primarily immigrants broke into the hospital to exact their own vigilante justice. As the "reporter" for *Jednota* related,

> With a roar our people on 13 August rushed toward the hospital, where the injured black man lay. . . . And so also there our nation waited . . . until they succeeded in penetrating the hospital, rushing and taking the black man out of there, even though he was tied in his bed. They carried him out of the hospital, making for a field, where they deposited him on a pile of straw and wood, and then burned him alive. Up to 5,000 people witnessed and took part in this terrible execution. . . . The blacks in our town are afraid of the residents. It's understandable that no one can possibly approve of the awful act of the crowd. The people don't have the right to take into their own hands the power of justice. But on the other hand, we must also acknowledge, that the people had reason to be indignant.[54]

The switches in language in *Jednota's* account suggest that in this case, immigrants in this heavily foreign-born town had done more than just read about lynching. The writer begins by describing the perpetrators of the deed as "our people" (*l'ud*) and then refers to them as "our nation" (*národ*), suggesting that immigrants not only sanctioned but participated in the harsh rituals of racialized justice. Or a Slovak affinity with other whites ("our people") is indicated. The reporter, though, pulls back and recognizes that such lynchings might be in need of condemnation—at which point he refers to the lynchers as a "crowd" (*davu*) but then concludes that "the people" (again *l'ud*) had every "reason to be indignant." By 1911, to many Slovak "reporters" or readers, burning a man alive by "our people" could be conceptualized as communal justice.

Slovák v Amerike reassured readers that the Coatesville lynchers were some of the most respectable citizens, with women insisting on taking part. Only after blacks demanded the extradition of one of the alleged lynchers did the paper report fears of a coming race war. Evidently blacks demanding protection of the law could by 1911 signify racial tumult. Coatesville residents rallied to a white man to protect him from the indignity of being tried for a lynching; they remained at best onlookers, if not participants, when a black man was burned alive.[55]

It was only the radical press that wrote unambiguously against lynching. *Rovnosť ľudu* (Equality for the people) was the organ of the Slovak Socialist Workers' Section. In its account, "Two Negroes Lynched," *Rovnosť ľudu* exhibited a degree of anger at the crime and skepticism toward assertions of black criminality that are difficult to find in other papers. "Hal Winton and an unidentified black person were savagely grabbed by a mob from the arms of town officials and lynched. Officials reported he had killed Willey P. Martin, manager of a plantation, but does anyone think that this was actually likely? Indeed, lynching is the worst form of barbarism. This travesty was executed with the complicity of the court, which knew of it, and yet permitted it."[56] *Rovnosť ľudu* also sneered at the morality of lynching in an article titled "Good Christians Approve of Lynching," referring to "Respectable and dear Christians." "They've organized into a 'fine' body, 'the Baptist Young People's Union.' The lynchings of blacks are justifiable, under certain conditions, their 34th national convention has decreed. . . . And these are Christians?!"[57]

Yet even at *Rovnosť ľudu,* editors were becoming more like those of mainstream nonimmigrant papers with regard to race. An English-language cartoon carried by the paper shows a lawyer telling his black bootlegger client, "You told me you were innocent, and I was able so to convince the squire— Now what do you think my services were worth?" The stereotypical shiftless, lying bootlegger replies, "Mistah Stone, Ise broke flatter'n a pancake. But ah kin bring you a quart ob dat liquor Ise bin sellin for leben dollars."[58]

To find this cartoon here is lamentable but not surprising. In Philadelphia, the Slovak Socialist Workers' Section met at Slovak Hall, which a social worker noted "was available for rental by all other groups, but Negroes were excluded because it was feared that their cleanliness standard would not measure up to that of other groups." This policy stood, even though the Slovak Socialist Workers' Section president managed the hall.[59]

The Slovak Socialist Workers' Section report suggests that radical Slovaks were not merely being prudent in barring blacks but acted on generally accepted "fears" of unclean *Čierny.* Certainly not every Slovak learned the same attitudes on race all at once. But lynching accounts in the Slovak press, in tandem with other cultural productions, provided immigrants with new ways of conceiving who they were and how they fit into their new homeland.

NOTES

1. John Bodnar, *The Transplanted: A History of Immigrants in Urban America* (Bloomington: Indiana University Press, 1987), xv; Ewa Morawska, *For Bread with Butter: The Life Worlds of East Central Europeans in Johnstown, Pennsylvania, 1890-1940* (New York: Cambridge University Press, 1985), 22–39; Mark Wyman, *Round Trip to America: The Immigrants Return to Europe, 1880-1930* (Ithaca, NY: Cornell University Press, 1993), 9–12; M. Mark Stolarik, *Immigration and Urbanization: The Slovak Experience, 1870-1918* (New York: AMS, 1989), 25, 36; Caroline Golab, *Immigrant Destinations* (Philadelphia: Temple University Press, 1977), 34.

2. Grace Elizabeth Hale, *Making Whiteness: The Culture of Segregation in the South, 1890-1940* (New York: Pantheon Books, 1998); Leon F. Litwack, "Hellhounds," in James Allen et al., *Without Sanctuary: Lynching Photography in America* (Santa Fe, NM: Twin Palms, 2000), 8–37.

3. For reports of lynch mobs stepping in when authorities proved ineffective, see, for example, *Slovák v Amerike*, July 7, 1903; July 21, 1905; September 6, 1910; August 29, 1911; October 26, 1911; January 21, 1913. For official leniency as the supposed cause of lynching, see Michael J. Pfeiffer, "Lynching and Criminal Justice in South Louisiana, 1878–1930," *Louisiana History: The Journal of the Louisiana Historical Association* 40, no. 2 (Spring 1999): 155–77; James W. Clarke, "Without Fear or Shame: Lynching, Capital Punishment and the Subculture of Violence in the American South," *British Journal of Political Science* 28, no. 2 (April 1998): 269–89. Excellent overall histories of lynching are Christopher Waldrep, *The Many Faces of Judge Lynch: Extralegal Violence and Punishment in America* (New York: Palgrave Macmillan, 2002); Hale, *Making Whiteness*; Amy Elizabeth Wood, *Lynching and Spectacle: Witnessing Racial Violence in America, 1890-1940* (Chapel Hill: University of North Carolina Press, 2009); Michael J. Pfeifer, *Rough Justice: Lynching and American Society, 1874-1947* (Urbana: University of Illinois Press, 2004). See, too, Rebecca N. Hill, *Men, Mobs, and Law: Anti-Lynching and Labor Defense in U.S. Radical History* (Durham, NC: Duke University Press, 2008), esp. 112–61.

4. For jokes on immigrants' first encounters with blacks, see *New Yorský denník*, June 4, 1921; August 12, 1922. Other jokes at the expense of blacks appeared in *Šidlo* (Dagger), *New Yorský denník*'s humor column, on February 26, May 28, and June 16 and 18, 1921; December 2, 1922; and March 17 and April 7, 1923. As Robert Orsi notes, some of these stories, especially those recalled decades later, may have been apocryphal, projecting later racial attitudes onto the moment of arrival. Such tales nevertheless reveal something of immigrants' learned sense of distance from blacks, and as noted, as early as 1921 immigrant papers provided articles, some humorous, some not, arguing that blacks were qualitatively different. Robert Orsi, "The Religious Boundaries of an In-Between People: Street Feste and the Problem of the Dark-Skinned Other in Italian Harlem, 1920–1990," *American Quarterly* 44, no. 3 (September 1992): 313–47.

5. *Slovák v Amerike*, June 26, 1903. For the lynching of White, see Yohuru R. Williams, "Permission to Hate: Delaware, Lynching, and the Culture of Violence in

America," *Journal of Black Studies* 32, no. 1 (September 2001): 3–29; and Philip Dray, *At the Hands of Persons Unknown: The Lynching of Black America* (New York: Modern Library, 2003), 144–45.

6. Hale, *Making Whiteness*, 199–215. Benedict Anderson has likewise written on how a sense of national affinity was often facilitated among middle-class newspaper readers, an "imagined community" via printing press. Benedict Anderson, *Imagined Communities: Reflections on the Origin and Spread of Nationalism* (New York: Verso, 1994).

7. It is difficult to determine whether "regular" immigrants created the neologism *lynčovat'* (to lynch) or if editors of immigrant newspapers introduced this loan word into Slovak and Rusyn. Most such news articles, though, were rewrites from English-language newspapers or wire services, which were translated by immigrant editors. This suggests editors coined the word when the Slavic words mentioned were regarded as insufficient to describe American collective violence. The first such accounts I found that refer to *lynčovania* are from 1894, a time when few Slavic immigrants lived near the scene of these southern public murders; this, too, suggests that editors coined the neologism. Other neologisms such as *štrajk* and *skébovat'* were created to refer to industrial job actions with which immigrants were more familiar.

8. *Slovák v Amerike*, August 27, 1896.

9. *Slovák v Amerike*, February 2, 1906. See Dray, *At the Hands of Persons Unknown*, 150–59.

10. *Národné noviny*, February 5, 1914.

11. *Amerikansky russky viestnik*, July 7, 1904. Likewise, *New Yorkský denník* reported on a lynching victim, William Bragg, who was burned alive with petroleum. *New Yorkský denník*, January 22, 1919.

12. *Národné noviny*, July 16, 1914. The headline was "Black Lady's Lynching."

13. See, for example, *Amerikansky russky viestnik*, October 25, 1894. Another early account of a lynching is *Amerikansky russky viestnik*, May 2, 1895, "A brief trial *[Krátky Process]*": "Parsons, Tenn.: 26 April—Along the Tennessee River, 6 miles downriver from this town, lived a married Negro farmer, Thomas Gray. Neighbors bordering his land soon confessed to each other to feeling a less than neighborly feeling toward him, and thus they came to an agreement, and shot him dead." *Slovák v Amerike* featured lynching stories as early as November 22, 1894.

14. Leon Litwack, *Trouble in Mind: Black Southerners in the Age of Jim Crow* (New York: Vintage Books, 1998). A brief survey of *Amerikansky russky viestnik* revealed more than forty articles on lynching between 1894 and 1906. The paper continued to feature lynching accounts in the 1910s and 1920s. *Jednota* ran forty-four lynching accounts between 1902 and 1906. *Národné noviny* had frequent articles on lynching, as did *Slovák v Amerike*. *New Yorkský denník* extensively covered lynchings into the 1920s.

15. *Amerikansky russky viestnik*, January 16, 1896; *Slovák v Amerike*, October 3, 1911. See, too, *Slovák v Amerike*, April 18, 1905. See also Matthew Frye Jacobson, *Whiteness of a Different Color: European Immigrants and the Alchemy of Race* (Cambridge, MA: Harvard University Press, 1998), 4, 55–62, 65, for cases in which Si-

cilian-black marriages were upheld as not necessarily violating antimiscegenation statutes. For fears of voluntary black-white partnerships spurring lynching, see J. William Harris, "Etiquette, Lynching, and Racial Boundaries in Southern History: A Mississippi Example," *American Historical Review* 100, no. 2 (April 1995): 387–410. See, too, Ray Stannard Baker, *Following the Color Line: American Negro Citizenship in the Progressive Era* (1908; reprint, New York: Harper and Row, 1964), 167–68.

16. Wood, *Lynching and Spectacle.* Lynch leaders from Stuttgart, Arkansas, asserted to a reporter that their lynching had been "humane." *Minneapolis Tribune,* September 3, 1916, cited in Molefi Kete Asante, "Litany of Horror: A Survey of Newspaper-Reported Lynchings," *Journal of Blacks in Higher Education* 43 (Spring 2004): 116–23. On lynch mobs' assertions to be acting in publicly sanctioned ways, see David Garland, "Penal Excess and Surplus Meaning: Public Torture Lynchings in Twentieth-Century America," *Law & Society Review* 49, no. 4 (December 2005): 793–833.

17. "Eight People Shot Dead," *Národné noviny,* October 2, 1913.

18. Litwack, "Hellhounds"; *Amerikansky russky viestnik,* July 7, 1904.

19. See *New Yorkský denník,* August 9, 1915; September 12, 1916; August 3, 1922; *Jednota,* August 2 and 30 and September 6, 1905; February 20, 1907; August 15, 1908; October 21, 1908; *Slovák v Amerike,* July 7 and 14 and November 13, 1903; May 10, 1904; July 21, 1905; August 14, 1906.

20. *Amerikansky russky viestnik,* February 15, 1906.

21. See *Slovák v Amerike,* March 30, 1900, for a similar lynching in Bel Air, Maryland.

22. *Slovák v Amerike,* February 2, 1906.

23. Wood, *Lynching and Spectacle;* Hill, *Men, Mobs, and Law,* 112–61. See, for example, *Slovák v Amerike,* August 29 and October 26, 1911; January 21, 1913.

24. Gunther Barth, *City People: The Rise of Modern City Culture in Nineteenth-Century America* (New York: Oxford University Press, 1980).

25. *Jednota,* October 23, 1918; *Národné noviny,* August 12, 1915; *New Yorkský denník,* April 17, 1919.

26. Thomas Bell, *Out of This Furnace* (1941; reprint, Pittsburgh: University of Pittsburgh Press, 1976), 5, 78, 327–30.

27. *Jednota,* October 15, 1902.

28. *Slovák v Amerike,* October 17, 1895; December 29, 1903.

29. See, for example, *Slovák v Amerike,* November 17, 1910; *New Yorkský denník,* February 9 and March 23, 1915; February 26 and July 20, 1916; May 8, June 16, and July 24 and 27, 1921; January 9, 1923; and *Jednota,* February 10, 1909.

30. *Slovák v Amerike,* June 26, 1903.

31. *Slovák v Amerike,* October 29, 1901.

32. *Slovák v Amerike,* July 14, 1903.

33. "Lynching as Theater" (*"Lynčovanie na divadle"*), *Slovák v Amerike,* April 25, 1911.

34. Hale, *Making Whiteness;* Wood, *Lynching and Spectacle.* See *New Yorkský denník,* August 9, 1915; September 12, 1916; August 3, 1922; *Jednota,* August 2 and 30 and

September 6, 1905; *Slovák v Amerike,* July 7 and 14 and November 13, 1903; May 10, 1904; July 21, 1905; August 14, 1906.

35. David Roediger, *The Wages of Whiteness: Race and the Making of the American Working Class* (New York: Verso, 1991), 6–12. The concept of "inbetween people" is useful for considering race and southeastern European peoples. See James Barrett and David Roediger, "Inbetween Peoples: Race, Nationality, and the 'New Immigrant' Working Class," *Journal of American Ethnic History* 16, no. 3 (Spring 1997): 3–44; and Dominic A. Pacyga, "To Live among Others: Poles and Their Neighbors in Industrial Chicago, 1865–1930," *Journal of American Ethnic History* 16, no. 1 (Fall 1996): 55–73. For "Mongolian" Magyars, see, for example, *Slovák v Amerike,* March 29, 1907; February 14, 1911; December 17, 1914; *Národné noviny,* August 12, 1915; July 4 and 25, 1918; March 5 and April 11, 1919; November 12, 1920. On the last date the paper editorialized on the subject, referring to the Hungarian government: "How foolish and benighted are these Asiatic Nobles of the Empty Cranium. . . . Thus we have the oddest thing in the world, worthy of Barnum's Side Show." "Mongols Always Remain Mongols," November 28, 1918. *Slovák v Amerike* suggested, "We should ship all the Magyars C.O.D. to Asia, let them all go" (December 3, 1912).

36. *Jednota,* November 2, 1904, 1. Hale, *Making Whiteness,* esp. 125–38, and Litwack, "Hellhounds," note that in spite of white supremacists' self-serving rhetoric, lynchings and Jim Crow measures were often directed not at uneducated or landless blacks but successful middle-class African Americans such as Blount, who were far more of a threat to the racialized status quo.

37. Baker, *Following the Color Line,* 221, 241–46, 248–50. For another case of a successful black's lynching in 1934 in Louisiana, see Adam Fairclough, "'Forty Acres and a Mule': Horace Mann Bond and the Lynching of Jerome Wilson," *Journal of American Studies* 31, no. 1 (April 1997): 1–17. See, too, J. William Harris, "Etiquette, Lynching, and Racial Boundaries in Southern History: A Mississippi Example," *American Historical Review* 100, no. 2 (April 1995): 387–410.

38. *Amerikansky russky viestnik,* August 13 and 20, 1903.

39. *Jednota,* August 24, 1904. For the Statesboro lynching, see Wood, *Lynching and Spectacle,* 19–23, 86–87, 90–92.

40. On the Philippines, see *Jednota,* August 27 and October 22, 1902; March 23 and July 20, 1904; December 9, 1908; November 10, 1909; *Amerikansky russky viestnik,* January 17 and 24 and April 4, 1901; *Slovák v Amerike,* March 23 and May 11, 1900; June 12, 1906; July 8, 1909; January 30, 1913. *Slovák v Amerike* and *Národné noviny* also published letters from Slovak-American soldiers stationed in the Philippines that spoke of the savagery of the natives. *Slovák v Amerike,* April 20, 1899; November 9, 1906; *Národné noviny,* August 7, 1911; October 26, 1911; March 28, 1912. For slighting references to Africans and "cannibalism," see *New Yorský denník,* February 9 and 10, 1915; November 4, 1917; May 28, 1921; and *Slovák v Amerike,* October 18, 1901; July 1, 1902. The *Slovák v Amerike* accounts refer to the "people-chewers" of Spanish West Africa and New Guinea. In African Guinea, too, natives resisting French colonizers were dismissed as "ceaselessly restless savages." *Slovák v Amerike,*

April 11, 1913. *Národné noviny* opined, "Africans, like our gypsies, don't really work" (February 9, 1915). *Jednota* dismissed restless Haiti in an editorial that ended, "This little republic of black citizens has supplied endless headaches to Uncle Sam" (December 9, 1908). For Polish, Yiddish, and Irish immigrant newspapers' coverage of America's imperial adventures, see Mathew Frye Jacobson, *Special Sorrows: The Diasporic Imagination of Irish, Polish, and Jewish Immigrants in the United States* (Berkeley: University of California Press, 2002).

41. *Slovák v Amerike*, August 29, 1905.

42. *"Zas lynčovanie"* (The practice of lynching), *Amerikansky russky viestnik*, July 9, 1903. *Jednota* reported on September 21, 1904, that "Blacks in the United States had established a national black political party, which they had named the 'National Liberty Party,' and had nominated as the candidate for president of that party the black man George Turner."

43. *Slovák v Amerike*, June 1, 1899.

44. *Jednota*, February 19, 1908.

45. *Slovák v Amerike*, March 21, 1895.

46. *Slovák v Amerike*, September 2, 1897. The same issue carried a story of a Macon, Georgia, lynching, headlined "Bestial Killing of a Black."

47. *New Yorkský denník*, March 31, 1920; *Slovák v Amerike*, August 29, 1911. A similar case in Jonesboro, Arkansas, in which a mob of four hundred hung Waldo Thomas from a telegraph pole on Main Street, was reported in *New Yorkský denník*, December 29, 1920.

48. *Slovák v Amerike*, November 24, 1905.

49. For the Chicago race riot, see *New Yorkský denník*, July 30 and 31 and August 1 and 2, 1919. For Tulsa, see *New Yorkský denník*, June 14, 1921. See, too, *Slovák v Amerike*, October 26, 1911, for a "race war" in Oklahoma after black landowners sought to defend their rights.

50. For 1910s and 1920s race riots, see, for example, *New Yorkský denník*, June 1 4, and 6, 1917 (East Saint Louis, Illinois); May 13, 1919 (Charleston, South Carolina); September 30 and October 1 and 2, 1919 (Omaha, Nebraska); September 22, 1920 (Chicago; headline: "Murder of Whites by Blacks in Chicago Causes Rioting"); June 3, 4, 5, 7, and 14, 1921 (Tulsa, Oklahoma); January 7, 1923 (Rosewood, Florida). See, too, *Slovák v Amerike*, March 24, 1905, covering white vigilantes expelling all blacks from Rankin, Pennsylvania, a city in which many Slavs worked; and *Slovák v Amerike*, November 13, 1903, for a similar expulsion of all blacks from Morgan City, Illinois. In Indiana County, Pennsylvania, too, all blacks were ordered by a vigilante mob to leave the county. *Amerikansky russky viestnik*, February 26, 1903.

51. *Jednota*, August 5, 1908; *Slovák v Amerike*, June 26, 1908; *New Yorkský denník*, July 4 and 6, 1917; July 30, 1919; *Slovák v Amerike*, June 30, 1905; August 9, 1907.

52. *Slovák v Amerike*, November 13, 1903; June 26, 1908. For other real-estate stories and ads, see *Slovák v Amerike*, June 25, 1908 (Metuchen, New Jersey); *Jednota*, July 8, 1908 (Cleveland); *New Yorkský denník*, July 2, 1917 (Somerville, New Jersey); and *Národné noviny*, August 15, 1918 (suburban Philadelphia).

53. R. Vladimir Baumgarten and Joseph Stefka, *The National Slovak Society: 100 Year History*, 1890-1990 (Pittsburgh: National Slovak Society, 1990), 269, 271.

54. *Jednota*, August 23, 1911. See, too, *Slovák v Amerike*, August 17 and 22, 1911; March 18, 1913. On the Coatesville lynching, see William Ziglar, "'Community on Trial': The Coatesville Lynching of 1911," *Pennsylvania Magazine of History and Biography* 106, no. 2 (April 1982): 245–70.

55. *Slovák v Amerike*, August 17 and 22, 1911.

56. "Two Negroes Lynched" (*Dvaja Černosi lynčovani*), *Rovnosť ľudu*, February 20, 1925.

57. "Good Christians Approve of Lynching" (*Dobri krest'ania suhlasia lynčovanim*), *Rovnosť ľudu*, July 31, 1925.

58. *Rovnosť ľudu*, September 11, 1925.

59. Christine Zduleczna, "The Czechoslovaks of Philadelphia," in *The Foreign-Born of Philadelphia* (Philadelphia: International Institute of Philadelphia, 1927). For a well-publicized case of a Finnish ethnic club in Harlem affiliated with the Communist Party U.S.A. that refused to serve blacks in 1931, see Jacobson, *Whiteness of a Different Color*, 248–56. *New Yorský denník* "humorously" commented on whites' fears of black uncleanliness when it ran a joke that began, "A nigger asked his son, 'Willie, why are you forbidden from swimming with the white boys?'" *New Yorský denník*, April 7, 1923.

British Public Debates and the "Americanization" of Lynching

SARAH L. SILKEY

S THE UNITED STATES EMERGED in the nineteenth century as a powerful economic rival to British interests, British politicians and social leaders struggled to determine what significance to attach to the prevalence of lynching in the United States. Rather than representing a specifically defined set of actions, *lynching* served as a flexible rhetorical construct employed to condone or condemn acts of mob violence.[1] Therefore, the malleable and often contested nature of the concept made it possible for British and American social and political leaders to advocate competing definitions of *lynching* throughout the nineteenth century. The moral implications they attached to lynching in these debates helped define the social limits of British and American culture.

Perhaps the most famous of these debates grew in response to the 1893–94 transatlantic antilynching campaign led by Ida B. Wells, an African American journalist and civil rights activist. At the end of the nineteenth century, the southern system of segregation depended upon strict race and gender boundaries, which were fostered by anxieties about black male sexual aggression toward white women and reinforced by lynching.[2] Lynching rhetoric, especially the myth of the black rapist, played a powerful role in maintaining national and international tolerance for this often brutal system of American race relations. Consequently, Wells sought to undermine social tolerance of mob violence by attempting to shift lynching discourse toward a critique of white supremacy. Through pamphlets, letter-writing campaigns, newspaper articles, and public meetings, Wells and her supporters stimulated a dynamic transnational debate on lynching during her 1893 and 1894 British speaking tours. This discourse represented the confluence of public debates about lynching that had existed on both sides of the Atlantic for nearly sixty years before Wells began her campaign.

Through these national and transnational debates, Americans and Britons defined lynching as an American institution, separate and distinct from the universal problem of mob violence. British commentators largely accepted American assertions that lynching was a product of the unusual conditions in which the new republic developed. Not only did American lynching apologists argue in favor of this distinction, but they also insisted upon their fundamental right to employ lynch law. In order to distance themselves from the practice, British critics of lynching reinforced these claims of American exceptionalism by arguing that their more sophisticated English culture would never tolerate mob violence. Consequently, the acceptance or rejection of lynching became woven into each country's national identity. Through nineteenth-century transatlantic discourse on mob violence, we can trace this process—the gradual "Americanization" of lynching.

During the summer of 1835, news of two Mississippi lynchings spread across the United States and Britain and launched the first significant transatlantic debate about the acceptability of this novel form of extralegal violence. Local citizens hanged five gamblers in an attempt to cleanse Vicksburg of their immoral influence.[3] Meanwhile, five white men and five African American slaves accused of fomenting insurrection were reported to have been sentenced to death and executed by a "lynch court" in Madison County.[4] Although the terms "Judge Lynch" and "Lynch law" had been used, at least informally, in the United States, British commentators appeared unfamiliar with the concept. These two cases, occurring only days apart, created a sensation in the United States and attracted the attention of the British press.[5] While violence had always been a part of American society, the Vicksburg and Madison County incidents established "Lynch law" as a part of American culture in British eyes.

From these early days, Americans defended their right to employ summary execution outside the system of judicial due process. In 1836, Thomas Shackelford published *Proceedings of the Citizens of Madison County, Mississippi, At Livingston, in July, 1835, in Relation to the Trial and Punishment of Several Individuals Implicated in a Contemplated Insurrection in this State*, a defense of lynching that anticipated arguments offered by future lynching apologists. Responding with "manly energy" in defense of their community, residents of Madison County reacted to an alleged slave insurrection conspiracy by substituting lynch law for legal due process. Shackelford, a local attorney, argued that the community had acted in self-defense to preserve "all which we hold most dear in this world." Relying upon hearsay and the inadmissible testimony of slaves who were hanged for their participation in the alleged plot, the evidence against the suspected white conspirators would not hold up to the rigors of the regular courts. Therefore, the residents of Madison County held "something like a *trial*" for the accused in a hastily formed lynch court. According to Shackelford's account, at least six enslaved African Americans and six white men were publicly hanged over the course of three weeks.[6]

Although Shackelford assumed his reasoned and carefully documented account would receive public approval, his attempt to present lynching as a necessary and honorable method of community defense met with disdain in Britain. As the incident had occurred just two years after the 1833 Emancipation Act abolished slavery throughout the British Empire, few British commentators had sympathy for American slaveholders who claimed the right to set aside the rule of law in order to protect their interests in human bondage. To a British audience, Shackelford's "evidence" of an imminent slave insurrection seemed ludicrous, almost hysterical. Although any discontent openly expressed by a slave would have immediately alarmed southern slave holders, the *Times* was not surprised that a slave might express being "tired of waiting upon the 'white folks'" or wanting "to be her own mistress." Charges against the alleged white conspirators appeared equally flimsy. While perhaps indicating regrettable personal preferences, "being out all night" without "satisfactory explanation," "being deficient in feeling and affection for his second wife," or "trading with the negroes . . . and enjoying himself in their society" hardly seemed to warrant death by hanging without legal conviction.[7] Shackelford's pamphlet clearly indicated that the participants in the Madison County lynchings acted with impunity, believing their actions were both necessary and just. Yet in British eyes, if residents had the time, organization, and forethought to hold "trials," record confessions, and conduct public executions, there seemed little excuse not to convene proper legal proceedings. If American lynching apologists wished to receive broad public approval, they needed to better substantiate the necessity of mob violence in American society.

Americans offered a variety of arguments in defense of lynching. However, these arguments largely rested on the assertion that American society was, at its core, wholly different from European society. Despite the dangers mob violence posed, the unprecedented history of the United States—a former British colony with seemingly limitless natural resources, a steadily growing population, and increasing political and economic power—required the adoption of new moral and social standards. For example, in *The Americans in Their Moral, Social, and Political Relations*, Francis Grund attempted to defend lynching as "a species of *common law*," deeply rooted in American colonial history and perfected during the Revolutionary War. In Grund's estimation, lynching was used not in "opposition to the established laws of the country . . . but rather as a supplement to them." By providing a time-honored commonsense solution to correct the imperfections and shortcomings of the legal system, lynching had "been productive of some of the happiest results."[8] Americans like Grund "seriously defended" lynch law as "the only law of which some portions of the Union are capable." Ultimately, it was the very "necessity of the case" that "bar[red] all discussion" or debate on the suitability of lynching.[9]

British commentators who accepted the premise of American exceptionalism found it difficult to question American assertions that lynch law was required to maintain order. "We have often in England made a great mistake," the *Penny Illustrated Paper* explained, "in supposing that Lynch law was necessarily either cruel, unjust, or unnecessary," for without it "there would be no law at all." The implementation of a rude "mode of organization in the outskirts of a spreading empire," the *Times* concurred, was simply a condition of territorial expansion; Americans could not adequately guarantee the defense of their property or the safety of their families without it.[10] Still in its infancy, the United States could not be fairly compared to European nations. As American society became more organized, the need for this rough form of justice would presumably diminish.

Americans' willingness to forgo fair trials in exchange for swift vengeance appeared symptomatic of the moral deficiencies of American society and did not sit well with British social leaders. Accordingly, tolerance of mob violence became a mark of distinction between the two societies in their eyes. To British observers, the United States was populated by "the canting zealots of liberty and lashes" whose "religious revivals" and "love-feasts" merged with "slave auctions" and "Lynch-law."[11] British commentators scoffed at the notion that a "country of lynch-law and negro slavery" thought itself "the home of justice and of equal right" when "the high principles maintained in England on the equal rights of all mankind" had been established firmly by the abolition of colonial slavery under the 1833 Emancipation Act.[12] American society did not meet British moral standards, and the continued tolerance of slavery and mob violence diminished the moral authority of the

United States. Consequently, Britons placed little stock in the opinions "of a slave-driving, Lynch-law, tar and feathering Yankee!"[13]

Conservative politicians, in particular, denounced lynching as evidence of the inferiority of American society. The Tory Party suffered a striking defeat after the 1832 Great Reform Act extended the franchise to the middle class and shifted the balance of power traditionally controlled by the landed aristocracy. Under the leadership of Robert Peel, the Tories reinvented themselves as the Conservative Party. During the 1830s and 1840s, Conservatives cultivated middle-class anxieties about the potential spread of American lawlessness to England in an attempt to rally opposition to further proposed British democratic reforms, particularly the redistribution of parliamentary representation and universal manhood suffrage advocated by the Chartist movement. To Conservatives, lynching was a symptom of the excesses of Jacksonian democracy. If Britons were to embrace universal suffrage, they, too, might become subject to an American-style "mobocracy." Therefore, it was the duty of Conservatives to defend England from falling prey to the anarchy that threatened to engulf the United States.[14] As Conservative member of Parliament Wilson Jones declared, "Let us thank God for the blessings we enjoy, and buckle on our armour, with a determination to preserve them."[15]

Despite the negative connotations of lynching put forward by Conservative politicians, British commentators who had witnessed American frontier conditions, particularly those in the gold fields of California, often defended the use of lynching and, in the process, defended their own participation in or tolerance of mob violence. In a letter to the editor of the *Times* recounting his participation in the California gold rush, William Kelly lauded the important role "the famous judge Lynch" played in deterring crime in American frontier communities. According to Kelly, the knowledge that any wrongdoing would result in summary violence had "stricken terror into the evildoers," and as a result, the "rude society" in the mining camps had assumed "a placable and honest air." Security of property was especially important in the remote tent communities of the mining districts and sudden, dramatic consequences for attempted thefts deterred future transgressions. The knowledge that attempts to steal another man's treasure might result in death or physical mutilation would make any would-be thief take pause. Consequently, "honesty, even though it may be constrained, pervades this region," and the fruits of a man's labor were "as safe in your canvas tenement as if deposited in a metal safe" with a pick-proof lock.[16] San Francisco reportedly assumed "a habitable condition" after residents began to apply lynch law "to a great extent." Correspondents applauded the San Francisco Vigilance Committee for accomplishing "more good in the detection of crime than could have been accomplished by the police in a lifetime."[17] Frontier residents who found state laws "inadequate" began to consider lynching "more operative than legal justice."[18] Although unfortunate, lynching appeared to be both effective and satisfying. "Popular feeling" quickly grew "in favour of Lynch law in preference to the uncertainties and delays of constitutional enactments."[19] In his American travel narrative, Frederick Marryat reported that, however distasteful, lynching "has occasionally been beneficial, in the peculiar state of the communities in which it has been practiced." Marryat described situations where "Lynch law was called in to *assist* justice on the bench," with mobs waiting outside courtrooms to ensure punishment where legal technicalities, reluctant jurors, or clever lawyers may have prevented successful convictions. Lynching could be used as a panacea for the perceived failings of the judicial system or in cases where "from excitement the majority will not wait for the law to act."[20]

By the 1850s, lynching had won a grudging respectability—at least as long as it was confined within the boundaries of the United States. Vigilance committees in California had waged a successful campaign to increase American acceptance of lynch law by arguing that, based on the principle of popular sovereignty, local citizens had the right to employ mob violence to establish order when unscrupulous gold seekers brought rampant lawlessness into frontier communities.[21] Overwhelmed by the migration of large numbers of single men seeking to attain quick wealth, Californians relied upon "a corps of volunteers . . . formed of respectable persons to preserve some degree of security against the outrages of the mobs of suspicious gentry who are flocking to this country from all quarters."[22] "In this aggregate of homeless, reckless, and lawless adventurers," Californians claimed, "an extemporized code of honour or honesty" supplied "the function of civil government."[23] After all, Americans insisted, lynching was not the act of wild mobs of drunken and disorderly men; it was "men of Anglo-Saxon blood, decent education, and respectable political training" who carried out the sentences of "Judge Lynch." These honorable men of good community standing lent credibility to the process and transformed what had once been viewed as "a barbarous process of vengeance or violence . . . into a recognized operation of popular justice." The administration of lynch law had become "so far naturalized" in some parts of the country that "American journals look with approval on these proceedings" even when lynching superseded "the ordinary administration of the law."[24]

This "remarkable movement of opinion" was not lost on British commentators—particularly those with interests in the Australian goldfields opened in 1851.[25] Arguing that the police force was both inadequate and corrupt, Australian settlers patterned their justification for resorting to lynch law after the claims made by Californians. The social disruption accompanying massive migration, they argued, led to increasing crime rates. Unable to rely upon an ineffectual police force for protection, the people of Australia were "crying out for Lynch law."[26] As in San Francisco, Australians in the mining districts reported the salutary effect lynch law had on local crime rates and argued that "the sooner it gets general" adoption "the better," for the sooner it would "get rid of the hordes of ruffians who are prowling about." Fears about the potential excesses of the mob did not appear to concern these commentators, for they asserted that "Lynch-law has no terrors for an honest man."[27] Some even claimed that British settlers could improve upon the practice. In Melbourne, for example, local citizens, displeased with the poor performance of the police, planned to form "a private rifle corps for the apprehension of thieves." Rather than inflicting summary punishment like the vigilance committees of California, however, these citizens planned to deliver suspected thieves "to the constituted authorities" for trial: "That," a reporter proudly concluded, "is how Englishmen realize the idea of Lynch law." Whether or not lynch mobs in the rest of Australia were as high-minded appears doubtful from the many reports of lynch law that surfaced throughout the gold mining regions.[28] Yet these attempts to make lynching appear safe and honorable underscore the continued reluctance of the British public to condone the practice.

Despite these lingering reservations over the tolerance of lynch law, British newspapers still labeled acts of mob violence in England as "lynchings" throughout the mid-nineteenth century. Just as in the American press, the term *lynching* could be applied to condone as well as to condemn these incidents. Despite concerns raised by lethal incidents of lynching in the United States, innovative or morally satisfying nonlethal demonstrations of extralegal punishment met with approval in the British press. None seemed more deserving of popular justice in the eyes of the British public than men who committed domestic abuse or took advantage of vulnerable young women. In one "horrid case of cruelty" reported in 1844, a man and his mistress were both threatened with mob violence after severely beating and starving the man's seven-year-old son. Mr. Potton, who had abandoned his wife to live with his mistress, was accused of participating in the neglect and physical abuse of his child. "With great difficulty," a police officer navigated Ann Webb, the mistress who allegedly beat and starved the young child, through the angry crowd that gathered around the Lambeth Street courthouse. Although Webb successfully stood trial without feeling the vengeance of the mob, Mr. Potton was not as fortunate. Before the police had detained Potton, his coworkers at a hearthrug weaving factory administered "what they termed a dose of 'Lynch law' . . . for having brought scandal upon his fellow-workmen by his shameful conduct." Potton was condemned by his coworkers "to be tarred and feathered," a sentence they carried out "with hearty good will into immediate execution" before releasing him to the police. Responding to another case of domestic violence in 1847, women in Sussex implemented their own form of "Female Lynch Law." Outraged after seeing a man humiliate his wife by spanking her in public, the women castigated the man by whipping him with switches cut from hops and stinging nettles. At length "they released the culprit, who . . . gladly availed himself of the opportunity to retire, looking as happy as if he had stumbled into a wasp's nest." The reporter for the *Times* took delight in describing how the man "suffered, not from the 'stings and arrows of outrageous fortune,' but from the equally smarting and more tangible effects of nettles and hop-bines."[29]

Although British cases of extralegal justice were often administered by working-class men and women, lynching was not circumscribed by class boundaries; those dressed as gentlemen also felt the wrath of Judge Lynch when they crossed moral boundaries. In a case of "Lynch law in St. James's Park" in 1862, "a well-dressed man" observed taking "liberties" with three young girls was pursued by a determined "mob of several hundred persons" intent upon dragging "the miscreant through the bushes" and tossing "him into the ornamental water." Before the mob could achieve its goals, however, the man fled to the safety of the York column and threw himself upon the mercy of the sentry on duty. There he sat, listening to the "fearful yells and execrations" of the crowd from the top of the monument, until an armed escort could be found to convey him to the Vine Street police station. In an "Extraordinary Scene" of "Lynch Law" three years later, another "gentleman," who had gained a reputation for exploiting the affections of ladies of comfortable wealth, was treated to similar humiliation. Lured to Wandsworth Common by a married woman posing as a single lady "possessed of £300 a year," the man was "seized by two rough-looking men," who dragged the scoundrel to the edge of a polluted pond to "chuck him into its waters." Covered in mud and his clothes ruined, the man "wallow[ed] out on all fours

. . . in a very deplorable condition." The sight quickly attracted a crowd that hooted and hurled both insults and "inodorous eggs" at the man as he ran from the scene. In 1867, a pickpocket disguised as a respectable gentleman was detected at the Derby Day events along Clapham Common and treated to a similar "Lynching." In response to a lady's complaint that the man had stolen her watch, a group of mechanics "collared the swell-mobsman," returned the watch to its owner, and then threw the thief in a pond. "As he came to the side the dose was repeated several times" until he was finally allowed to skulk off "amidst the hooting and laughter of the crowd of spectators."[30]

Even officers of the law were not immune to the authority of Judge Lynch. For example, a police inspector was threatened with lynching in 1845 for the wrongful death of a prisoner under arrest. When the suspect calmly refused to relinquish disputed property, the inspector drew a club from his pocket and dealt the "deceased a violent blow" to his head, causing "him to stagger" and complain about "how bad his head was." Community outrage grew and began to show "symptoms of administering Lynch law upon the inspector" after the prisoner succumbed to the needlessly inflicted wound. Demands for summary justice were calmed only by the speedy indictment and arrest of the inspector on the charge of manslaughter.[31]

British lynching incidents were often not as violent as those reported in America and sometimes were averted before coming to fruition. The British press identified such acts as "lynch law" even when the mob was dispersed or otherwise thwarted. It was the spirit of extralegal "justice," not the particular actions of the mob or the alleged crimes committed, that defined lynching for Britons in the mid-nineteenth century. Lynch law filled a perceived gap in the judicial system by addressing cases that were unlikely to result in trial and conviction. Then as now, domestic violence and child neglect were often considered private affairs; young girls would not have wanted to lodge formal complaints against a molester for fear that confirming such incidents might reflect badly on their character; similarly, ladies who had fallen prey to a philanderer would not have wanted to make their disgrace known; and even pickpockets, who clearly broke the law and whose victims held no such fears of public shame, frequently went undetected. By ensuring delivery of a publicly satisfying punishment through threat or action, lynchings sent a clear message to both the transgressor and the community about what behaviors were considered socially unacceptable in Britain. Even those who held positions of power, such as a police inspector, were not immune from prosecution when city officials feared an outbreak of mob violence if they failed to act.

In many ways, lynching fulfilled similar social and rhetorical functions in both countries; however, the form of Judge Lynch's sentences varied considerably on each side of the Atlantic. "Lynching" was a fluid concept that could be tailored to the purposes of the one who invoked the word. Depending upon the needs of the community and severity of the presumed infraction against the public peace, lynching could encompass everything from public humiliation, flogging, or burning in effigy to hanging, shooting, or burning alive. Even so, public perceptions of lynching began to solidify over the course of the nineteenth century: while lynching became more frequently associated with acts of public humiliation or *threatened* violence in England, lynching in the United States became tantamount to extralegal execution.

By the 1850s, British commentators began to draw a sharp distinction between British and American applications of lynch law. Although lynching may have been excusable to some degree on the American or Australian frontiers, mob violence in England was still considered "a disgrace" by many.[32] Put simply, to become more like the United States was to regress as a civilization. While it might still be acceptable for a British community to drag a rogue through the mud or duck him in a pond, any form of more serious mob violence would have been considered unsporting. As one commentator explained, honorable men faced their opponents "one to one." "The English love of justice," therefore, restrained British mobs from engaging in the kind of violent confrontations so frequently reported in the United States.[33] Moral superiority was an important part of British national identity in the nineteenth century and remained a recurrent theme in the British press. "We are remarkably moral, self-restrained, and well-conducted people," the editor of the *Times* pronounced in 1851. "All opinions concur in rendering this acknowledgment to our national virtues."[34] While younger nations might resort to mob violence to control crime, Britons "take care to punish offences committed under our flag" properly in a court of law.[35] Although mob violence might save "a world of trouble" in "the back-woods" of the United States, lynch law was simply "not adapted for our state of society."[36]

As the term became more closely associated with lethal measures after the Civil War, British reporters became increasingly reluctant to apply the label to incidents in Britain. For example, in 1873, the *Graphic* assured its readers that "Lynch law does not flourish upon English soil."[37] Americans, by contrast, had long been perceived to be prone to lawlessness and excessive violence. "Gouging and Lynching appear[ed] to be exclusively free-soil products," and "the land of the free" remained the only place "where an accidental 'difference' results in permanent mutilation."[38] British moral character simply would not tolerate such aberrations. The *Times* regretted that "America has not arrived at the same standard of morality."[39]

While labeling incidents of mob violence as lynchings gradually fell out of fashion in Great Britain, British reporters continued to report lynchings in developing nations, as well as those European nations presumed, like the United States, to be less refined than England. Having previously accepted claims that prospectors in California and Australia required lynching to keep the peace, British readers would not have been surprised to read reports that lynch law had been adopted by settlers in the goldfields of South Africa. However, the British press also reported incidents of "Lynch law" in France, Italy, Germany, Spain, Portugal, Hungary, Mexico, and Turkey.[40] Lethal incidents of extralegal violence were reported with increasing disapproval in the British press by the 1880s. For example, British reporters were "shocked" by "specimens of Spanish 'lynching,'" which were considered "all the more terrible" for the "business-like" manner in which they were executed and warned that France was in danger of being "disgraced" as "a country governed by lynch-law." The disapproval evident in these press reports decreased British sympathy for European nations that resorted to lynch law and further distanced British culture from lynching.[41]

The British press continued to "Americanize" mob violence in the late nineteenth century by withholding the label "lynching" from events in England. British mobs even began to equate lynching with "American" justice, reportedly demanding, "let us have American law" in their frenzy.[42] Although the temptation to lynch continued to run high at times, by the 1880s mob violence was neither seriously advocated nor widely tolerated in Britain. As the midcentury economic boom of the Industrial Revolution began to decline and concerns about rising unemployment and working-class discontent grew, British commentators became less inclined to glorify mob violence for fear that it might be seen as an acceptable method for expressing public dissatisfaction with government power. In cities such as Carlisle, Grimsby, and London, local authorities made consistent efforts to defuse threats of mob violence and defend prisoners from angry crowds.[43] By making certain that such demands for summary justice went unfulfilled while still reporting lethal acts of lynching in the United States, the British press demonstrated the disparity between British and American social standards.

Embracing this distinction, British commentators and social leaders began to joke about applying lynch law to disreputable persons in England, feeling confident that middle-class Britons would share in the desire for retribution but not act upon such fantasies. For example, during a tense meeting responding to the unscrupulous management of the Rock Investment Trust, Mr. Palmer, one of the many investors who had lost money, declared that it was a pity none of the trust's directors had attended the meeting, since "there was such a thing as 'lynching,' and he would have liked to have assisted at a practical exposition of the art." His remarks were met with cheers and laughter from the audience.[44] As lynching became an increasingly distant and foreign concept, it became easier to forget the realities of the practice and instead begin to romanticize it along with other fading parts of the great American frontier adventure.

As the American frontier gradually gave way to settled communities and farmland after the Civil War, transatlantic popular culture sought to capture and preserve the spirit of the Wild West. The concept of lynching as a form of frontier justice became entwined within the larger cultural mythology about the American frontier that flourished in the 1870s and 1880s. Dime novels relating "true" stories of the Wild West became popular reading in both the United States and Britain during this period. In their pages, brave lawmen and vicious outlaws became powerful images of the American frontier. With the growth of frontier mythology, Britons began to admire the rugged individualism required by settlers to protect their families and build "civilized" communities in a harsh and hostile environment filled with dangerous outlaws and wild "Red Indians."[45] Lynching as frontier justice began to appear honorable, even admirable, as a result. Not only did Britons begin to criticize Americans less for lynching in the years following the Civil War, they became fascinated by American lynching stories.

One of the principal ambassadors of American frontier mythology during this period was Buffalo Bill Cody, whose traveling Wild West show repeatedly toured Europe beginning in 1887. His first British tour coincided with Queen Victoria's Golden Jubilee celebrations. With more than 2.5 million people attending performances in London, the Wild West show became an instant success.[46] British appetites grew for tales of lynching as part of the authentic American experience. By the time of his "Farewell Visit to Europe" in 1892, Cody had incorporated "TWO NEW PICTURES of historical interest" entitled "Lynching a Horse Thief" and "Burning at the Stake" into his spectacular presentation of Sioux Indians, American cowboys, bucking horses, and wild buffalo. The show received favorable reviews, and audiences were "entranced by these vivid representations of lynch law . . . in the Far West."[47]

Likewise, British authors relayed their encounters with lynch mobs as colorful adventure stories about rural American folkways. A. H. Paterson told British audiences in an 1887 edition of *Macmillan's Magazine* about his participation in a lynch party, composed of the area's most respected citizens, formed to protect their small western community from the threat of murderous anarchy. Confident in the morality of his actions, Paterson described at length the deliberate process involved in the lynching. After an allegedly corrupt jury acquitted two accused murderers, upstanding citizens of the small western community met in secret to deliberate the fate of the two men. Holding a second "trial," the secret court convicted the two men by authority of "Judge Lynch" and promptly hanged them. Afterward, the lynchers swore they had acted honorably and "given judgment without malice toward any one." R. B. Townshend's "true" account of frontier lynching in *The Nineteenth Century* was set in a Colorado community with no law-enforcement facilities. The community organized itself into a "people's court" and conducted an impromptu trial within hours of an alleged murder. The accused was quickly found guilty and hanged, prompting "many of the worst characters in town" to leave the same night. Townshend claimed the lynching he witnessed purified "the moral atmosphere of Morgan City" and prevented further criminal activity.[48] Although British commentators had been appalled by the use of a lynch court in Madison County in 1835, by the 1880s lynching had become part of transatlantic popular culture. The British public craved thrilling tales of life on the American frontier and eagerly received such accounts.

Depictions of lynching as an honorable form of American frontier justice affirmed the delight with which British audiences consumed these tales. Lynching as "frontier justice" no longer offered any moral ambiguity to British audiences. Although lynching might no longer be appropriate in England, the "best citizens" of American frontier settlements still required popular justice to impose law and order, even as the frontier began to close. Thus lynching revealed not the lawlessness of American society or the weakness of American character but the moral fiber of brave pioneers.

While lynching as frontier justice might be celebrated in transatlantic popular culture, the vast majority of American lynching reports reaching Great Britain by the early 1890s did not fit this description. Lynchings in settled areas were becoming ever more frequent, and fears that lynching might undermine the judicial system began to trouble British observers. Such fears appeared justified after the March 14, 1891, lynching of Italian nationals in a New Orleans prison. Thousands of local citizens, displeased with the verdict of a murder trial, "broke" into the city jail and killed eleven Italian immigrants. Sparking an international controversy and creating a diplomatic crisis between the United States and Italy, the New Orleans lynching shocked Great Britain. The legal authorities admitted that they had known the intentions of the lynchers, but they made no attempt to stop the lynching. This was not some remote frontier community with limited access to the court system; New Orleans was a thriving port city. Several of the victims had been legally tried and acquitted but remained in jail awaiting trial on lesser charges. Claims made by lynching apologists that extralegal violence maintained social order appeared ludicrous when that violence nullified the authority of a working judicial system.[49]

Despite threats and appeals from the Italian government for legal redress against the lynchers, the federal government washed its hands of the affair, maintaining it had no constitutional mandate to interfere in what was essentially a matter for the State of Louisiana. U.S. secretary of state James G. Blaine provoked angry responses from the international community when he argued that the murdered Italians had been afforded the same rights and privileges as any American citizen. Indignant British journalists derided the secretary's position, asking whether "liability to lynch law" should be considered "a right and privilege" that all foreign visitors must "enjoy."[50]

While the majority of British newspaper and journal articles expressed outrage, or at least disgust, with the impotence of the U.S. government to uphold even a semblance of legal order, a minority approved of the lynching. Citing interference by the mafia in the original trial, some British commentators concluded that the citizens of New Orleans were justified in bypassing the corrupted legal system and reasserting their authority. To reassure British travelers who feared they might be at risk of meeting a similar fate, some observers emphasized the alleged criminality of the lynch mob's victims as justification for the Italians' deaths. In a surprising twist, a small, outspoken group of British commentators chastised the mob for lynching the wrong people—they should have murdered the corrupt judge and jury instead.[51]

While Britons grappled with the social and political aftermath of the New Orleans lynching, reports of another horrific case of lynch law came out of Paris, Texas. On February 1, 1893, as many as ten thousand spectators participated in the torture and burning alive of Henry Smith, a black man accused of raping and murdering a four-year-old white girl. Newspaper reports in the British press detailed the elaborate preparations made for the lynching. Announcements had been made throughout the region days in advance, and special excursion trains brought spectators from neighboring districts into the town. Schools were dismissed, and a scaffold was built to provide the entire crowd with an unobstructed view of the proceedings. The family of the alleged victim was given the honor of torturing Smith with red-hot irons for forty minutes before he was set alight. Although lynching apologists claimed that such terrible violence was required to satisfy community outrage over the violation of white women and children by black men, the bloodthirsty revelry of the crowd scandalized British readers and brought their assumptions about American lynching further into question.[52]

Once again, reports of a high-profile American lynching that bore little resemblance to "frontier justice" flooded British newspapers. This time, however, confusion and disgust over the racist arguments used in support of the lynchers dominated British public debates. The *Daily News* marveled at the depravity of the Texas mob, which tried to repay Smith's violence "with interest" by burning him alive, while the *Daily Chronicle* expressed disgust at "the most terrible revenge" inflicted by the white citizens of Texas. In response to the concerns raised by British commentators, Ida B. Wells was invited to act as a spokesperson for the Society for the Recognition of the Brotherhood of Man (SRBM), a nascent British organization dedicated to "improving inequality and wrongs" committed against "the struggling helpless races in America, India, Africa, and Australia."[53] Still unsettled by the lingering New Orleans controversy and stunned by the lynching in Texas, British audiences were primed to hear Wells's critique of American race relations. Wells sought to mobilize the remnants of the British antislavery and freedmen's aid associations when she traveled to Great Britain under the SRBM's umbrella in April 1893. Although her first tour was plagued by an acrimonious dispute within the SRBM's central leadership, her second tour, beginning in March 1894, allowed Wells to gain access to influential religious leaders, newspaper editors, and the national May Meetings of various religious and reform organizations in London.[54]

Through her interviews and speaking engagements, Wells argued that lynching was a form of terrorism used by racist whites to oppress African Americans. Cultivating fear to discourage black economic and social advancement, lynchers sought to restore the social and economic power enjoyed by southern whites before the Civil War. Wells presented American press clippings and personal testimonials about her own encounters with mob violence to support her claims that lynching was racially and economically motivated. She told how three successful black entrepreneurs in her hometown, Memphis, Tennessee, were arrested for defending their property from armed attack. While awaiting formal charges, the men were taken from the jail and brutally shot. In "typical" fashion, the morning newspapers "gave full accounts of the lynching" within hours of the attack yet still claimed the identity of "the lynchers to be unknown." Rather than an attempt to protect white women from sexual assault, the Memphis lynching served only to eliminate a thriving business and intimidate the growing black middle class. When Wells published an editorial in her newspaper, the *Free Speech and Headlight,* denouncing "the old thread-bare lie that Negro men rape white women," the "leading citizens" of Memphis destroyed her press, threatened Wells with mutilation, and forced her into exile from the South. Wells argued that such abuses would continue as long as lynching was used to deny African Americans due process.[55]

As British audiences struggled to understand what lynching in the United States had become, Wells sought to undermine the assertions made by American apologists that lynching was used only in response to rape. Therefore, in her speeches and newspaper interviews, Wells highlighted the shocking cases of cruelty and torture committed by lynch mobs against women and children—those held to be incapable of rape. She told of a Tennessee woman wrongly accused of poisoning her white employer who was "dragged out of gaol, every stitch of clothing torn from her body, and . . . hanged in the courthouse square in sight of everybody." When a black man in Louisiana refused to confess to the murder of a local white man, he was forced to watch as a mob hanged first his son and then his young daughter as punishment for his obstinacy. The ingenuity and cruelty of lynch mobs, she declared, "can scarcely be believed." In Texas, a "mob laid hold of" a woman accused of poisoning, forced her into a barrel filled with spikes and rolled her down a hill. "Howling furiously," the mob ran after the barrel, kicking it to speed it along its deadly path. At last, "they knocked it open again, dragged off the spikes a mass of ragged skin and bones and bloody clothes, hanged it—for there was little semblance to a human being then—upon a tree and shot it as it hung."[56] These harrowing tales made Americans appear capricious and cruel. Stripping women in the courthouse square, executing innocent children for the "crimes" of their parents, torturing and mutilating women to death—this was certainly not the behavior of honorable men.

The vehemence of American attacks upon Wells's campaign led British editors to sympathize with her cause. For example, when Georgia governor William J. Northen wrote a letter to the editor of the *Daily Chronicle* attempting to defend the South by fervently attacking Wells's character, the editor admonished Northen's misguided attempt to deflect attention from the real issue. For when the American press "literally teemed with accounts of the most brutal lynchings," he declared, Americans had already indicted themselves before the world. The detailed depictions reported in American newspapers of the torture and burning of Henry Smith in Paris, Texas, and the lynching of Italians in New Orleans were simply too horrible to have been invented. Nevertheless, Elizabeth L. Banks attempted to deny the veracity of such reports in an article for the *Sun,* claiming "that fully one-half the reported lynchings are purely imaginary." As an American, Banks sided with white southerners, whom she felt were unfairly maligned in the British press and "far more deserving of sympathy than . . . filthy, lazy, and impudent" black men.[57] An Englishman living in Tennessee concurred with Banks, arguing in a letter to the *Spectator* that the British press should "not condemn us without knowing what we have to put up with." "The negro," he insisted, "is not a human being in the same sense as the white man"; African Americans were "constitutionally dishonest, hopelessly lazy, and devoid of any idea of sexual morality," leading to the criminal behavior that prompted communities to lynch them. The poise with which Wells carried herself in her personal interviews and public appearances belied such arguments, but even if that were not the case, "Our correspondent misses the point," the *Spectator* complained. "Nobody argues that inferior races may not need severe disciplinary laws," only that they "should be heard in their own defence, and should be convicted by Judges who intend to be impartial"—something "mobs do not."[58] Furthermore, these criticisms of the black community did not conform with British experiences in the "West Indian, and African colonies," where it was not "necessary to burn negroes alive to ensure due protection to white women."[59]

As Wells won the editorial support of British newspapers, the romantic image of lynching as frontier justice began to fade in the shadow of the brutal oppression of African Americans. After weighing her testimony, the *Bradford Observer* determined that "there seems to be nothing irrational or impossible in the plea that [African Americans] ought not to be branded and burned alive and rolled in nailed casks, or even hanged on a tree, at the whim and sport of a mob." The *Newcastle Daily Leader* sneered at America's "boasted forwardness in civilisation," which in reality amounted to a "chamber of horrors" for African Americans. The *Daily Chronicle* did not pull punches in its denunciation of the South. The editor deemed that while "race prejudice" may be "one thing; the horrible tortures, not only described by Miss Wells, but admitted and almost gloried in by the Southerners themselves, are quite another." British commentators were disturbed by the salacious details of lynchings unabashedly reported in the American press and the vehemence with which Americans defended their right to lynch. "When we read of such atrocities," the editor of the *Daily Chronicle* despaired, "we ask ourselves whether the Southern States are really fitted for self-government."[60]

Such powerful denunciations of lynching cemented the divide between British and American cultures drawn in earlier debates over American tolerance of mob violence. By dispelling the illusion that there was honor in lynch law, Wells encouraged Britons to distance themselves from Americans, particularly white southerners. Regardless of whether lynching had been essential to the early development of American society, it seemed wholly inappropriate for a thriving modern nation to tolerate mob violence at the end of the nineteenth century, and Britons would not have wished to associate themselves with any culture that demonstrated so little respect for propriety.

Wells's campaign and the contentious public debates it inspired reinforced British assumptions that lynching was an American phenomenon and that British national identity might be defined, in part, by its intolerance for mob violence. By the late 1890s, the British public considered lynching to be synonymous with "American law," and British authorities were reported to take successful measures to protect prisoners from angry crowds. Although *lynching* occasionally appeared in other contexts, the British press overwhelmingly applied the term, with its lethal and racial connotations, to events in the United States after Wells's campaign.[61] Wells's depictions of lynching as racist violence, and the distasteful defenses of mob violence offered by southern apologists, removed any remaining luster from lynch law. With nothing left to admire, Britons relinquished lynching to the Americans. Thus, by the end of the nineteenth century, lynching had become permanently, and negatively, linked to American culture.

NOTES

Portions of this essay have been published previously in Sarah L. Silkey, "Redirecting the Tide of White Imperialism: The Impact of Ida B. Wells's Transatlantic Antilynching Campaign on British Conceptions of American Race Relations," in *Women Shaping the South: Creating and Confronting Change*, ed. Angela Boswell and Judith N. McArthur (Columbia: University of Missouri Press, 2006).

1. Christopher Waldrep, *The Many Faces of Judge Lynch: Extralegal Violence and Punishment in America* (New York: Palgrave Macmillan, 2002), 2–6.

2. Jacquelyn Dowd Hall, *Revolt against Chivalry: Jesse Daniel Ames and the Women's Campaign against Lynching* (New York: Columbia University Press, 1993), 145–49.

3. "Lynch Law," *Times* (London), August 25, 1835; "Lynch Law," *Jackson's Oxford Journal*, August 29, 1835; Foreign Miscellany, *Preston Chronicle*, August 29, 1835.

4. Editorial, *Times*, August 28, 1835; "Slavery," *Brighton Patriot and Lewes Free Press*, September 1, 1835; Weekly Epitome, *Hull Packet*, September 4, 1835; Foreign News, *Cobbett's Weekly Political Register* (London), September 5, 1835.

5. "Express from Tamworth," *Times*, September 5, 1835; "Grand Dinner to Sir Robert Peel," *Derby Mercury*, September 9, 1835; Waldrep, *Many Faces of Judge Lynch*, 27–29, 46.

6. Thomas Shackelford, *Proceedings of the Citizens of Madison County, Mississippi, At Livingston, in July, 1835, in Relation to the Trial and Punishment of Several Individuals Implicated in a Contemplated Insurrection in this State* (Jackson, MS: Mayson and Smoot, 1836), iii–iv, 8, 11–13, emphasis in original.

7. "Lynch Law Term Reports," *Times*, November 5, 1836.

8. Francis J. Grund, *The Americans in Their Moral, Social and Political Relations* (1837; reprint, with introduction by Robert Berkhofer Jr., New York: Johnson Reprint, 1968), 178–79, 180, emphasis in original.

9. Editorial, *Times*, October 1, 1845.

10. "Lynch Law," *Penny Illustrated Paper* (London), January 18, 1862; editorial, *Times*, October 1, 1845.

11. "Conservative Dinner at Wrexham," *Times*, September 15, 1837; editorial, *Times*, July 28, 1836.

12. "America Compared with England," *Times*, January 25, 1849; editorial, *Times*, November 27, 1833.

13. Miles, "England and America," letter to the editor, *Times*, October 4, 1843.

14. Rohan McWilliam, *Popular Politics in Nineteenth-Century England* (London: Routledge, 1998), 17–18, 49; Paul Adelman, *Peel and the Conservative Party, 1830-1850* (Harlow: Pearson Longman, 1990), 13; Robert Blake, *The Conservative Party from Peel to Major* (London: Heinemann, 1997), 10–12; editorial, *Times*, April 5, 1837; editorial, *Times*, January 26, 1846.

15. "Conservative Dinner at Whexham," *Times*, September 15, 1837.

16. William Kelly, "California, Ho!," letter to the editor, *Times*, November 30, 1849.

17. America, *Times*, July 30, 1851; America, *Times*, August 26, 1851.

18. America, *Times*, April 7, 1851; America, *Times*, December 12, 1850.

19. The United States, *Times*, August 26, 1851.

20. Frederick Marryat, *A Diary in America, with Remarks on its Institutions* (Paris: Baudy's European Library, 1839), 1:316–18, 323–24, emphasis in original.

21. Waldrep, *Many Faces of Judge Lynch*, 56–61, 65–66.

22. "State of California," *Times*, October 3, 1849.

23. Editorial, *Times*, September 7, 1849.

24. Editorial, *Times*, August 27, 1851.

25. Ibid.

26. The Unfortunate Owner, "The 'Government' in Australia," letter to the editor, *Times*, December 22, 1852.

27. "The Australian Gold Diggings," *Times*, August 20, 1852.

28. "The Australian Goldfields," *Times*, November 8, 1852. For other examples, see "The Australian Gold Mines," *Times*, April 6, 1852; "The Australian Goldfields," *Times*, December 16, 1852; editorial, *Times*, December 24, 1852; Australia, *Times*, July 26, 1855; Australia, *Times*, April 3, 1858.

29. Lambeth-Street, *Times*, August 31 and September 2 and 5, 1844; "Female Lynch Law," *Times*, October 6, 1847.

30. "Lynch Law in St. James's Park," *Times*, 2 August 1862; "Lynch Law at Wandsworth: Extraordinary Scene," *Penny Illustrated Paper*, September 2, 1865; "Derby Delinquents," *Penny Illustrated Paper*, June 1, 1867.

31. "Manslaughter by a Police Inspector," *Times*, November 17, 1845.

32. Anti-Lynch, letter to the editor, *Times*, December 31, 1850.

33. "Lynch Law at Wandsworth: Extraordinary Scene," *Penny Illustrated Paper*, September 2, 1865.

34. Editorial, *Times*, October 27, 1851.

35. Editorial, *Times*, October 11, 1860.

36. Editorial, *Times*, November 24, 1849.

37. Topics of the Week, *Graphic* (London), September 6, 1873.

38. Editorial, *Times*, October 27, 1851.

39. Editorial, *Times*, October 11, 1860.

40. For examples, see "The Cape of Good Hope," *Times*, February 24, 1872; "France," *Times*, December 20, 1883; Ouida, "Romance and Realism," letter to the editor, *Times*, October 12, 1883; "A Berlin Convent," *Times*, August 21, 1869; "The Revolution in Spain," *Times*, October 14, 1868; "Portugal," *Times*, December 2, 1884; "Austria-Hungary," *Times*, September 24, 1891; "The Assault on President Diaz," *Times*, September 18, 1897; "Turkey," *Times*, January 22, 1881.

41. "A Madrid Anniversary," *Times*, May 8, 1873; "French Racing," *Times*, April 19, 1892; "Lynch-Law in Paris," *Times*, January 9, 1885; "The Riots in Belgium," *Times*, March 30, 1886.

42. Police, *Times*, January 25, 1897.

43. McWilliam, *Popular Politics*, 18–19. For examples, see "The Alleged Cruelty at Sea," *Times*, January 29, 1885; "Murder by Burglars in Cumberland," *Times*, October 31, 1885; Police, *Times*, January 25, 1897.

44. "The Rock Investment Trust (Limited)," *Times*, February 11, 1892.

45. Joy S. Kasson, *Buffalo Bill's Wild West: Celebrity, Memory, and Popular History* (New York: Hill and Wang, 2000), 5–8; Heather Cox Richardson, *West from Appomattox: The Reconstruction of America after the Civil War* (New Haven, CT: Yale University Press, 2007), 270–72.

46. Kasson, *Buffalo Bill's Wild West*, 65–66, 75, 77–82; Louis S. Warren, *Buffalo Bill's America: William Cody and the Wild West Show* (New York: Alfred A. Knopf, 2005), 283–90, 302.

47. Buffalo Bill's "Wild West" Show, advertisement, *Graphic*, August 6, 1892, emphasis in original; "Fresh Attractions at the 'Horty,'" *Penny Illustrated Paper*, July 30, 1892.

48. A. H. Paterson, "Lynch Law," *Macmillan's Magazine* 55 (March 1887): 347; R. B. Townshend, "A Trial by Lynch Law," *Nineteenth Century* 32 (August 1892): 252.

49. N. J. D. Kennedy, "Lynch," *Juridicial Review* 3 (July 1891): 216; "The Lynching Affair at New Orleans," *Spectator* 66 (March 21, 1891): 401; Jessie White (Vedova) Mario, "Italy and the United States," *Nineteenth Century* 29 (May 1891): 703. For a well-articulated example of British concerns, see "Lynching in America," *Chambers's Journal*, May 17, 1890, 317–19.

50. N. J. D. Kennedy, "Lynch II—Its International Aspect," *Juridicial Review* 4 (January 1892): 46, 48; "Lynch Law," *Saturday Review* 71 (May 30, 1891): 643.

51. "The Lynching Affair at New Orleans," 401; Kennedy, "Lynch," 217.

52. "Sensational Lynching Affray in State of Texas," *Glasgow Herald*, February 2, 1893; "More Lynching Tragedies—Scenes of a Horrible Nature," *Glasgow Herald*, February 2, 1893; "Sensations: 'A Man and a Brudder,'" *Star* (London), February 2, 1893; "Lynch Law in Texas," *Daily News* (London), February 3, 1893; editorial, *Daily Chronicle* (London), February 3, 1893; The United States, *Times*, February 8, 1893.

53. "Lynch Law in Texas," *Daily News*, February 3, 1893; editorial, *Daily Chronicle*, February 3, 1893; "Unity Our Aim," *Fraternity* 1 (July 1893): 1.

54. For Wells's description of the breakdown in the SRBM, see Alfreda M. Duster, ed., *Crusade for Justice: The Autobiography of Ida B. Wells* (Chicago: University of Chicago Press, 1970), 103–5, 109–11, 124.

55. "Black versus White," *Labour Leader* (London), May 12, 1894; Ida B. Wells, *United States Atrocities: Lynch Law* (London: Lux, 1893), 1–2, 9, 11–13.

56. "Lynch Law in America," *Daily Chronicle*, April 28, 1894; "Lynching in the United States," *Newcastle Daily Leader*, April 20, 1894; "Miss Ida B. Wells," *Sun* (London), May 31, 1894.

57. William J. Northen, letter to the editor and editor's note, *Daily Chronicle*, June 5, 1894; Elizabeth L. Banks, "The Negro Problem," *Sun*, July 6, 1894.

58. H.E.S., "Lynch Law in America," letter to the editor and editor's note, *Spectator* 73 (July 7, 1894): 16; "Aberdeen—Lynch Law in America," *Aberdeen Daily Free Press*, April 25, 1893; "Lynch Law in the Southern States," *Scottish Pulpit* (Glasgow), May 10, 1893; *Lady's Pictorial* 25 (May 20, 1893): 809.

59. Philip C. Ivens, "Colour Prejudice," letter to the editor, *Sun*, July 9, 1894.

60. Editorial, *Bradford Observer*, May 11, 1894; "Lynching in the United States," *Newcastle Daily Leader*, April 20, 1894; editorial, *Daily Chronicle*, April 28, 1894.

61. For examples of *lynching* defined as "American law," see "Midnight Affray in a Flat," *Lloyd's Weekly Newspaper* (London), January 24, 1897; Police, *Times*, January 25, 1897; "Midnight Affray," *Illustrated Police News* (London), January 30, 1897. Although rare, a few incidents outside the United States were reported as "lynchings" in the British press during the early twentieth century. For examples, see "Alleged Lynching in Johannesburg," House of Commons, *Times*, August 2, 1904; "The Condition of Russia," *Times*, August 18, 1905; "The Lynching of Five Generals," *Times*, January 30, 1912.

Lynching across the Pacific

Japanese Views and African American Responses in the
Wartime Antilynching Campaign

FUMIKO SAKASHITA

O N JANUARY 25, 1942, a mob lynched Cleo Wright, an African American
cotton mill worker in Sikeston, Missouri, for rape. Described by antilynching organizations as "the first lynching after Pearl Harbor," the
Sikeston lynching became a new symbol for African Americans' two-front
war—fighting fascism abroad while fighting Jim Crow at home. On February 26, a month after the incident, the Saint Louis and Saint Louis County
branches of the National Association for the Advancement of Colored People
(NAACP) protested the Sikeston lynching with a silent parade. The *Pittsburgh Courier* reported that the protestors carried several antilynching signs
with such messages as "Stop Lynching and Pass the Anti-Lynch Bill" and "V
for Victory Abroad and V for Victory at Home." A picture captured the protestors and their signs, one of which read: "'Remember Pearl Harbor' But
Don't Forget Sikeston."[1]

The strategy of placing domestic injustices in an international context
had long been utilized by African American antilynching activists, dating
back to Ida B. Wells's campaign in Britain in 1893–94 that aroused British
public sentiment against lynching to influence American society. Such efforts mounted in the 1930s and 1940s as the country fought Nazism and
fascism. The black press and leaders constantly reminded the public that international audiences, particularly those in enemy countries, saw lynching
as an American disgrace. They warned the government that lynching armed
Hitler and his allies—Italy and Japan—with a powerful propaganda weapon
against the United States.

But did these enemy countries in fact use lynching for Axis propaganda, as antilynching activists claimed? The purpose of this essay is to explore Japanese views on the issues of lynching and race in the United States from the late 1910s to the 1940s and African American responses to them. How did the wartime enemy countries see American lynching? How were their views on lynching formed over time? And in what way did African Americans react to their reporting of American lynching? The Japanese people today, who use the word *rinchi* ("lynch" in Japanese pronunciation) to describe collective violence in general, have little awareness of the term's original American context. In the early twentieth century when lynching was a contemporary social problem in the United States, however, Japanese books, newspaper accounts, and editorials kept the nation well informed about American lynching and racial friction. Ongoing international developments, such as the defeat of Japan's racial equality proposal at the Paris Peace Conference in 1919, the Japanese Exclusion Act of 1924, and the Manchurian incident in 1931, helped promote Japanese interest in American lynching. Diverse Japanese commentators from leftists to ultranationalists criticized lynching from their own perspectives. While the Japanese media paid only intermittent attention to American lynching, it nevertheless proved an effective tool in promoting Japan's domestic and international political goals.

After reviewing various Japanese narratives on American lynching, I further demonstrate how African Americans' antilynching discourse changed as their country moved toward war with Japan. Black newspapers and periodicals strategically shifted their antilynching rhetoric as their view of Japan changed from "a leader of the darker races" to wartime enemy. Admittedly, unlike Wells's campaign, which physically crossed over national boundaries, most antilynching efforts discussed in this essay were transnational only on the discursive level. However, the wartime antilynching discourse, just like other antiracist utterance, helps us understand how African Americans created the discursive counterpublic sphere in which they struggled to redefine the black body as both black and American. The unique wartime status of the Japanese and their antilynching views played a complex yet important role in forming African American antilynching narratives.

EARLIER JAPANESE VIEWS ON AMERICAN LYNCHING

A concept of lynching had existed in Japan long before the Japanese learned the American term *lynching*, according to the leftist journalist Gaikotsu Miyatake, who in 1922 published a book entitled *Shikei Ruisan* (Compiled story on lynching), a collection of stories on reported lynching mainly in Japan but also around the world. Miyatake stated that "shikei" (私刑), which literally meant private persecution in Japanese, originated in China, reaching Japan by the 1680s. He further explained to his readers that in Europe and America "it [shikei] was generally called 'lynch' or 'lynching,'" and quoted its definition from *Encyclopedia Britanica*.[2] It was around the 1920s when the American term *lynching* became interchangeable with the Japanese term *shikei*, and Miyatake used both in *Shikei Ruisan*. Newspapers often printed *lynching* in Japanese kana letters alongside Chinese characters for *shikei,* and the term *rinchi* (lynch) alone became recognizable in many Japanese media. An article in the newspaper *Yomiuri* in 1922, for example, stated: "You already know what shikei, rinchi, or lynching means . . . it is a private persecution."[3]

Japanese newspapers cited the occurrence of lynching in the United States as early as 1886, but it was not until the first decades of the twentieth century that these reports gained attention of the Japanese.[4] In 1919 and 1921, the press reported major race riots in Chicago; Washington, DC; Knoxville, Tennessee; New York; Omaha, Nebraska; Helena, Arkansas; and Tulsa, Oklahoma, under such headlines as "A Fight between Black and White" and "Another Race Riot Occurred."[5] Most of those cases included the lynching of black men either as their cause or effect, and several newspapers mentioned that black men's assaults on white women had caused the lynching. The report of the newspaper *Tokyo Nichinichi,* for instance, described the Omaha riot in 1919 as follows: "While the Omaha, Nebraska, riot raged out of control, the mob finally killed a black man named William Brown, who had allegedly attempted to rape a white woman. This supposed rape caused the riot."[6] Likewise, the newspaper *Tokyo Asahi* reported that the Tulsa riot of 1921 "began on May 31 when a young black man was arrested for raping a white girl. About twenty-five whites rushed into the criminal court to lynch him."[7]

Although the articles mentioned "black rapists" and such images were widely printed in Japanese newspapers, journalists paid more attention to the brutality of the white mobs than to the alleged black criminals. In its report on the Knoxville riot of 1919, which was headlined "White Mob," the *Osaka Asahi* depicted a frenzied white mob who "attacked the jail to lynch" a black man suspected of murdering a white woman. Failing to find the suspect, the mob instead found many gallons of whiskey forfeited as a violation of the prohibition law. "They gulped down cup after cup instantly," the report continued, "and rushed to the black residential area to start hunting black people."[8]

Such stories of white Americans' cruelty against blacks prompted sympathy toward African Americans among Japanese intellectuals. In 1920, Fumimaro Konoe, who was one of the delegates to the Paris Peace Conference of 1919 and later prime minister (1937 to 1941), published a book titled *Ōbei Kenbun Roku* (Personal experiences in Europe and America). In it, he explicitly condemned lynching in the South but saw race friction as a problem throughout the United States. Attributing American rioting to white brutality, Konoe sympathized with black protests against white bigotry, writing that after "huge conflicts between whites and blacks in Washington and Chicago last year, it is now clear that black rage against white persecutions and insults is reaching its peak." He recalled a young black man, a servant for his train compartment on the way from Chicago to Seattle, who frequently came up to Konoe with teary eyes and told him how brutal whites were.[9]

Many Japanese saw such racial conflicts as contradictory to American ideals of freedom and democracy. In 1919, an essay entitled "Kokujin Kaihō Ron" (Black liberation) appeared in the leftist journal *Kaihō* (Liberation) after major race riots broke out. The author was the university professor Shinjirō Kitazawa. Briefly mentioning that he actually saw two lynchings during his stay in the United States, Kitazawa wrote: "When we see that the United States, one of the world's most civilized nations, still frequently allows such barbaric atrocities even in the daytime, we keenly realize how awful racism is."[10] Likewise, the *Yorozu Chōhō*, a paper known for its yellow journalism, began its report on another race riot in Chicago: "American citizens, who have shouted freedom while advocating justice and humanity, are lynching the black race everywhere in public, even in the daytime."[11] Takeo Gotō, a Washington correspondent for the *Jiji Shimpō*, published *Saikin Beikoku no Shinsō* (The truth about recent America) in 1922, in which he devoted one whole chapter, "Beikoku Kokujin no Gyakutai" (Abuse against American blacks), to examining lynching and violence against black people. In the first section of the chapter, titled "Sangyaku na Byōkan" (Miserable pathology), he declared:

> The United States' citizens possess great spirits. Many of them believe that American civilization, which was established particularly based on justice and freedom, has its own superiority different from European and Asian civilizations. . . . However, it is a shame for such a law-abiding civilization that the most

hateful pathology is sweeping through the society. . . . It has revealed the greatest defect in American civilization. . . . Emancipation by Lincoln was certainly good news to all the human races. . . . But have black Americans, freed for sixty years, been blessed with comfortable lives under such American spirit?[12]

Such a view was also shared in a four-part series of reports on lynching in the newspaper *Yomiuri* on August 29, 30, 31, and September 1, 1922. The writer, Fusae Ichikawa, was a prominent Japanese woman suffragist who stayed in New York and Chicago from 1921 to 1924 to study the American women's movement. Her article "Bunmei no Ojoku, Jindō no Zoku" (The disgrace to civilization, outrage against humanity) covered diverse issues of lynching from its statistics, causes, specific cases, the black media working for the antilynching campaign, the NAACP's efforts, and the ongoing debate on the Dyer antilynching bill. While seeing lynching primarily as a black, southern problem, Ichikawa also introduced its diverse characteristics by mentioning female victims and by including a picture of three white immigrants lynched in California.[13] The article began by noting a keen irony: "the United States, which loves to win the world's best, has the world record in lynching as well."[14] For the Japanese, lynching served as one of the best examples to pinpoint American racial hypocrisy.

The fact that Japanese intellectuals sympathized with black people, however, does not mean all of them were free from racial prejudice toward blacks. In 1922 a series of three articles in the *Tokyo Nichinichi*, for instance, forester Keiji Uehara revealed his own prejudice when he commented: "It is obvious even in the eyes of a layman that they [blacks] are not a superior race. . . . Some have no ability to count to twenty, much less the sense of morality or virtue."[15] Even the aforementioned left-minded Gotō, while sympathetic to the state of blacks, advanced a similar view: "the color of black people, which is in fact revolting, might cause their filthy living conditions."[16]

White supremacist ideology engendered such imagery. The era of Japan's modernization and Westernization in the late nineteenth century coincided almost exactly with the period when pseudoscientific racism dominated in Europe and America. "Scientific" racial theory helped Japanese people create their own version of racial hierarchy in the nonwhite world, in which they were superior to other darker races. Their racist attitudes toward other Asian nationals, as well as other ethnic and social minority groups within Japan— including the Ainu (indigenous people), the Okinawans, and the Burakumin (the descendants of outcaste group categorically created in the seventeenth century)—were based on a strong belief in Japanese ethnic homogeneity and the purity of the Japanese race. This myth of homogeneity helped convince many Japanese nationalists that they had a duty to mediate between the Western world and "lesser" Asian nations. While American ideals did not protect people of color, Japan believed that its new status could help redress this problem and thus the nation could become the "true" inheritor of the ideals America had abandoned.[17]

The Japanese perception of lynching also reflected such contemporary Japanese racial ideology of the nonwhite world. In Japan lynching was sometimes linked with Japanese political and social issues discussed in contemporary racial terms. Some intellectuals saw America's racial conflicts in relation to the racial equality proposal offered by Japanese delegates at the Paris Peace Conference in 1919. Although the rejection of the proposal disappointed many Japanese and even led to anti-American sentiment among them, they were at the same time very proud of their status as the only nonwhite nation among the "first-class" nations in the world. Introduced within the context of imperialist diplomacy, Japan urged racial equality in order to achieve its imperial ambitions more than to attack white supremacy. The proposal, as the historian Yuichiro Onishi observes, "ironically became an effective tool to strengthen Japan's position within the global racial polity in attaining 'white' imperial power status."[18] In this context, condemnation of lynching turned in a strange way into a self-congratulatory appraisal of Japanese leadership in the nonwhite world. One such case was that of Sei Kawashima, the Chicago correspondent for *Tokyo Nichinichi*. In 1919, he mentioned the racial equality proposal in a long article entitled "Kuro Shiro Sensō" (Black-white war). Providing a detailed report on the Chicago race riot, Kawashima observed that a "white mob attacked blacks, poured gasoline over them and burnt them to death. . . . We can hardly imagine such brutality has occurred in the big city of a civilized country." Asking "why in the world white perceptions of black people have not changed at all since the slavery era, despite the fact that blacks are now fully American citizens . . . and have acquired equal rights with whites on the surface," he explained to Japanese readers that black people had ardently desired to abolish racial discrimination for a long time. Then he abruptly raised the issue:

> It was Japan's proposal of abolishing racial discrimination at the peace conference that gave black people a great psychological impact at that time. *After Japan*

made the racial equality proposal, black trust in Japan has remarkably increased and
they [blacks] have shown much respect to Japanese people. At the same time
they regret that China did not make an effort to pass the proposal with Japan.
. . . Some blacks believe that this October [in 1919] Japan would take action
again with the same proposal, and boast that it is the time when they should
start a much more severe race war. *Not a few of them regard the Japanese as a
leader of the colored races.*[19]

Kawashima thus attempted to use America's racial conflicts as evidence that
the colored races could overcome such worldwide prejudice under Japanese
leadership.

Kametarō Mitsukawa, a distinguished right-wing and pan-Asianist intel-
lectual, echoed Kawashima's argument in a more dramatic manner. His 1925
book *Kokujin Mondai* (Issues surrounding black people) devoted a chapter
to the history of American lynching. For Mitsukawa, lynching powerfully
demonstrated the cruelty of white people. In the chapter "Kokujin Shikei
Mondai" (The problem of lynching of blacks), he discussed the Ku Klux
Klan (KKK), lynching, and race riots, before concluding that "the violence
of white people who advocate justice and humanity is beyond description."[20]
Particularly remarkable were two pictures of lynching Mitsukawa included
in the book, each of which portrayed a number of whites with the burned
corpse of a black body. Although no identification is attached to the pictures,
the captions tell us how Mitsukawa saw these lynchings. The description of
the first photo, which appears to depict the lynching of William Brown in
Omaha in 1919, read: "Lynching of a black by Americans (1): a horrific scene
where they forced the victim to sit on a pile of wood, poured gasoline on
him, and burned him to death." The second photo—the lynching of Jesse
Washington in Waco, Texas, in 1916—was captioned "Lynching of a black by
Americans (2): at the gallows the body they burned to death was displayed."[21]

Written in 1922 and published three years later, *Kokujin Mondai* dealt
with history of black people—in Africa, Europe, and America—as an international human rights movement. Inspired by the Garvey movement, Mitsukawa's interest in the race problem came out of his view that blacks shared
with Asians an experience of Western colonialism. In his preface, Mitsukawa
stated that he had long engaged himself in helping liberate Asian people from
Western oppression, and because of that, he was heartbroken to learn about
"Africa being exploited as badly as Asia and black people who are oppressed

as much as yellow people."[22] Mitsukawa believed that the Japanese should become "the champion of the darker races" whose oppression they had once shared. In the 1925 preface, Mitsukawa began by asking:

> Why do black people exhibit the portrait of our baron Nobuaki Makino [who made the racial equality proposal at the Paris Peace Conference] alongside that of the liberator Abraham Lincoln on the walls of their houses? Although Japan's proposal of abolishing racial discrimination was defeated by pressure from the Great Powers at the Paris Peace Conference, it was surely a bombshell dropped against the white autocracy base. . . . They advocate the League of Nations and international cooperation. What kind of human love or world peace is possible while excluding the oppressed colored people? . . . The Japanese race . . . must keep their eyes on black people.[23]

Mitsukawa indeed published the portraits of Lincoln and Makino side by side on the page following the table of contents. The caption read: "Two portraits exhibited and respected in black families."[24] This anecdote seems to have been widely shared among Japanese nationalists. In 1920, prior to the publication of Mitsukawa's *Kokujin Mondai*, the *Yomiuri* carried a news account headlined "Our Baron Makino, Who Is Worshipped by Ten Million Blacks." It reported on a speech delivered by the law professor Shinkichi Ue-sugi to a nationalist gathering, where he related his firsthand experiences with African Americans: "I have met several key [black] figures, and everybody is counting on Japan. [I saw] two pictures displayed in their Far East headquarters office. One was the portrait of . . . their president, Mr. Lincoln, and the other, that of our Baron Makino, who proposed the racial equality clause at the peace conference."[25] For pan-Asianists and their apologists, the proposal's rejection symbolized the West's disdain for Japan, and in this context, Kawashima and Mitsukawa saw the American race problem as an experience all oppressed people of color shared. Mitsukawa added: "Those who question if there is any relationship between the Japanese and blacks, imagine how huge the influence of 150 million blacks would be if the second world war happened in the Pacific. Those who are myopic stating that the problem of the Pacific is the problem of California, the postwar problem of the Pacific is . . . expanding even to include the Indian Ocean and the African continent."[26] Kawashima and Mitsukawa situated American lynching and racism in the broader context of white racism and urged all colored people to follow Japanese leadership. Their very belief, along with Uesugi's, that the Japanese should be a leader of other races of color, however, shows the emerging imperialist intentions among Japanese intellectuals.[27]

Also promoting such an expansionist idea was the *Asian Review,* an English monthly published in Japan between 1920 and 1921 by the Kokuryū-kai (Black Dragon Society), one of the most notorious nationalist organizations during the interwar period.[28] The journal intended to introduce Japan to the world as the champion of "people's diplomacy," as the organization announced in its Japanese magazine, *Ajia Jiron* (Asia chronicle). Although the *Asian Review* denied Japan's imperial ambition in Asia, Japanese imperialism was in fact what the Kokuryū-kai primarily advocated. *Ajia Jiron* further explained the purpose of starting the *Asian Review* as follows: "Not only do we [the Kokuryū-kai] hold a humanitarian mission of justice to abolish any discriminatory treatment against the human race; we also have to propagandize our nation's grave obligation to protect and advance the rights and happiness of the Asian race in particular."[29] The rhetoric used here is reminiscent of the "Greater East Asia Co-Prosperity Sphere," the Japanese version of Manifest Destiny, formally introduced in 1940 to justify Japanese imperialist expansion, or of similar ideas (such as "Asia for Asiatics" and "East Asian New Order") that had been in place for many years. In the first edition of the *Asian Review* the editors expressed their wish to see "our colored brothers of all shades of opinion to present a united front" on racial equality, and although mostly dealing with issues on Japan and Asia, the journal paid considerable attention to the problems that black Americans faced. The journal published such articles as "Treatment of the Negroes in the United States," "Awakening of the Negroes," "Lynching in America," and "Race-War in the United States."[30] Citing a report on lynching by the NAACP, "Treatment of the Negroes in the United States," for instance, commented: "Indeed the tale [of lynching] unfolded above is horrible. It is inconceivable that any human being is capable of imposing such revolting cruelties upon his fellow beings. . . . Americans boast that they have a democratic country. But when one considers the barbarous excesses committed by them, one cannot but come to the only possible conclusion that America is a land of 'Mobocracy.' . . . They have not a word for the most outrageous crimes of their co-religionists in America, Africa and other coloured countries!"[31]

In "Race-War in the United States," the writer added to "the horror-provoking chapter of the vile deed" an account on the lynching in Tulsa that caused the riot. In conclusion, the author asserted, "The facts stated above prove clearly that the whites were the guilty party. Let us see what deterrant [*sic*] punishments are inflicted on them by the government authorities who are at least expected not to have one standard of justice for the whites and another for the colored people."[32] Although Kokuryū-kai's condemnation of white racism seemed sincere, the historian Marc Gallicchio observes that the journal "served the interest of the Japanese government to remind Americans of their own failings," noting that the Japanese Ministry of Foreign Affairs as well as many political leaders supported the journal. As Gallicchio points out, in the 1920s Japanese nationalists like the Kokuryū-kai produced "a rhetorical defense of Japanese imperialism" that rebuked the West and simultaneously appealed to colonized people around the world.[33] Reference to lynching served as one of the best rhetorical defenses of Japan's imperialist policy.

The Rise of Anti-American Sentiment and the Changing Views on Lynching in Japan

The year 1924 became a watershed for the Japanese view on lynching. While American lynching had been well publicized in Japan before 1924, it was through the conditions of Japanese immigrants, particularly on the West Coast, that the Japanese people became more aware of American racism and mob violence. In 1924, despite of Japan's diplomatic effort to prevent it, the U.S. Congress passed the Immigration Act, better known in Japan as the Japanese Exclusion Act. While the act restricted immigration into the United States to 150,000 people a year based on a quota system, it achieved statutory Japanese exclusion by the constructed concept of "persons ineligible to citizenship" and thus imposed complete Asiatic exclusion.[34] Lumping Japanese people together with other Asians who were inferior in the Japanese racial ideology, the act infuriated Japanese intellectuals, who were proud of Japan's status as the only non-Western great power. Not a few of them became disillusioned with America as a land of democracy.[35]

As W. E. B. Du Bois told an audience during his visit to Japan in 1936, the American policy of Japanese exclusion resulted from political bargaining between Republican senators from the South and the West, by which the former endorsed the Exclusion Act proposed by the latter in exchange for opposing the 1924 federal antilynching bill.[36] Japanese readers understood that such political deals too often prevented passage of antilynching bills. In 1922, the *Yomiuri, Yorozu Chōhō, Tokyo Nichinichi,* and *Kokumin* reported that, in choosing between giving up the whole session to a filibuster or going ahead with the regular business of the session dealing with other legislation, the U.S. Senate decided to abandon the Dyer Anti-Lynching Bill. The Senate's majority leader was Henry Cabot Lodge, a vocal supporter of immigration restriction who played a crucial role in the passage of the Japanese Exclusion Act of 1924.[37] As early as 1920, the *Yomiuri* observed the relationship between anti-Japanese measures and antiblack violence in the United States; the paper juxtaposed two headlines—"Impossible to Prevent the Anti-Japanese Law [California's Alien Land Law of 1920]" and "Lynching of a Black Person"—as if to call particular attention to the malicious racial prejudice in the United States.[38] So did Kijūrō Shidehara, then ambassador to the United States, who had been a major negotiator to solve the problem regarding Japanese immigrants. In July 1920, Shidehara sent the Japanese foreign minister copies of the *Congressional Record* and the *House of Representatives Report* containing debates on the Dyer Anti-Lynching Bill.[39] The issues of lynching reminded the Japanese people of the racially hostile conditions that they had to face.

In 1924, lynching and the discrimination against the Japanese merged into one issue when Japanese newspapers picked up the stories about the murder of two Japanese immigrants and the attempted lynching of another that occurred on June 19 and 20 in California. The attempted lynching in Los Angeles, which allegedly involved KKK members tarring and feathering the victim, particularly attracted considerable attention among the Japanese media. Under such headlines as "Barbaric Lynching against Japanese for the First Time," "Horrific Lynching by Japanophobe Mob," and "Mob Rushed for Lynching Japanese," the papers devoted full pages to detailed explanations of lynching and the Klan. Carrying a picture of a KKK meeting, the *Tokyo Asahi* stated that "tarring and feathering was a horrible password for lynching."[40] The *Kokumin* published a picture of the KKK leader H. W. Evans and explained that tarring and feathering was the KKK's unique method of lynching to ensure white supremacy.[41] In an account headlined "Tarring and Feathering: The Lynching Method beyond Brutality," the *Osaka Asahi* asked, "Who on earth invented such a cruel punishment? While such a penalty had been used in European countries in the Crusades, in the twentieth-century world only a few American states continue such malicious lynching."[42]

Japanese ultranationalists' hostility toward the lynching of African Americans became even more militant when white Americans lynched a Japanese immigrant. The *Kokumin* carried Mitsuru Tōyama's furious denunciation of the incident. The prominent right-wing political leader Tōyama charged, "Americans are really unconcealed savages. It is said that when they lynch black people, they burn them to death. . . . We must let the government arouse public sentiment. We must teach Americans that outraged people are the most formidable."[43] Through the incident, the law professor Uesugi saw American racism against all people of color: "Americans look down on the Japanese completely. This is clear if we recall their inhuman, brutal lynchings of black people from year to year. . . . Conflict between Japan and America will be inevitable."[44]

While lynchings of African Americans functioned as a crucial reference point for the treatment of the Japanese in the United States, Japanese anti-lynching sentiments began to change its character by the 1930s. In that decade, anti-American sentiment in Japan kindled by the Japanese Exclusion Act and the rough treatment of Japanese immigrants caught fire. With the rise of Japanese militarism, intellectuals increasingly fended off America's criticism of Japan's imperialist expansion in East Asia by denouncing American racism. To accomplish this they merely had to refer to lynching. In 1933, future prime minister Konoe, in his defense of Japan's imperialist policy in Manchuria, charged, "They [Americans] call it barbarity that Japanese soldiers kill native people in Manchuria, but is it a real civilization that permits white Americans to tie black citizens to trees, burn them, and call that lynching?"[45] NAACP secretary Walter White disgustedly recalled that the Japanese translation of his *The Fire in the Flint* (1924), first published in 1935 with the literally translated title *Hiuchi-ishi no Hi*, and later renamed *Shōsetsu Rinchi* (Lynching: a novel) in 1937 to propagandize against the United States: "Unwittingly and unwillingly, I was also utilized through the medium of *The Fire in the Flint* in Japan. . . . Later, when American indignation over Japan's invasion of China mounted, a new Japanese edition, with the title changed to *Lynching*, was brought out. The new edition sold in fantastic numbers, due to a publicity campaign by the Japanese government pointing out that the novel pictured the kind of barbarities which were tolerated and even encouraged in the democracy which had the temerity to criticize Japan for her acts in China."[46]

It is not clear if the Japanese government indeed publicized the book to the Japanese audience as White claimed, but he was not the only American author to see his work converted to propaganda uses by Japanese publishers. The Japanese translation of Scott Nearing's *Black America* (1929) appeared in 1931 with the title *A History of Black Oppression: Lynching Story*.[47] The translator of *The Fire in the Flint* was Yasuichi Hikida, a Japanese independent scholar who had resided in New York since 1920 and was sympathetic to African Americans. Columbia-educated and Christian (he went to a local black church in Harlem), Hikida did indeed work as a government agent for the Japanese consulate from 1938 to 1942, but that was after the publication of *Shōsetsu Rinchi*.[48] In the preface, Hikida commented with apparent sincerity, "In this present time the issues of colored races are particularly studied and discussed, and attract the public interest in my home country Japan. It would be my greatest pleasure if this translation helps the readers understand the current conditions of American Negroes who are suffering in the depth of despair."[49]

White's friendship with Hikida must have deepened his sense of betrayal over the Japanese translation of *The Fire in the Flint*. In his 1933 letter to James Weldon Johnson, White introduced Hikida as "my very good friend" and "one of my most esteemed friends," who "has done already a very great deal through the writing of articles for Japanese publications to set before the people of Japan the real facts regarding the Negro in the United States." White also told Johnson that Hikida was trying to arrange a Japanese translation of *The Fire in the Flint*.[50] He wrote Johnson to forward a letter from Hikida asking Johnson for permission to translate Johnson's famous "Lift Every Voice and Sing." Hikida enthusiastically told Johnson that the Japanese translation of the song would "bring a significant result in years to come." Unsatisfied with the current situation, in which the Japanese "are contented with worthless publications that come through white agents with the white man's view point of Negroes," Hikida thought that the translation would "eventually contribute toward creating a sentiment and promote understanding of American Negro among Japanese."[51]

As a member of the NAACP for decades, "the ubiquitous Yasuichi Hikida" (so described by the historian Reginald Kearney) actively involved himself in the African American political scene in Harlem and elsewhere. He maintained a close relationship with prominent black leaders including White, Johnson, Du Bois, Arthur Schomburg, Alain Locke, Rayford Logan, Carter G. Woodson, and Nannie Burroughs.[52] By 1941 the FBI had concluded from decoded messages between the foreign office in Tokyo and Japanese embassies and consulates that Hikida spoke for the Japanese government. One decoded message discussed plans to hire an espionage agent living among African Americans in New York.[53] Although the person's name was deleted by the Department of Defense, it was Hikida according to Harlem's black newspaper the *Amsterdam Star News*, which reported that the FBI intended to investigate some black leaders on charges of bribery by the Japanese government and that the FBI had singled out Hikida as a key person on the Japanese side.[54] Hikida's involvement in espionage was also confirmed by a Japanese report on the wartime conditions of African Americans, *Sensō to Kokujin* (War and blacks), whose preface stated that the report was written by Hikida, "who had been mainly responsible for this operation [propagandizing among blacks] at the Japanese Consulate in New York."[55] When authorities apprehended Hikida as an "alien enemy" on January 13, 1942, they seized his large collection of African American literature, which led the FBI to conclude that "Hikida had been in charge of Japanese propaganda among the negroes for four or five years and had formerly been employed by the Japanese Consulate to spread propaganda among the negroes."[56]

Sensō to Kokujin, a report of more than one hundred pages that Hikida wrote after he returned to Japan, provided the Japanese government with comprehensive, up-to-date information on the status of African Americans following the opening of the war in the Pacific. Quoting a number of white- and black-oriented newspapers, periodicals, and articles describing African Americans' wartime demands and views, the report rightfully concluded that blacks "were caught between love for their own race and love for their country." For instance, the report quoted Emmett J. Scott, a longtime personal secretary of Booker T. Washington and the highest-ranking African American official in Woodrow Wilson's administration, who insisted that the United States would not need to worry about whether African Americans believed in fascism or communism or whether they were interested in the Japanese plot about skin color if it abolished lynching, accepted political rights for African Americans, and treated them as citizens of the democratic nation. The report also mentioned how African Americans utilized the famous slogan "Remember Pearl Harbor" as "their own weapon" in January and February 1942, quoting the black journalist George S. Schuyler. After the lynchings in Alexandria, Louisiana, and in Sikeston, Missouri, Schuyler wrote that African Americans were lifting their united voice to "Remember Alexandria" and "Remember Sikeston" while America raised a united voice of "Remember Pearl Harbor."[57]

These accounts of African Americans' wartime frustration with mob violence and racism at home convinced the Japanese government that it could effectively agitate among blacks. In 1943, the government assigned Hikida to write another report on African Americans but this time more particularly on wartime espionage. Entitled *Senji Kokujin Kōsaku* (Wartime black propaganda operations), the report explained in its preface how African American antipathy against domestic racism was the greatest obstacle for the United States in claiming it fought for democracy. Hikida insisted on the importance of developing propaganda aimed at blacks based on his belief that African Americans felt a particular friendship for Japan. The report outlined a three-part propaganda program consisting of (1) information gathering, (2) use of black prisoners of war, and (3) shortwave radio broadcasts. Sections 2 and 3 provided detailed plans for recruiting black POWs for a Japanese propaganda campaign and using them in broadcasts aimed at blacks in the United States and abroad. For recruitment, Hikida suggested creating propaganda leaflets targeting black POWs, including pictures of lynchings carried out on U.S. Army facilities, reports on racial frictions in the United States, and propaganda that uncovered the American intention to have black servicemen particularly fight the Axis armies of color. The shortwave radio broadcasts would cover "matters that the black intellectuals and others find pertinent," "matters that blacks want to know about," "matters that should please blacks," "specific matters that should arouse blacks' attention," and "matters that should attract blacks' interests." Under these headings, the report proposed propagandizing that American and British "democracy" was nothing but "hypocrisy" and that Japan was fighting for the advancement of the colored races.[58]

As the historians Masaharu Sato and Barak Kushner have pointed out, Japan's propaganda to African Americans, contrary to much of its propaganda during the war, did not need to rely on fabrication but accurately reported the ongoing lynchings and racial discrimination in the United States. Even before the Japanese government officially launched its radio propaganda campaign, according to Sato and Kushner, the racial thread in Japanese propaganda had been picked up by the American Foreign Broadcast Intelligence Commission Service. One of the broadcasts portrayed America as barbaric on the grounds that outside the United States, "notorious lynchings are a rare practice even among the most savage specimens of the human race."[59] Similarly, regarding "specific matters that should arouse blacks' attention" in the shortwave broadcasts, Hikida proposed first pointing out to African Americans the stark contrast between their contribution to World War I and how white Americans treated them in postwar U.S. society. He did not forget to include lynching as an example of such unfair treatment of blacks.[60]

While Japanese intellectuals often countered American criticism of Japan's imperialistic expansion by exposing American racial hypocrisy, Japanese propaganda activities intentionally employed racial themes particularly targeting African Americans to justify Japan's war to liberate the colored races from Western colonialism. Nothing served this purpose better than the subject of lynching.

AFRICAN AMERICAN RESPONSES TO JAPANESE ANTILYNCHING PROTESTS

Before starting their rhetorical campaign pointing out that the lynching in the United States was playing into the hands of Axis propagandists, the black press reported favorably on Japanese antilynching propaganda. In 1919, when reports of U.S. race riots and related lynching incidents appeared in Japanese newspapers, the *Cleveland Advocate* published an article headlined "Japanese Paper Takes a Fling at Uncle Sam" that included the Japanese newspaper *Yamato*'s criticism of the United States for hypocritically advocating justice to "the weaker peoples of the world." It described the *Yamato* as "one of the leading Japanese newspapers" before stating that the paper "accused Americans of lynching and discriminating against Negroes in open defiance of the Constitution." The paper also introduced the *Yamato*'s prediction that "unless the federal lynch law was passed to prevent such depraved and outlawed occurrences the United States would face the most serious crisis in history." The *Advocate* thus cited international criticism in order to shame the public into supporting the federal antilynching legislation.[61] Likewise, in 1921, Cincinnati's black weekly newspaper the *Union,* under a headline that read "Japan Considers American Lynchings," reported the NAACP's announcement that a Japanese periodical (Kokuryū-kai's *Asian Review*) had condemned American lynching. It introduced the periodical's call for strong public condemnation throughout the world "in order to bring sufficient pressure to bear on the American government to adopt effective measures" to stop lynching.[62] These papers show how blacks tried to let the public know that American racial politics had to respond to international attention, not only from Japan but from other countries as well. In 1925, an Indian activist living in Japan forwarded a copy of Mitsukawa's *Kokujin Mondai* to Marcus Garvey.[63] Though sympathetic to Japan, Garvey could not read Japanese and therefore had only limited access to the book's overall message, but its visual images—not only the lynching photos but also one of the Universal Negro Improvement Association's pan-African flag on the title page—probably told him enough.[64]

The irony, however, is that Japanese imperialists wrote the *Yamato, Asian Review,* and *Kokujin Mondai* articles. As pan-Asianists, they implicitly justified the idea of Japanese expansion in Asia by linking lynching with Western oppression against nonwhite people and promoting Japan's role as liberators. To some extent, African American intellectuals were aware of Japan's imperialistic policies in the Far East, but for them, Japan's status as a victim of racism, its criticism of American racism, and its support of racial equality outweighed any negative aspects of Japanese imperialist foreign policy. As many scholars have pointed out, a number of African American intellectuals and leaders sided with Japan as "a leader of the darker races" or at least looked to Japan for inspiration.[65] Among them were Booker T. Washington and Mary Church Terrell, who praised Japan's victory over Russia,[66] and James Weldon Johnson, who stated in 1919 that Japan was "perhaps the greatest hope for the colored races of the world."[67] In the same year, when the Japanese delegation stopped in New York en route to the Paris Peace Conference, an African American delegation including Ida B. Wells-Barnett, William Monroe Trotter, Madam C. J. Walker, and A. Philip Randolph visited the Japanese representatives to show their support for Japan's racial equality proposal.[68] As early as 1918, Garvey, an advocate of "Asia for the Asiatic" as well as "Africa for the Africans," warned that "the next war will be between the Negroes and the whites unless our demands for justice are recognized. . . . With Japan to fight with us, we can win such a war."[69] Du Bois, who visited China, Manchuria, and Japan in 1936, was convinced that despite Japan's imperialism in Manchuria, a "lynching . . . would be unthinkable" there. With high admiration of Japan as "a country of colored people run by colored people for colored people," he remained a strong advocate of Japan's pan-Asianism until the 1940s.[70]

As World War II approached, the image of the Axis powers—Germany, Italy, and Japan—as enemies of American democracy offered the African American antilynching struggle a variety of opportunities. While black newspapers and periodicals began to make direct parallels between American racism and the atrocious deeds of these enemy countries, prior to the war in the Pacific they focused mainly on Nazism. Hitler and the swastika became symbols as strong as the KKK and the noose in the antilynching campaign. In June 1934, the *Crisis* published a cartoon of a hooded KKK figure with a rope in his hand looking across the Atlantic at Europe, whence the words "Nazi persecution of Jews and Negroes" are flaming up. The caption "Giving Him Some Fresh Ideas" clearly suggests the resemblance between racial atrocities by Nazis and the KKK.[71] A similar motif was used in the September 1934 issue of the *Crisis* to criticize the hypocrisy of a governmental figure, General Hugh S. Johnson, the director of the New Deal's National Recovery Administration. The cartoon featured Johnson looking at Europe where swastika flags were waving, while standing on American soil covered by graves of lynching victims. The caption cited the speech Johnson had made on July 12: "A few days ago, in Germany, events occurred which . . . made me physically sick."[72] Such visual comparison enabled African Americans to condemn the hypocrisy of American democracy.

Black leaders' comments in letters to the White House, in speeches, and in the press echoed the idea embedded in these cartoons. Particularly at a time when white southerner senators repeatedly filibustered antilynching bills, they used Nazism to urge the Senate and the president to take immediate action. On July 31, 1935, a day after "the tenth lynching" of that year

"Giving Him Some Fresh Ideas." *Crisis,* June 1934. (Courtesy of the Crisis Publishing, Co., Inc.)

occurred at Louisburg, North Carolina, Walter White wrote to President Franklin Roosevelt. Informing Roosevelt that the lynching had happened in the state of "one of the most vociferous leaders of the filibuster" against the Costigan-Wagner Bill, White wrote that the "situation necessitates your urging upon Congress that it act without delay to pass the Costigan-Wagner bill. Our country cannot with good grace denounce barbarism in Nazi Germany as long as these mob outrages disgrace America."[73] Carl Murphy, the president of the *Baltimore Afro-American*, wrote to a secretary to the president: "It is not doing us as a [Democratic] party any good to have the *Congressional Record* and the public press filled, day after day, with anti-Negro propaganda matching in bigotry and prejudice anything published in Germany, Russia

" 'A few days ago, in Germany, events occurred which . . . made me . . . physically sick.' —General Hugh S. Johnson's speech at Waterloo, Ia., July 12." *Crisis,* September 1934. (Courtesy of the Crisis Publishing, Co., Inc.)

or Italy against Jews, Catholics and aliens."[74] NAACP field secretary William Pickens stated in a radio address that American Hitlerism revived "ku-klux-ism in Georgia . . . vigilantism in California, and . . . lynching in Mississippi." Likewise, in his antilynching speech at the NAACP's annual meeting, White reminded the audience that "a counterpart of Hitlerism ha[d] existed in the United States for many generations."[75] In commenting on the lawlessness African Americans faced in American society and the Senate's refusal to pass a federal antilynching bill in 1940, the *Crisis* editor Roy Wilkins stated:

> The Crisis is sorry for brutality, blood, and death among the peoples of Europe, just as we were sorry for China and Ethiopia. But the hysterical cries of the preachers of democracy for Europe leave us cold. We want democracy in Alabama and Arkansas, in Mississippi and Michigan, in the District of Columbia— *in the Senate of the United States.*
>
> It is not important (if true) that there have been "only a few" lynchings. It is supremely important for this democratic process we say we revere that Constitution, and not the emotional whims of hoodlums, be known as the law of the land. Until that is made unmistakably clear, the only essential difference between a Nazi mob hunting down Jews in Central Europe and an American mob burning black men at the stake in Mississippi is that one is actually encouraged by its national government and the other is merely tolerated.[76]

Wilkins quoted the *New York Times* as saying, "Nothing that can happen in this country is better grist for the Nazi propaganda mill than a lynching" and continued, "America is marching to war for the purpose of stopping brutalities overseas, but apparently our government does not choose to stop lynching within its own borders, or even within the borders of its army camps."[77]

While making Nazism an important component of their antilynching language, African Americans still held a mixed feeling toward Japan, the only Axis enemy of color. On December 6, 1941, the eve of the Japanese attack on Pearl Harbor, the *Baltimore Afro-American* published an opinion column entitled "In Fighting Japan Our Own Hands Are Not Clean." In it, the author noted that it is "a great mystery to many people why we insist on a Monroe Doctrine and deny to Japan similar political leadership in Asia" before giving a brief overview of the American history of slave trading and westward and colonial expansion. The column concluded: "No, we can't preach morality and consistency to the Japanese. They want to know why we, who have slaughtered the reds and the blacks, have so suddenly become Christian crusaders for the yellows of China."[78] Although in the following week the paper's editorial tone changed dramatically, with more overtly patriotic sentiments and reference to the Japanese as "Japs," this column shows that African Americans remained ambivalent about Japan's imperialist expansion. The writer may no longer have seen Japan as a liberator of the colored race from Western colonialism, but he at least questioned whether the United States had a right to criticize Japan's version of the Monroe Doctrine. They were well aware of the hypocrisy of American democracy, something wartime lynching and racism best represented.

After the Pearl Harbor attack, the image and iconography of Japan joined that of Hitler in antilynching narratives. Black newspapers used a similar motif in their cartoons, showing Japanese figures favorably observing the lynching of Cleo Wright that occurred in Sikeston, Missouri, on January 25, 1942. A week later, the African American newspaper the *Louisville Defender* published a cartoon that depicted Hitler, Mussolini, and the Japanese emperor Hirohito peeking into a white mob burning a black man and Hitler telling Mussolini and Hirohito: "Boys! That's Democracy a la USA."[79] Likewise, the *Baltimore Afro-American* carried a cartoon entitled "Defending America Our Way," in which a grinning Hitler and a smiling slant-eyed Japanese soldier witness the hanging and burning of the Sikeston lynching.[80] These cartoons well captured the contradictory situation that African Americans had long faced, where the "war for democracy" was reverberating throughout the country, while the very same "democratic" society perpetuated rampant racial violence and segregation. Depicting the parallel between lynching and Nazism and fascism visually was a useful tactic for African Americans to show the contradiction that American society entailed, and the image of Japanese imperialism finally joined to serve their antilynching cause.

Just as they used these cartoons, African Americans employed rhetorical strategy to unveil the paradox of American democracy in their efforts against mob violence. Two weeks after the Sikeston lynching, the *Pittsburgh Courier* columnist Joseph D. Bibb stated: "While we are remembering Pearl Harbor, we are not forgetting the race riots that ran rampant over the nation after the armistice was signed. We remember the racial clashes in Washington and Chicago. We never forget how soldiers were lynched, flamed and mutilated in the South."[81] Perhaps "War Quiz for America," a three-page, call-and-response prose piece by the journalist Frank Marshall Davis that appeared in the *Crisis*, best represented the wartime view of African Americans. The piece opened with a leading voice asking, "Who am I?," followed by three responding voices naming African American figures in history from Crispus Attucks to Dorie Miller, a hero celebrated for "shooting down four Jap planes with a machine gun" at Pearl Harbor. A chorus chanted: "I am four of nine Scottsboro boys still rotting in Kilby prison in Alabama[.] I am Cleo Wright lynched at Sikeston, Missouri, while you cried for national unity in the face of Jap savagery." Another voice posed a question to Uncle Sam: "Why did you send me against Axis foes . . . / Without shielding my back / From the sniping Dixie lynchers / In the jungles of Texas and Florida?" Responding to black soldiers' skepticism about democracy, the leading voice stated:

> If it [democracy] works in lands I never saw before
> Against strangers with faces new to me

Louisville Defender, January 31, 1942.

Then it must be the right thing to use

Against all foes of freedom

Against all apostles of fascism

Against some people I know

Right here in America.

Then the following voices immediately responded:

> VOICE: I know more about Biblo than I do about Tojo
>
> VOICE: I've heard about Hitler but I have also lived in Georgia when Talmadge was governor
>
> VOICE: Talk about Mussolini if you want to, but did you ever hear Rankin rave in Congress?

Defending America Our Way

Baltimore Afro-American, January 31, 1942. (Courtesy of the Afro-American Newspapers Archives and Research Center)

VOICE: Tell me the Black Dragon Society is just a foreign nightmare but I have
been beaten and murdered by the Ku Klux Klan[82]

By comparing the Axis figures (Japanese prime minister Hideki Tojo, Hitler, and Mussolini) to racist southern politicians (Senator Theodore G. Bilbo,
Governor Eugene Talmadge, and Senator John E. Rankin) and the Japanese
imperialist society Kokuryū-kai to the KKK, Davis skillfully unveiled the
double standard of the nation's "democracy against fascism" slogan. Bibb and
Davis, among many African Americans, utilized the idea of the "war for democracy" to win their struggle against lynching and racism.[83]

On February 7, 1942, the *Pittsburgh Courier* embarked on its famous
"Double V Campaign"—victory over fascism abroad and victory over Jim
Crow at home.[84] But as we have seen, the idea of "double victories" had been
introduced prior to the *Courier's* official launch of the campaign. In 1941,
Mary McLeod Bethune, a member of President Roosevelt's "black cabinet,"
declared: "We have the dual task of defeating Hitler abroad and Hitlerism at
home."[85] African American leaders and the black press shared a similar perspective with their audience and utilized such wartime rhetoric to advance
their cause at home. Admittedly, during the war, the domestic effort was
aimed mainly at ending segregation and discrimination in the U.S. armed
forces.[86] But lynching was an equally urgent issue. In October 1943, for example, the Alabama state convention of the Congress of Industrial Organizations adopted a resolution urging support of the Gavagan Anti-Lynching
Bill and pledged the organization's funds and efforts to promote an intensive
campaign for the passage of the legislation "as an essential program for winning the war."[87]

Under the "Double V" banner, African American leaders repeatedly
warned the American public and the government that lynching provided
perfect propaganda for the Axis powers. On January 26, 1942, the day after
the Sikeston lynching, the NAACP wired President Franklin Roosevelt re-
questing immediate legislation giving authority to the federal government to
proceed against lynch mobs and lynching. The telegram stated: "We are certain that Japanese propagandists are already citing this lynching as evidence
of what colored races of the Far East would suffer if the democracies win."[88]
On October 19, 1942, a week after another three lynchings occurred in Mississippi, the National Negro Congress, a popular front organization created
by the Communist Party of the United States of America in 1935, sent a telegram to President Roosevelt to protest the incident. Calling these lynchings

"traitorous crimes," the organization stated that the lynchings provided "a comfort to Hitler and the Axis enemies of the United Nations" that represented "a direct challenge to our national government and the win-the-war policies of our Commander-in-chief, by the white supremacy forces in this country, acting for Hitler."[89] Referring to the Sikeston lynching and the Mississippi lynchings, the *Crisis* affirmed that "in this war time a community that stages a lynching is working for Hitler and Tojo." "These lynchings," the article continued, "are sabotaging our war effort, making it easier for Japan to influence the hundreds of millions of colored peoples in the Far East against the United Nations. American mobs make our ally, China, suspicious of the democracy of white people."[90] The *Pittsburgh Courier* reprinted an editorial from the leftist New York City paper *PM* that observed: "Axis propagandists know how to use a little ugly truth when we hand it to them. We hand it to them every time an American mob lynches a Negro, every time we discriminate against a Negro soldier."[91]

The editorial's claim was not groundless. As we have seen, the Japanese government did launch a wartime propaganda operation targeting African Americans and often used lynching as an example of the hypocrisy of American democracy. Although African American newspapers continued to pay attention to Japanese views on lynching, after Pearl Harbor they were more interested in how Japan used the news on American lynching. And these messages of foreign and domestic oppression surely reached the African American masses as well. In February 1942, Archibald MacLeish, director of the War Department's Office of Facts and Figures, received a letter from a white woman in New York who had listened on the radio to his address to the National Urban League. As a head of the newly established agency to disseminate information about the wartime defense efforts to the general public, MacLeish shared with his black audience his naïve assertion of African Americans' support for the ongoing war. The concerned white woman detailed what she had heard through her maid and several other black friends. "I learn that all Negroes, from menial laborers to professional people are unconvinced they have in fact, a stake in this country," she told MacLeish. "They wonder whether living under the domination of the Japanese or even under Hitler, could be worse than living under the fascism as practiced in the southern states. They wonder if the brutality of the storm troopers is any worse than the brutality of a mob in Sikeston, Mo."[92] While African Americans' "Double V" campaign may have picked up middle-class male voices of dissent more often than others, the letter clearly revealed that skepticism about American democracy was shared among African Americans across class and gender.

The "Double V" ideology helped African Americans condemn lynching without risking being labeled "un-American." Since Americans lumped Japan together with Italy and Germany, African Americans tried to distance themselves from the Japanese, who had been their colored comrades for decades. In the May 1942 issue of the *Crisis*, Benjamin E. Mays, then the president of Morehouse College, insisted that African Americans "must and will be loyal to [their] country in the present crisis." One of the reasons, according to Mays, was that Japan's intentions did not serve black interests. He concluded:

> One fact became clear to me. Japan has no particular love or interest in the darker people of the earth. Japan is for Japan. And she will seek to suppress and does suppress her darker brothers in the same way as imperialistic white nations. The idea that existed some years back that Japan would be the nation around which the darker races of earth might rally and look to for guidance is utter nonsense. Japan is interested in Japan. The American Negro therefore need have no sympathy for Japan. His destiny is in the United States of America and his salvation must be worked out here where the ideals are democratic and the religion is Christian.[93]

African Americans may have had, as Mays insisted, no interest in sympathizing with Japan, but they did remain sympathetic with Japanese Americans, the only group incarcerated because of their Axis ancestry. Less than a week after Pearl Harbor, in opposition to the governmental plan of Japanese internment, Seattle's black newspaper *Northwest Enterprise* reminded African Americans: "The same mob spirit which would single them [Japanese Americans] out for slaughter has trailed you through the forest and to string you up at some crossroad."[94] In "Americans in Concentration Camps," the *Crisis* attributed the incarceration of Japanese Americans to American racism by pointing out that neither German Americans nor Italian Americans were put into internment camps. It further predicated: "What has happened to these [Japanese] Americans in recent months is of direct concern to the American Negro. For the barbarous treatment of these Americans is the result of the color line."[95] "This may be a prelude to our own fate," George Schuyler concluded. "Who knows?"[96]

In his exploration of enemy images both in Japan and America during

World War II, the historian John Dower has pointed out that "the Japanese were well informed about segregation and the lynching in the United States."[97] As we have seen, in fact the Japanese publicized American racial conflicts well before World War II. As in the United States, in Japan lynching provided a powerful symbol of American racism that contradicted the image of America as "a land of democracy and freedom." Almost all the intellectuals and media mentioned in this essay never forgot to point out the contradiction. Ideology and background controlled how Japanese writers approached lynching. While some intellectuals and journalists criticized lynching as an infringement on basic human rights, others saw lynching in the context of Japanese political discourse. Race rioting after the 1919 Paris Peace Conference spurred Japan's racial equality proposal encouraged Japanese pan-Asianists to link American racism with Western oppression of nonwhite people. These pan-Asianists announced that Japan had a mission to liberate them, thus implicitly justifying Japanese expansion in East Asia. Furthermore, increased diplomatic friction between the United States and Japan encouraged the Japanese to find in lynching an effective means of deflecting American criticism of Japanese actions in China and elsewhere. Such tendencies culminated in Japan's propaganda operation among African Americans during the war in the Pacific.

The antilynching movement along with Japanese criticism of lynching reflected the unique racial politics of African Americans in wartime. African Americans' shift toward publicizing the Japanese antilynching responses before Pearl Harbor showed how they negotiated their wartime status as both black and American. In their "Double V" two-front war, they struggled to find an answer to what it meant to be "American," yet Japan's paradoxical status as a colored imperialist power gave African Americans ambivalent feelings about Japan and the Japanese, thus complicating their identity politics. Their contradictory views of Japan and the Japanese further revealed how African Americans faced their "double consciousness." To position themselves as Americans, African Americans had to consider imperial Japan the enemy, but at the same time, as people of color, they still sympathized to some extent with the Japanese as allies against Western imperialism and white supremacy. The Japanese case offers us an example of African Americans' continuous struggles to form a wartime national identity in relation to other racialized subjects during the U.S. wars in East Asia in the decades that followed.

NOTES

This essay owes a great debt to those who offered valuable comments and suggestions for its improvement. I acknowledge with gratitude the support I received from Pırıl Hatice Atabay, Darren Lee Brown, Gavin James Campbell, Pero Gaglo Dagbovie, the late Aimé J. Ellis, Tiffany Willoughby Herard, Darlene Clark Hine, Masahiro Hosoya, Robin D. G. Kelley, James H. Madison, Kenichi Mizutani, Sayuri G. Shimizu, David W. Stowe, and Christopher Waldrep. I also wish to thank Crisis Publishing, the publisher of the magazine of the National Association for the Advancement of Colored People, for the use of cartoons first published in the June and September 1934 issues of *Crisis* magazine.

1. *Pittsburgh Courier,* February 28, 1942; visual materials from the NAACP, Prints and Photographs Division, Library of Congress, lot 13093, no. 24. For a detailed study of the Sikeston lynching, see Dominic J. Capeci Jr., *The Lynching of Cleo Wright* (Lexington: University Press of Kentucky, 1998). The following studies also mention the Sikeston lynching and the Pearl Harbor analogy: Neil A. Wynn, *The Afro-American and the Second World War* (New York: Holmes and Meier, 1993), 100; Ernest Allen Jr., "Waiting for Tojo: The Pro-Japan Vigil of Black Missourians, 1932–1943," *Gateway Heritage,* Fall 1995, 39; Marc Gallicchio, *The African American Encounter with Japan and China: Black Internationalism in Asia, 1895-1945* (Chapel Hill: University of North Carolina Press, 2000), 127–28; Gallicchio, "Amerika Kokujin no Tainichi-kan no Kioku: Sono Bōkyaku to Saisei" [Memory and the lost-found relationship between black Americans and Japan], trans. Yūko Itō, in *Kioku to shiteno Pāru Hābā* [Pearl Harbor as memory], ed. Chihiro Hosoya, Akira Iriye, and Ryō Ōshiba (Tokyo: Minerva Shobō, 2004), 240; Gallicchio, "Afurika-kei Amerikajin no Sensō-kan, Ajia-kan" [African Americans and the Asia-Pacific war], trans. Yūko Itō, in *Ajia Taiheiyō Sensō* [The Asia-Pacific war], vol. 3, *Dōin, Teikō, Yokusan* [Mobilization, resistance, collaboration], ed. Aiko Kurasawa et al. (Tokyo: Iwanami Shoten, 2006), 253.

2. Gaikotsu Miyatake, *Shikei Ruisan* (Tokyo: Hankyō-dō, 1922), 5.

3. *Yomiuri,* August 29, 1922. In this essay, I standardize usage as "lynching" except in translations of Japanese book titles.

4. For earlier newspaper accounts on lynching, see *Yomiuri,* January 27, 1886 (on the lynching of Alexander in Mobile, Alabama); June 29, 1899 (on the lynching of Sam Hose in Palmetto, Georgia); January 8, 1900 (on the lynching of Richard Coleman in Marysville, Kentucky).

5. See, for instance, *Tokyo Nichinichi,* July 31, 1919; *Kokumin,* September 3, 1919; *Osaka Asahi,* September 3 and 19, 1919; *Tokyo Nichinichi,* October 1, 1919; June 24, 1920; and *Tokyo Asahi,* June 24, 1920; June 3 and 4 and August 5, 1921.

6. *Tokyo Nichinichi,* October 3, 1919.

7. *Tokyo Asahi,* August 5, 1921.

8. *Osaka Asahi,* September 4, 1919.

9. Fumimaro Konoe, *Ōbei Kenbun Roku* (Tokyo: Chūō Kōron-sha, 1920), 145–46.

10. Shinjirō Kitazawa, "Kokujin Kaihō Ron," *Kaihō,* October 1919, 74.

11. *Yorozu Chōhō,* August 1, 1920.

12. Takeo Gotō, *Saikin Beikoku no Shinsō* (Tokyo: Mita Shobō, 1922), 338–39.

13. *Yomiuri*, August 30, 1922.

14. *Yomiuri*, August 29, 1922. Miyatake cites Ichikawa's widely covered report in *Shikei Ruisan.*

15. *Tokyo Nichinichi*, January 29, 1922.

16. Gotō, *Saikin Beikoku no Shinsō*, 341.

17. John W. Dower, *War without Mercy: Race and Power in the Pacific War* (New York: Pantheon, 1986), 203–4; Gallicchio, *African American Encounter*, 61. For a brief historical overview of the black image among the Japanese, see John G. Russell, "Narratives of Denial: Racial Chauvinism and the Black Other in Japan," *Japan Quarterly* 38, no. 4 (October 1991): 3. For a detailed analysis of the idea of Japanese ethnic purity, see Dower, *War without Mercy*, chapter 8.

18. Yuichiro Onishi, "The New Negro of the Pacific: How African Americans Forged Cross-Racial Solidarity with Japan, 1917–1922," *Journal of African American History* 92, no. 2 (Spring 2007): 194.

19. *Tokyo Nichinichi*, September 3, 1919. Emphasis in original.

20. Kametarō Mitsukawa, *Kokujin Mondai* (Tokyo: Niyū Meicho Kankō-kai, 1925), 244.

21. Ibid., between pp. 240 and 241. The identification of the first picture is not certain, but it seems to be a picture of the same lynching as depicted in a well-known picture of the Omaha lynching, taken from a different angle. See James Allen et al., eds., *Without Sanctuary: Lynching Photography in America* (Santa Fe, NM: Twin Palms, 2000), photo no. 97.

22. Mitsukawa, *Kokujin Mondai*, preface of 1922, 3. Written in 1922, the manuscript was once lost during the turmoil after the Great Kantō Earthquake of 1923 and was not found until 1925 when the book finally came out. For the influence of the Garvey movement on Mitsukawa, see Yukiko Koshiro, "Beyond an Alliance of Color: The African American Impact on Modern Japan," *Positions: East Asia Cultures Critique* 11, no. 1 (Spring 2003): 187; Hiromi Furukawa and Tetsushi Furukawa, *Nihonjin to Afurika-kei Amerikajin: Nichibei Kankei-shi ni okeru Sono Shosō* [Japanese and African Americans: Historical aspects of their relations] (Tokyo: Akashi Shoten, 2004), 105.

23. Mitsukawa, *Kokujin Mondai*, preface of 1925, 1–2.

24. Ibid., 9.

25. *Yomiuri*, December 16, 1920.

26. Mitsukawa, *Kokujin Mondai*, preface of 1925, 2.

27. Naoko Shimazu, *Japan, Race, and Equality: The Racial Equality Proposal of 1919* (New York: Routledge, 1998), 176.

28. Yoshiki Sakurai, "Kokuryū-kai to Sono Kikanshi" [Kokuryū-kai and its journals], in *Kokuryū-kai Kankei Shiryō-shū* [Materials related to Kokuryū-kai] (Tokyo: Kashiwa Shobō, 1992), ix–x. Kokuryū-kai, literally "Black Dragon Society," was in fact named after the Amur River located between northeastern China and Russian Far East. "Amur" means "cupid" in Russian but is rendered in Chinese as "Kokuryū Kō" (Black Dragon River), which is the origin of the Japanese organization's name. This coincidental denotation led some African Americans to favor Kokuryū-kai.

29. "The Purpose of Publishing the *Asian Review*," *Asia Jiron* 3, no. 9 (November 1, 1919): 83.

30. "Coloured and Whites," *Asian Review* 1, no. 5 (July 1920): 459, quoted in Gallicchio, *African American Encounter*, 60.

31. "Treatment of the Negroes in the United States," *Asian Review* 1, no. 7 (October 1920): 693.

32. "Race-War in the United States," *Asian Review* 2, no. 5 (July–August 1921): 434–35.

33. Gallicchio, *African American Encounter*, 59–60. Among its supporters were the aforementioned Nobuaki Makino, former foreign minister Kikujirō Ishii, Navy Minister Admiral Tomosaburō Katō, and Prime Minister Takashi Hara.

34. Mae M. Ngai, "The Architecture of Race in American Immigration Law: A Reexamination of the Immigration Act of 1924," *Journal of American History* 86, no. 1 (June 1999): 67–70, 80–81.

35. Kimitada Miwa, "Taibei Kessen eno Imēji" [Imaging the war against the United States], in *Nihon to Amerika: Aitekoku no Imēji Kenkyū* [Japan and America: A study of mutual images], ed. Hidetoshi Katō and Shunsuke Kamei (Tokyo: Nihon Gakujutsu Shinkō-kai, 1991), 229.

36. Reginald Kearney, "Pro-Japanese Utterances of W. E. B. Du Bois," *Contributions in Black Studies* 13–14 (1995–96): 208; Gerald Horne, "Tokyo Bound: African Americans and Japan Confront White Supremacy," *Souls* 3 (Summer 2001): 20. For the Immigration Act of 1924 and the process of political bargaining, see Toshihiro Minohara, "Kariforunia-shū ni okeru Hainichi Undō to 1924-nen Imin-hō no Seiritsu Katei: Imin Mondai wo meguru Nihibei Kankei, 1906–1924-nen" [The development of the anti-Japanese movement in California and the Immigration Act of 1924: Japanese-U.S. relations on the immigration problem, 1906–1924] (Ph.D. diss., Kobe University, 1998), chapter 5. For African American views on the anti-Japanese movement, see David J. Hellwig, "Afro-American Reactions to the Japanese and the Anti-Japanese Movement, 1906–1924," *Phylon* 38, no. 1 (1st qtr. 1977): 93–104.

37. *Yomiuri, Yorozu Chōhō, Tokyo Nichinichi,* and *Kokumin,* December 5, 1922.

38. *Yomiuri,* September 1, 1920.

39. Kijūrō Shidehara, "Beikoku ni okeru Shikei ni taisuru Kokujin Hogo-hōan Sōfu no ken" [On sending copies of the U.S. bill protecting blacks from lynching], Gaimushō Kiroku [foreign ministry record], 1–6–3, Gaikō Shiryō-kan [Diplomatic Record Office of the Ministry of Foreign Affairs of Japan], Tokyo.

40. *Tokyo Asahi,* June 22, 1924.

41. *Kokumin,* June 22, 1924.

42. *Osaka Asahi,* June 22, 1924.

43. *Kokumin,* June 22, 1924.

44. *Yorozu Chōhō,* June 22, 1924.

45. Quoted in Junichirō Shōji, "Konoe Fumimaro no Taibei-kan" [Fumimaro Konoe's views on America], in *Taishō-ki Nihon no Amerika Ninshiki* [Japanese views of America in the Taisho period], ed. Yūichi Hasegawa (Tokyo: Keiō Gijuku Daigaku Shuppan-kai, 2001), 93.

46. Walter White, *A Man Called White: The Autobiography of Walter White* (1948; reprint, New York: Arno, 1969), 69; Furukawa and Furukawa, *Nihonjin to Afurika-kei Amerikajin,* 95.

47. Furukawa and Furukawa, *Nihonjin to Afurika-kei Amerikajin,* 110.

48. Kearney, "Pro-Japanese Utterances," 211; Kearney, *African American Views of the Japanese: Solidarity or Sedition?* (Albany: State University of New York Press, 1998), 83–84; Gallicchio, *African American Encounter,* 103–4; Horne, "Tokyo Bound," 22; Furukawa and Furukawa, *Nihonjin to Afurika-kei Amerikajin,* 161–69; Yasuhiro Idei, *Kokujin ni Mottomo Aisare, FBI ni Mottomo Osorerareta Nihonjin* [The Japanese who was loved most by blacks and feared most by the FBI] (Tokyo: Kōdan-sha, 2008), 204–8, 214–15.

49. Yonezō Hirayama [Yasuichi Hikida], preface to *Lynching: A Novel* (Tokyo: Ni-hon Kōron-sha, 1937).

50. Walter White to James Weldon Johnson, September 25, 1933, James Weldon Johnson and Grace Nail Johnson Papers, box 24, folder 542, Yale Collection of American Literature, Beinecke Rare Book and Manuscript Library, Yale University, New Haven, CT.

51. Hikida to Johnson, September 26, 1933, James Weldon Johnson and Grace Nail Johnson Papers, box 9, folder 206.

52. Kearney, *African American Views,* 83; Yasuichi Hikida to James Weldon Johnson, September 26, 1933, and October 11, 1935, James Weldon Johnson and Grace Nail Johnson Papers, box 9, folder 206; David Levering Lewis, *When Harlem Was in Vogue* (1979; reprint, New York: Penguin Books, 1997), 302; Furukawa and Furukawa, *Nihonjin to Afurika-kei Amerikajin,* 162–63; Idei, *Kokujin ni Mottomo Aisare,* 204, 218–19, 231.

53. Kichizaburō Nomura, Ambassador to the United States, to the Ministry of Foreign Affairs, July 4, 1941, MAGIC (decoded Japanese intelligence files) intercept, quoted in Idei, *Kokujin ni Mottomo Aisare,* 205–6.

54. *Amsterdam Star News,* January 3, 1942, quoted in Idei, *Kokujin ni Mottomo Aisare,* 238–39.

55. Gaimushō Chōsabu Dairokka (Ministry of Foreign Affairs, Research Section, Department Six), preface to *Sensō to Kokujin: Nichibei Kaisen Igo no Kokujin no Dōkō oyobi Sono Haikei* [War and blacks: Activities of blacks and their background since the outbreak of the Japan-U.S. War], October 1942, in Minzoku Mondai Kankei Zakken: Kokujin Mondai [Documents related to racial issues: Issues on blacks], Gaimushō Kiroku, I 460–1–3. The preface also stated that the operation had been conducted "since the second Sino-Japanese War [of 1937] by the Japanese Consulate in New York and elsewhere."

56. "Japanese Influence and Activity among the American Negroes," in *The FBI's RACON: Racial Conditions in the United States during World War II,* ed. Robert A. Hill (Boston: Northeastern University Press, 1995), 509–10.

57. *Sensō to Kokujin,* 88, 67–68, 48–49.

58. Yasuichi Hikida, *Senji Kokujin Kōsaku* (Wartime black propaganda operations), January 1943, Gaimushō Kiroku, S1700–25, pp. 14–43. For a detailed study

on Japan's shortwave radio propaganda operation aimed at African Americans, see Masaharu Sato and Barak Kushner, "'Negro Propaganda Operations': Japan's Short-Wave Radio Broadcasts for World War II Black Americans," *Historical Journal of Film, Radio, and Television* 19, no. 1 (March 1999): 5–26.

59. Sato and Kushner, "Negro Propaganda Operations," 9.

60. Hikida, *Senji Kokujin Kōsaku*, 29.

61. *Cleveland Advocate*, September 27, 1919.

62. *Union*, July 30, 1921.

63. Ernest Allen Jr., "When Japan Was 'Champion of the Darker Races'": Satotaka Takahashi and the Flowering of Black Messianic Nationalism," *Black Scholar* 24, no. 1 (Winter 1994): 29.

64. Furukawa and Furukawa, *Nihonjin to Afurika-kei Amerikajin*, 105.

65. See, for example, Kearney, "Pro-Japanese Utterances," 201–17; Allen, "Waiting for Tojo"; Brenda Gayle Plummer, *Rising Wind: Black Americans and U.S. Foreign Affairs, 1935-1960* (Chapel Hill: University of North Carolina Press, 1996), 69–71; Horne, "Tokyo Bound," 16–28; Horne, *Race War! White Supremacy and the Japanese Attack on the British Empire* (New York: New York University Press, 2004), 84, 145, 258, 306, 330; Gallicchio, *African American Encounter*, chapters 1–4; Gallicchio, "Amerika Kokujin no Tainichi-kan no Kioku," 229–39; Gallicchio, "Afurika-kei Amerikajin no Sensō-kan, Ajia-kan," 249–50; George Lipsitz, "'Frantic to Join . . . the Japanese Army': Beyond the Black-White Binary," in *The Possessive Investment in Whiteness: How White People Profit from Identity Politics*, rev. and expanded ed. (Philadelphia: Temple University Press, 2006), 189–96. Some African Americans, including A. Philip Randolph, Chandler Owen of the *Messenger*, and Langston Hughes (who visited Japan in 1933 and interacted with Japanese leftists) were critical of Japanese imperialism during the interwar period. Daniel Widener, "'Perhaps the Japanese Are to Be Thanked?': Asia, Asian Americans, and the Construction of Black California," *Positions* 11, no. 1 (2003): 158–59; Koshiro, "Beyond an Alliance," 194; Onishi, "New Negro of the Pacific," 200–202.

66. Allen, "Champion of the Darker Races," 29; Furukawa and Furukawa, *Nihonjin to Afurika-kei Amerikajin*, 89–90; Lipsitz, "Frantic to Join," 191; Kearney, *African American Views*, 20.

67. *New York Age*, March 29, 1919, quoted in Kearney, *African American Views*, 57. Yukiko Koshiro points out that Johnson, after having visited Japan in 1929, became cautious about the alliance with the Japanese because of Japan's dualistic racial identity. "Beyond an Alliance," 186–87.

68. Kearney, *African American Views*, 54–55; Widener, "Perhaps the Japanese," 157–58. For African Americans and the racial equality proposal, see Plummer, *Rising Wind*, 15–20; and Onishi, "New Negro of the Pacific," 191–213.

69. Allen, "Champion of the Darker Races," 29; Horne, "Tokyo Bound," 18.

70. *Pittsburgh Courier*, February 13 and March 20, 1937, reprinted in W. E. B. Du Bois, *Newspaper Columns* (White Plains, NY: Kraus-Thomson, 1986), ed. Herbert Aptheker, 1:167, 182. For Du Bois's East Asia trip, see Kearney, "Pro-Japanese Utterances," 204–9; Kearney, *African American Views*, 19, 87–91; Koshiro, "Beyond an

Alliance," 187; Lipsitz, "Frantic to Join," 191; Furukawa and Furukawa, *Nihonjin to Afurika-kei Amerikajin,* 93–94.

71. *Crisis,* June 1934, 158.

72. *Crisis,* September 1934, 257.

73. Walter White to President Roosevelt, July 31, 1935, in George McJimsey, ed., *FDR and Protection from Lynching, 1934-1945,* vol. 11 of *Documentary History of the Franklin Roosevelt Presidency* (Bethesda, MD: University Publications of America, 2003), 251.

74. Carl Murphy to Marvin McIntyre, February 5, 1938, in McJimsey, *FDR and Protection from Lynching,* 523–24.

75. Jonathan Rosenberg, *How Far the Promised Land? World Affairs and the American Civil Rights Movement from the First World War to Vietnam* (Princeton, NJ: Princeton University Press, 2006), 112–13.

76. *Crisis,* July 1940, 209.

77. *Crisis,* June 1941, 183.

78. *Baltimore Afro-American,* December 6, 1941.

79. *Louisville Defender,* January 31, 1942.

80. *Baltimore Afro-American,* January 31, 1942.

81. *Pittsburgh Courier,* February 7, 1942.

82. "War Quiz for America," *Crisis,* April 1944, 113–14, 122.

83. For the racist politics of Bilbo, Talmadge, and Rankin, see White, *A Man Called White,* 268; Harvard Sitkoff, *A New Deal for Blacks: The Emergence of Civil Rights as a National Issue,* vol. 1, *The Depression Decade* (Oxford: Oxford University Press, 1978), 106–7, 117–18, 122, 292; Robert L. Zangrando, *The NAACP Crusade against Lynching, 1909-1950* (Philadelphia: Temple University Press, 1980), 150.

84. The *Courier* explained on February 14: "Last week, without any public announcement or fanfare, the editors of The Courier introduced its war slogans—a double 'V' for a double victory to colored America. We did this advisedly because we wanted to test the response and popularity of such a slogan with our readers. The response has been overwhelming." *Pittsburgh Courier,* February 14, 1942.

85. Rosenberg, *How Far the Promised Land?,* 137.

86. Zangrando, *NAACP Crusade against Lynching,* 166–67. Zangrando observes that when the NAACP's activities expanded in the 1940s, the antilynching bill ceased to be the organization's primary legislative objective.

87. *Pittsburgh Courier,* October 30, 1943.

88. *Baltimore Afro-American,* February 7, 1942.

89. National Negro Congress Papers, part 1, reel 23, Schomburg Center for Research in Black Culture, New York. In spite of their antilynching efforts, especially in response to the Sikeston lynching, African Americans witnessed the defeat of several federal antilynching bills. On February 7, 1942, for example, the *Baltimore Afro-American* reported on the death of eight antilynching bills that were introduced in the House of Representatives a year earlier in the first session of the 77th Congress. The paper was critical of the fact that no comments were made in the Congress on the Sikeston lynching by Missouri senators or representatives, including then Sena-

tor Harry S. Truman, or by President Franklin D. Roosevelt. *Baltimore Afro-American,* February 7, 1942.

90. *Crisis,* November 1942, 343.

91. *Pittsburgh Courier,* February 14, 1942.

92. Barbara Dianne Savage, *Broadcasting Freedom: Radio, War, and the Politics of Race,* 1938-1948 (Chapel Hill: University of North Carolina Press, 1999), 109–10.

93. *Crisis,* May 1942, 160, 165.

94. Quintard Taylor, "Blacks and Asians in a White City: Japanese Americans and African Americans in Seattle, 1890–1940," *Western Historical Quarterly* 23, no. 4 (November 1991): 425.

95. *Crisis,* September 1942, 281, 284.

96. *Pittsburgh Courier,* April 25, 1942, quoted in Horne, "Tokyo Bound," 26.

97. Dower, *War without Mercy,* 208.

U.S. Lynch Law and the Fate of the Soviet Union

The Soviet Uses of American Racial Violence

MEREDITH L. ROMAN

HITE AMERICAN BUSINESSMEN who visited the Soviet Union in the early 1930s often expressed frustration to U.S. consulate officials in Riga, Latvia, that Soviet citizens associated America with the "lynching" of blacks. One man, for instance, complained that the daughter of a Moscow University professor had asked him, "Don't you people in the 'free' United States of America lynch negroes?"[1] This essay explores why, in the decades between the two World Wars, inhabitants of the Soviet Union became acquainted with the acts of mob violence that Americans called lynching. In interrogating the coverage of American racial violence in the USSR, it pays special attention to how Soviet authorities used the term *lynching*. As will be shown, in the interwar era, and from 1928 through 1932 in particular, the "lynching" of black men in the "'free' United States of America" was central to representations of the Soviet Union as an enlightened, modern society where such "barbaric" racial violence was absent.[2]

Before the Nazis came to power in Germany, U.S. racism was identified in the Soviet Union as the most egregiously horrific aspect of Western capitalism, and the extralegal execution of black men was portrayed as its most defining feature. In 1926, Vladimir Maiakovskii, the preeminent revolutionary poet, informed readers of *My Discovery of America* that white American men subjected any Black man who glanced at a white woman to lynch law (*sud Lincha*), which meant, he elucidated, that they "tear off his arms and legs and roast him alive over a bonfire."[3] Despite this and similar references in Soviet publications to mob violence against African American men during the first decade of Bolshevik rule, it was in the late 1920s and early 1930s that these acts received the most sustained attention in the USSR, becoming a focus of political education campaigns and frequent newspaper articles, photographs, and cartoons. Two corresponding shifts in domestic and Comintern policy help explain this development.[4] By 1929 central authorities abandoned the New Economic Policy (1921–27), which sought to attain socialism through capitalist practices and launched a campaign to build socialism through rapid industrialization as outlined in the First (1928–32) and Second (1933–37) Five-Year Plans. At the same time that Soviet leaders praised U.S. industry as a model of development and recruited a substantial number of American and other foreign workers to help eradicate the country's industrial inferiority, they used American racial violence to insist on the moral superiority of the anticapitalist world they were building.[5]

Moscow's heightened interest in condemning U.S. racism was simultaneously motivated by the ascendancy of the Comintern's militant "Third Period" (1928–35). In 1928 authorities of the Third International posited that the "gradual and partial stabilization" of capitalism characteristic of the "Second Period" (1924–28) was being replaced by an impending crisis in capitalism that would bring with it a proliferation of revolutionary opportunities. To capitalize on these opportunities, Comintern leaders ordered communist parties around the world to abandon their policies of coalition with working-class parties while they assessed the revolutionary potential of black Americans.[6] As a result of this assessment, Comintern officials declared African Americans an oppressed nation with the right to national self-determination at the Sixth World Congress in 1928 and anointed them the revolutionary vanguard among colonized nations. This decree made American blacks "indispensable allies" of the USSR at a time when the country was building socialism in what Soviet leaders depicted as an extremely antagonistic capitalist world.[7] Thus, while the Comintern spoke of U.S. racism as an impediment to the international revolutionary movement, in the Soviet Union it was condemned as a threat, albeit indirect, to the country's national security.[8] Since the most sensationalized acts of violence were committed against black men, Soviet antiracism elided black women and gendered African American militancy (and that of the Soviet Union's allies) as male.

This essay examines three major manifestations of Soviet antiracism that represented Soviet citizens as committed to racial equality and appalled by American racial violence: a 1930 trial of two white American assailants of a black worker in Stalingrad; a two-year nationwide campaign (1931–32) to liberate nine African American teenagers in Scottsboro, Alabama; and the dissemination of visual images of mob violence against black men. As the Stalingrad trial, Scottsboro campaign, and central press reveal, Soviet officials most often adopted the terms *"linchevat'"* (to lynch) and *"sud Lincha"* (lynch law) rather than the Russian term *samosud* (mob law or, literally, "judging by oneself") to describe the extralegal executions of African American men.[9] Soviet citizens were therefore introduced to the vocabulary of U.S. racism and encouraged to understand that "lynching" (*linchevanie*) was a particularly heinous act of violence peculiar to the advanced capitalist society of the United States, where race hatred had reached its most depraved form.

Certainly, exposing the violence perpetrated against bourgeois America's black male citizens was meant to confirm for inhabitants of the Soviet Union that their mission of building an anticapitalist society was a noble one.[10] It also served as an obvious distraction from the various forms of violence committed against Soviet citizens.[11]

AMERICAN RACIAL VIOLENCE ON TRIAL

In late July 1930, Lemuel Lewis and William Brown, two white American laborers who were working at the Stalingrad tractor factory, inadvertently provided Soviet trade union authorities with an unprecedented opportunity to represent the Soviet Union as a society intolerant of American racial violence. The two men threatened and then physically assaulted Robert Robinson—the only black worker at the plant. The Soviet press connected Lewis and Brown's conduct with that of white Americans who murdered African Americans. Newspaper headlines condemned the assailants as the "Followers of Lynch at the Tractor Factory," articles addressed "Who is lynched in the USA," and photographs and cartoons showed black American men subjected to what editors overwhelmingly identified as lynch law (*sud Lincha*) in the United States.[12]

Yet Soviet authorities also highlighted an important distinction between the actions of the two white Americans in Stalingrad and the conduct of the white American mob in the United States. For example, at the Fifth Congress of the Red International of Trade Unions in mid-August 1930, Elena Stasova, the head of Mezhdunarodnaia Organizatsiia Pomoshchi Bortsam Revoliutsii (MOPR), or the International Organization for Assistance to Revolutionary Fighters, remarked, "Naturally, the white Americans here did not dare to attempt to lynch the Negro."[13] As Stasova's comment suggests, the purported enlightenment of inhabitants of the Soviet Union made "lynching" impossible on Soviet soil—a fact that even ignorant, "counterrevolutionary" white Americans like Lewis and Brown intuitively recognized.

The central press provided consistent evidence of this impossibility. Whereas the white American assailants of black men in the United States were shown escaping moral reprobation, let alone punishment, workers throughout the Soviet Union appeared united in their outrage at the racially motivated assault on their "brother." With headlines that read "This Is Not Bourgeois America," "In the USSR There Is No Place for Racial Enmity," and "The USSR Is the Fatherland for the Black, Yellow and White Races," Soviet newspapers reported that laborers around the country were enthusiastically attending protest meetings, issuing proposals that a brigade of Soviet and foreign laborers serve as the public prosecutors at the trial, inviting Robinson to join their factory families, and incessantly demanding that "the followers of Lynch" be expelled from the Soviet Union.[14]

George Padmore, the pan-African leader who was living in Moscow at the time of the assault on Robinson, testified to authorities' effectiveness at portraying the trial of Lewis and Brown as the product of Soviet citizens' widespread indignation. In 1941, seven years after he had been expelled from the Comintern and become a staunch anticommunist, Padmore nevertheless recalled that "the Russian workers were so indignant at white men treating a fellow-worker in that fashion simply because of his race, that they demanded their immediate expulsion from the Soviet Union."[15] In the late evening of August 29, 1930 (after six days of testimony from witnesses, the defendants, and the plaintiff), the Stalingrad court upheld what was scripted as the workers' demand, sentencing Lewis and Brown to banishment from the Soviet Union. As the public prosecutors emphasized during the trial, Lewis and Brown's act of racial violence threatened to impede the construction of socialism, the tempo of which was made possible only by upholding "equality of all people."[16] The deportation of two white American assailants of a black worker served as a powerful statement "to America, to the perpetrators of lynching," decried one newspaper headline, that the racist mores that sanctioned violence against black workers in the United States had no place in the first workers' state.[17]

While the campaign against and trial of Lewis and Brown were intended to exhibit as fact the superior racial enlightenment of Soviet citizens in juxtaposition to their American counterparts, it was also intended to teach or

model for those same citizens the proper "Soviet" response to American racial violence. This is most effectively evidenced in the workers' trial of V. M.
Tsiprus, which *Rabochaia gazeta* (Worker newspaper) organized on August
17 (five days before the trial of Lewis and Brown convened in Stalingrad).
Tsiprus, who had lived in the United States for thirty-six years, supposedly
expressed approval rather than indignation at the assault on Robinson. According to the press, Tsiprus said during a protest meeting held at the Moscow textile factory where he worked: "Negroes are snakes. They should
all be lynched [*linchevat'*]." Newspapers reported that Tsiprus's statements
roused "all kinds of indignation among workers of the Soviet Union," who
demanded that trade union officials punish Tsiprus. For his racist comments
or failure to "speak antiracism," a workers' court expelled Tsiprus from the
union for three months or until he was able to demonstrate, through community service, that he had replaced his "American" attitude toward blacks
with an enlightened (i.e., Soviet) perspective.[18]

AMERICAN RACE HATE IN BLACK AND WHITE

If the enlightened racial consciousness of the New Soviet Man and Woman
rendered mob violence against black workers beyond the realm of possibility in the USSR, "a lynched Negro," as one Soviet periodical claimed in November 1928, was "the monument of American civilization."[19] A cartoon that
Rabochaia gazeta published on the front page in 1931—without any articles
regarding U.S. racism—made this point explicit. The image showed the grim
reaper disguised as the Statue of Liberty. Hanging from Lady Liberty's skel-
etal arms were ten nooses with black victims dangling at the end of five of
them. The headline explained that this was "American 'Democracy,' as It Really Is," while the caption noted that "For Negro-workers in 'free' America
there are many free nooses."[20] The cartoon's reference to "many free nooses"
and depiction of five corpses visually reinforced the Soviet press's emphasis
that this distinctively American monument of "civilization"—the murdered
black worker—was becoming an even more common feature of the U.S.
landscape. In addition to cartoons like this one, photographs confirmed as
factually correct reports that the number of extralegal executions of black
men had escalated in response to African Americans' growing militancy.[21]

Like the "American 'Democracy'" cartoon, photographs of African American male victims of mob violence were published in Soviet newspapers with
only brief captions amid unrelated articles. They were just as likely to ac-

company reports concerning the latest achievements in the First Five-Year Plan and the recent production figures of a particular Soviet factory as they were to appear alongside news items that addressed U.S. race relations. Often readers were expected to know intuitively that the photographs had been taken somewhere in the United States, the details of which were inconsequential—just another example of horrific racial violence in capitalist America. A superimposed American flag sometimes served as the primary visual cue. The dissemination of such gruesome images in this manner no doubt points to the sensationalist function they served in the Soviet Union.[22] At the same time, by not disclosing the location of the execution, the date when it occurred, or the name of the victim, the photographs conveyed a message similar to those printed on postcards and sold at Moscow kiosks: these extralegal murders occurred with such frequency in America that they could happen to any black man (read "worker") at any time and under the pretext of any "crime."[23] "For Negro-workers in 'free' America," in other words, "there are many free nooses."

The photograph that appeared most often in Soviet newspapers and on the front pages of *Trud* (Labor) and *Komsomol'skaia pravda* (Komsomol truth) depicted the August 1930 Marion, Indiana, double murder of Abraham Smith and Thomas Shipp. Despite the photograph's relatively wide circulation, minimal information concerning the execution was disclosed. The standard caption simply stated, "The trial by lynching [*sudom Lincha*] of two Negroes." The crowd of well-dressed white men and women posing and smiling shamelessly at the camera beneath the two black men's corpses made it especially appealing to print. Their jovial ignorance spotlighted the moral depravity of U.S. modernity and provided the ideal contrast to the progressive, antiracist, "Soviet" consciousness that all inhabitants of the first workers' state allegedly possessed.[24] Photographs in the central press that showed Russian factory workers and journalists embracing—in "brotherly unity"—African American male Communists like James Ford and Isaiah Hawkins make this particularly evident.[25]

On those few occasions when the photograph's caption provided greater detail than "a trial by lynching," editors distorted or fabricated information to make the point explicit that the victim had been murdered because he was black and class conscious. For instance, the caption of a photograph on the front page of *Komsomol'skaia pravda* in August 1930 described the victim as "a Negro-worker, victim of mob law [*samosud*] at the hands of a band of white landowners in Marion (America)," who was "hanged simply because he [together with other Negroes] actively participated in preparations for a strike. Police appeared only after the murderers finished their 'work.'"[26] The editors erred in reporting that this man had been executed by mob law in Marion. Thomas Shipp and Abraham Smith, the aforementioned double-murder victims, whose photograph the youth paper had published days earlier and described simply as "lynch law," were Marion's only recorded victims of mob violence, and neither had been involved in labor activity. Yet this inaccuracy was immaterial. By identifying the black male victims as labor activists, the photograph furthered the representation of U.S. blacks as the revolutionary vanguard whose mobilization was met with barbaric violence by the same "white landowners" who sought to destroy the Soviet Union.

A cartoon in *Komsomol'skaia pravda* reinforced this message. A bare-chested black man was shown with his mouth contorted in agony and a noose around his neck. While the caption called on "Workers! To Struggle against the lynching of your Negro-proletarian brothers!," the headline promised that through this unity, "We will chop off the clutches of the Hang man." The "hangman" assumed the familiar form of an extremely fat, white male capitalist wearing a top hat. With a gun holster around his waist, he was depicted posting a sign above the victim's head that warned black workers, "Do Not Dare to Struggle for Your Rights."[27] By using the standard image of the capitalist, the cartoon made clear that African Americans and Soviet citizens were fighting the same enemy and that black men were the frontline casualties in a war that would eventually be directed at the USSR.[28] The Soviet press thus used "lynching" to convince readers of the superiority of Soviet society, while also reminding them of the need to work more diligently for its construction in the face of a growing threat of imperialist war.

Legal Racial Violence

The Soviet Scottsboro protest constituted the most elaborate, concerted effort to condemn the violence committed against African American men and connect it to the fate of the USSR. On April 9, 1931, an all-white jury in Scottsboro, Alabama, condemned to death eight African American male teenagers (and sentenced a ninth to life imprisonment) on trumped-up charges of raping two white women.[29] Newspaper articles emphasized that a mob—"the knights of Lynch"—had surrounded the courthouse to ensure that justice would be served, and cartoons alluded to the collusion between the mob and the American justice system.[30] To illustrate, one image showed a wire that could easily be mistaken for a rope spelling "U.S.A." Yet in the places where there should be knots to form each letter, the graphic artist, V. Federovskii, drew the heads of the Scottsboro prisoners with the rope-wire looped around each of their necks. The headline appealed to onlookers to "Snap the Wire of the Electric Guillotine." As this cartoon indicates, the wire of the electric chair—modern bourgeois civilization's improvement on the guillotine—was equivalent to the rope used to extralegally execute African American male workers; both were "barbaric" tools used to suppress revolutionaries and uphold "lynch justice" in the "U.S.A."[31]

In the spring of 1931, the Soviet section of MOPR, the propaganda organization known more popularly abroad as International Red Aid (IRA), launched a two-year nationwide campaign to "Snap the Wire of the Electric Guillotine" and liberate the Scottsboro prisoners.[32] From May 1931 through the fall of 1932, these young black American men were the subject of pamphlets, banners, news articles, poems, protest resolutions, rallies, cartoons, and photographs—all of which depicted them, as the "electric guillotine" cartoon suggests, as revolutionaries. The transformation of the nine black teenagers—referred to as the "Scottsboro Boys" in other countries—into class-conscious proletarians who had "rallied black and white workers for the struggle against the unbridled terrorism of the maddened bourgeoisie" was strategic. It rendered the Scottsboro defendants allies of the Soviet Union and their impending execution the initial step in the "maddened bourgeoisie's" plot to attack the USSR.[33]

Accordingly, though MOPR's affiliate organizations orchestrated wide-scale protests in Europe, the United States, and Latin America, leaders in Moscow believed that it was the duty of the Soviet people, as citizens of the first country building socialism, to raise the most massive, far-reaching Scottsboro protest and inspire toilers around the world to follow their example.[34] Maksim Gor'kii, the illustrious Russian writer, established a defense committee of seventeen "distinguished representatives of science, literature and society," otherwise known as the "Committee to Save the 9 Negroes," to help lead the Soviet campaign.[35] Gor'kii also penned the pamphlet *Terror against the Negro Workers in America*, three million copies of which were supposedly released in twenty-four areas of the Soviet Union in the summer 1931. Gor'kii warned that the Scottsboro death sentence and the increased violence against African American workers that it signaled constituted the bourgeoisie's efforts "to scare Negroes" back into their proper subservient place.[36]

In an essay in *Izvestiia* (News), Soviet novelist Aleksei Tolstoi similarly warned that the U.S. bourgeoisie had become even more desperate and violent as a result of the mobilization of black workers. At the same time, he condemned the white American masses for blindly supporting the bourgeoisie's efforts. Specifically, Tolstoi lamented that they would have accused the Scottsboro defendants of whatever "crime" necessary to justify their execution—regardless of its preposterous, baseless nature. The accusation of rape, he insisted, was no more sound than charging that the nine African American proletarians had "stolen the moon from the sky."[37] To this point, lecturers at protest rallies were instructed to inform attendees that false allegations of rape (of white women) had been used to justify the lynching or extralegal murder of black men since their emancipation from slavery.[38] A twelve-page lecture guide titled "The Lynching and Persecution of Negro Workers in the U.S.A." (*Linchevanie i presledovanie negritianskikh trudiashchikhsia v SASSh*) encouraged lecturers to emphasize that "*in the course of two centuries incidents of violence committed by black men against white women are not only rare, but are completely unknown.*"[39]

In a lengthy essay in *Komsomol'skaia pravda,* Anatolii Lunacharskii, the former "commissar of enlightenment," likewise ridiculed the absurdity of white Americans' racist mores. He posited that even the more open-minded white Americans who opposed the death sentence on the grounds that the black defendants had been denied a fair trial nevertheless believed that if they had "made advances" at the two white women, then they deserved to be deprived of their lives. This was because, Lunacharskii argued, by white Americans' logic "the black dogs" needed to "understand that it was entirely impermissible for them to raise their eyes to white women, whom their white brothers in Christ can acquire for a few dollars."[40] In a poem in *Literaturnaia gazeta* (Literary newspaper) titled "A Song about Alabama," Nikolai Aseev, a leading poet of the Russian avant-garde of the 1920s, also disparaged white Americans' perverse notions of what constituted a crime punishable by death on the part of black men. Aseev explained that in Alabama, if a Black man, above whose head constantly hangs a "long, sturdy noose," even smiled at a white woman, then lynch law ensured he would be "burned alive" by the legal means of the electric chair or the extralegal means of a noose and bonfire. He emphasized that this systematic terrorism against blacks, whom whites in Alabama still considered slaves, was inseparable from the threat of imperialist war against the Soviet Union.[41]

The central press (and MOPR's organizational records) represented Soviet citizens from "all corners of the USSR" as exhibiting an enlightened awareness that their fate as inhabitants of the workers' state was connected to that of their nine black comrades in Scottsboro.[42] Specifically, Russian and non-Russian workers, collective farmers, Red Army soldiers, and students were shown attending protest rallies en masse and pledging to form shock brigades, sow extra plots of land, and collect donations in support of the joint goal of building socialism and liberating the Scottsboro prisoners.[43] In a representative protest resolution that appeared on *Komsomol'skaia pravda*'s front page on July 4, 1931 (amid several other statements of solidarity), Ufa laborers declared: "Having listened to a report about the preparations for the execution of eight Negro comrades, we are creating a new shock brigade named for the eight Negro comrades to struggle by all means possible for the fulfillment of the Five-Year Plan in four years, and for strengthening the power of the USSR—the fatherland of the world proletariat."[44] At a time of tremendous upheaval and unrest in the Soviet Union related to rapid industrialization, the collectivization of agriculture, and famine, the Scottsboro campaign depicted the Soviet populace as unified around a higher cause of the defense of justice and human rights.[45]

While acknowledging that the Scottsboro protest (like the August 1930 trial of Lewis and Brown) was the result of official state action rather than popular initiative as Soviet authorities claimed, this essay does not discount that some Soviet citizens may have been outraged by the death sentence against the eight black teenagers and sincere in their expressions of solidarity with them.[46] Scholars of the Soviet Union have demonstrated that many individuals during the 1920s and 1930s possessed a strong desire to act as "the agents of historical progress" and help inaugurate a new, superior society where racial and national hatred was absent—a desire that the Soviet state no doubt harnessed.[47] As the historian Maxim Matusevich argues, it was not until after the Second World War that Soviet citizens' enthusiasm for antiracist rhetoric had worn thin, as many increasingly saw the state's indictment of American racism as having become just another dimension of the Cold War struggle with the United States.[48]

In the late 1920s and early 1930s racial violence against African American men was central to representations of the Soviet Union as the morally superior antithesis to bourgeois America.[49] The Soviet press and political education campaigns depicted black American men as eliciting greater violence and repression because of their increased politicization and alliance with the USSR. Quite paradoxically, then, representations of the injured black male body came to signify not only the enormity of U.S. racism and superiority of Soviet society but also African Americans' growing militancy. By portraying Black American men as militant revolutionaries, Soviet antiracism challenged the dominant, historically Western image of blacks as criminals, savages, fools, or clowns.[50] Yet because blacks' politicization was met with intense violence, Soviet citizens were primarily exposed to representations of their valued allies—except when shown on Soviet soil—as persecuted, and in some cases, defeated victims.[51] The simultaneous image of black men in the United States as heroic revolutionaries and tragic victims was arguably driven by a desire to represent the Soviet Union as a promised land and the Soviet people as fulfilling a paternalistic, pseudomessianic role rather than having a conscious desire to relegate African American men to a perpetually subordinate, inferior position.[52]

To be sure, African Americans who visited and worked in the USSR assumed an indispensable role in forging these representations and teaching Soviet officials and citizens about U.S. "lynch law." They spoke at protest rallies and factories, wrote articles for the Soviet press, posed for photographs with Soviet workers, contributed to the compilation of MOPR lecture guides and informational directives, and were depicted as sharing equally in the responsibility of liberating their black brothers in the United States who were "awaiting our help."[53] Regardless of the degree of opportunism that motivated the Soviet indictment of U.S. racism, these African Americans recognized that it raised critical awareness of the routine violation of human rights that black Americans suffered in spite of their status as U.S. citizens and challenged the prevailing white supremacist notion—dominant throughout Europe and the globe—that blacks were biologically inferior and unworthy of equality with whites.[54] Soviet antiracism also translated into a guarantee of physical safety (or freedom from violence) that many African Americans in the USSR equated with feelings of genuine freedom and full humanity. Even those individuals who became disillusioned with the Soviet experiment continued to espouse the practical humanizing benefits that Soviet antiracism had on the lives and psychological well-being of black men in an age of Judge Lynch.[55]

Consistent with the paternalistic, pseudomessianic vocation of the Soviet people, the dominant image of white Americans that emerged from the Soviet indictment of U.S. racism was ambiguous at best. As evidenced in the writings of Soviet intellectuals like Tolstoi and Lunacharskii, white Americans were imaged overwhelmingly as a blind, ignorant lot, the "knights of

Lynch" who played an integral role in executing their black comrades, and thereby in furthering the cause of the counterrevolution. This unfavorable depiction of white American toilers stood in direct contradiction to the contemporary Comintern line on revolution, which maintained that white American workers were increasingly recognizing their common plight and uniting with black Americans. Yet it was most effective for illuminating the alleged superior enlightenment of the Soviet people.[56] Revolution in the United States, or the liberation of black and white American workers, was hence portrayed as impossible without the intervention in some way, albeit undefined, of the heroic first workers' state.[57]

Since Soviet antiracism was motivated first and foremost by the objective of celebrating Soviet "exceptionalism," it did not retain its intensity or priority status beyond the early 1930s. Accordingly, Soviet authorities suspended the Scottsboro liberation movement in the USSR in 1933, long before all nine defendants were released from prison.[58] In November 1932, as a result in no small part to the protests that MOPR organizations staged around the world, the U.S. Supreme Court had ordered a new trial for the Scottsboro defendants on the basis that their right to due process, as guaranteed by the Fourteenth Amendment, had been violated. In the wake of this monumental legal decision, the protest resolutions, rallies, poems, essays, and cartoons condemning the Scottsboro death sentence disappeared from the Soviet press and MOPR literature and records.[59] And although there were incidents in which mobs murdered African Americans in spectacular fashion in 1934 and 1935 in the United States, photographs and cartoons of the black victims ceased to appear on postcards and the front pages of major Soviet newspapers.[60]

The Japanese occupation of Manchuria and the Nazis' assumption of power in January 1933 played a major role in dethroning U.S. racial violence from the central place it had occupied in Soviet propaganda of the preceding years. "Suddenly threatened on two sides," as the historian Norman Saul puts it, Soviet leaders were especially anxious to establish diplomatic relations with the United States, which the election of Franklin D. Roosevelt to the U.S. presidency in November 1932 made a distinct possibility. Soviet authorities assumed correctly that propaganda would be one of the new president's primary points of contention, and in November 1933, rapprochement was achieved.[61] Henceforth, U.S. racism garnered more subtle, "soft-line" approbation reflective of the policies of the Popular Front era (the effects of which informed Soviet propaganda prior to the Comintern's adoption of it as official policy in 1935).[62] The few instances when the term *lynching* was mentioned in the Soviet press in the mid–1930s, it was identified as a practice with which Soviet citizens were already familiar, implying that it required no further elaboration.[63] The racial policies and practices of Nazi Germany had become the graver threat to Soviet civilization with which the masses needed to become acquainted. Germany had replaced the United States, in other words, as the quintessential "Country of Racial Bigotry" against which Soviet enlightenment was juxtaposed.[64] Therefore, even though Grigorii Aleksandrov's 1936 film *Circus* (Tsirk) was ostensibly about a white American woman and her black baby finding refuge in the Soviet Union, the film's main villain was the very Nazi-looking German manager, Franz von Kneishits.[65]

In the decades after the Second World War "lynch law" would not regain the prominent place it had occupied in Soviet propaganda of the early 1930s. In contrast to the era of American isolationism, propagandists no longer needed to rely primarily on violence against African American men to establish America as the imperial, belligerent aggressor. They could and often did spotlight U.S. actions around the globe to challenge its leaders' claims to be *the* defender of the Free World. This is not to deny the critical role that American race relations played in the Cold War, especially with the emergence of the modern U.S. Civil Rights Movement in the 1950s.[66] To be sure, it did not take long for major Soviet newspapers like *Pravda* (Truth), *Izvestiia*, and *Trud* to report on the escalation of "Anti-Negro Terror" in the United States in the mid–1940s, which in many instances targeted war veterans.[67] However, the tone and function of these reports had changed. The era of "the spectacle lynching" had ended, and the Soviet press highlighted how various "progressive" and "democratic" organizations in the United States were demanding that federal and state officials punish the instigators of and participants in mob violence against blacks.[68] Since an increasing number of white Americans had begun to conceive of extralegal executions of African Americans as an exercise in terror rather than justice, widespread outrage over "lynch law" could no longer be scripted as uniquely "Soviet" or as evidence of the exceptional, antiracist consciousness of the New Soviet Person. Moreover, officials in Moscow used the "Rise in Anti-Negro Terror" in the second half of the 1940s and in the 1950s to expose the hypocrisy of U.S. democracy but *not* to signal an imminent imperialist war against the first workers' state.

The torture and murder of fourteen-year-old Emmett Till in Money, Mississippi, in late August 1955 most effectively illustrates that the extralegal execution of African Americans had lost its central importance in propaganda of the early Cold War. Many white Americans, including (at least initially) editors of southern U.S. newspapers, expressed outrage and embarrassment at the actions of Ray Bryant and his half-brother J. W. Milam, and the European press provided extensive coverage of the case.[69] But in the wake of Till's murder and Bryant and Milam's subsequent acquittal, the major Soviet newspapers were remarkably silent. This included *Pravda, Izvestiia,* and *Komsomol'skaia pravda,* the youth organ that, as this essay demonstrates, was at the forefront of the Soviet indictment of the legal and extralegal violence perpetrated against black men.[70] As a further contrast to the early 1930s, Soviet novelists and poets did not compose agitational literature condemning Till's murderers, and no nationwide campaign was organized to represent Soviet citizens as outraged at the heinous crime or to politicize the late Till as a revolutionary and valued ally of the USSR.[71] As the minimal Soviet coverage of the Till murder makes especially clear, after the Second World War U.S. racial violence was no longer scripted as a threat to the USSR's national security and thus did not carry the same sense of urgency or meaning for Soviet citizens. Their fate, in other words, was no longer represented as inseparable from that of U.S. blacks.

Certainly, African Americans continued to be identified as friends of the Soviet Union, as exhibited in the fanfare surrounding the visits of Paul Robeson and W. E. B. Du Bois to Moscow.[72] Yet because of changes in the international climate and political exigencies of the Soviet state, they had lost their exclusive interwar status as the Soviet Union's valued allies or revolutionary vanguard among oppressed nations. By the mid–1950s, Soviet leaders expressed interest in winning the esteem of Asians, and especially Africans, for which they were competing with the United States for influence. The unprecedented number of African dignitaries and students who traveled to the USSR in the wake of decolonization is indicative of the alliance that Moscow sought to forge with leaders of these new nations.[73] As the competition between these two new superpowers went global after the Second World War, the Soviet indictment of racism assumed a more international (rather than primarily American) focus. While African Americans had been instrumental in forging the identity of this emerging world power in its bid to establish an alternate, more progressive and humane model of modernity, Soviet leaders expanded upon their commitment to and "friendship" with the African continent to consolidate and secure it.[74]

NOTES

Reprinted in revised form from *Opposing Jim Crow: African Americans and the Soviet Indictment of U.S. Racism, 1928-1937* by Meredith L. Roman by permission of the University of Nebraska Press. © 2012 by the Board of Regents of the University of Nebraska.

1. *Records of the Department of State Relating to Internal Affairs of the Soviet Union, 1930-1939*, 861.5017—Living Conditions/623.

2. On Soviet leaders' interest in portraying the USSR as a superior, modern society amid the rise of fascism and the Great Depression, see Stephen Kotkin, *Magnetic Mountain: Stalinism as a Civilization* (Berkeley: University of California Press, 1995), 2, 151–52.

3. Vladimir Maiakovskii, *Maiakovskii ob Amerike: stikhi, ocherki gazetnye interv'iu* (Moscow: Sovetskii pisatel', 1949), esp. 120–21; and Maiakovskii, *My Discovery of America*, trans. Neil Cornwell (London: Hesperus, 2005), 83.

4. The indictment of U.S. racism was elevated from a "soft line" to a "hard line" or priority policy after 1928. See Terry Martin, *Affirmative Action Empire: Nations and Nationalism in the Soviet Union, 1923-1939* (Ithaca, NY: Cornell University Press, 2001), 83, 122–23.

5. For a discussion of socialism as "the antidote to capitalism," see Kotkin, *Magnetic Mountain*, 149–55. On Russian attitudes toward Western technology in tsarist and early Soviet history, see Hans Rogger, "*Amerikanizm* and the Economic Development of Russia," *Comparative Studies in Society and History* 23, no. 3 (July 1981): 382–420; and Alan Ball, *Imagining America: Influence and Images in Twentieth-Century Russia* (Lanham, MD: Rowman and Littlefield, 2003). According to Sergei Zhuravlev, during the most intensive phase of industrialization, nearly thirty-five thousand foreign workers, specialists, and their families were living in the Soviet Union, most of whom were Germans, followed by Americans. See Sergei Zhuravlev, "*Malen'kie liudi*" *i "bol'shaia istoriia": Inostrantsy moskovskogo Elektrozavoda v sovetskom obshchestve 1920-kh–1930-kh gg* ["Little people" and "big history": Foreigners of Moscow's electrical factory in Soviet society, 1920s–1930s] (Moscow: Rosspen, 2000), 29–31.

6. On the militant Third Period, see especially Geoff Eley, *Forging Democracy: The History of the Left in Europe, 1850-2000* (New York: Oxford University Press, 2002), 251–67.

7. On the decree's significance for the black freedom struggle, see Robin D. G. Kelley, *Hammer and Hoe: Alabama Communists during the Great Depression* (Chapel Hill: University of North Carolina Press, 1990); Mark Naison, *Communists in Harlem during the Depression* (New York: Grove, 1983), 17–20; Cedric J. Robinson, *Black Marxism: The Making of the Black Radical Tradition* (1983; reprint, Chapel Hill: University of North Carolina Press, 2000), 220–22; and Mark Solomon, *The Cry Was Unity: Communists and African Americans, 1917-1936* (Jackson: University Press of Mississippi, 1998), esp. 85–89.

8. Soviet leaders similarly connected the fate of the loyalists in the Spanish Civil War with the security of the USSR. See Daniel Kowalsky, *Stalin and the Span-*

ish Civil War (New York: Columbia University Press, 2004). On the siege mentality characteristic of this period of Soviet history, see Gábor Tamás Rittersporn, "The Omnipresent Conspiracy: On Soviet Imagery of Politics and Social Relations in the 1930s," in *Stalinism: Its Nature and Aftermath*, ed. Nicholas Lampert and Gábor Tamás Rittersporn (Armonk, NY: M. E. Sharpe, 1992), 101–20; and Daniel Peris, *Storming the Heavens: The Soviet League of the Militant Godless* (Ithaca, NY: Cornell University Press, 1998), 102–17.

9. On the history of the term *lynching* in the United States, see Christopher Waldrep, *The Many Faces of Judge Lynch: Extralegal Violence and Punishment in America* (New York: Palgrave Macmillan, 2002). On the U.S. Communist Party's definition of mob violence against black men as a "capitalist phenomenon," see Rebecca Hill, *Men, Mobs, and Law: Anti-Lynching and Labor Defense in U.S. Radical History* (Durham, NC: Duke University Press, 2008), 209–36. On *samosud* as a form of popular rural justice, see Cathy Frierson, "Crime and Punishment in the Russian Village: Rural Concepts of Criminality at the End of the Nineteenth Century," *Slavic Review* 46, no. 1 (Spring 1987): 55–69; and Stephen P. Frank, "Popular Justice, Community, and Culture among the Russian Peasantry, 1810–1900," *Russian Review* 46, no. 3 (July 1987): 239–65. On instances of *samosud* during collectivization, see Lynne Viola, *Peasant Rebels under Stalin: Collectivization and the Culture of Peasant Resistance* (New York: Oxford University Press, 1999); and Hiroaki Kuromiya, *Freedom and Terror in the Donbass: A Ukrainian-Russian Borderland, 1870s-1990s* (New York: Cambridge University Press, 1998).

10. On the Soviet press's role in convincing readers of the superiority of Soviet society in relation to capitalist countries in the 1920s, see Jeffrey Brooks, "Official Xenophobia and Popular Cosmopolitanism in Early Soviet Russia," *American Historical Review* 97, no. 5 (December 1992): 1431–48.

11. See, for example, Oleg Khlevniuk, *The History of the Gulag: from Collectivization to the Great Terror* (New Haven, CT: Yale University Press, 2004); and R. W. Davies and Stephen G. Wheatcroft, *The Years of Hunger: Soviet Agriculture, 1931-1933* (New York: Palgrave Macmillan, 2004).

12. *Trud*, September 5, 1930; *Komsomol'skaia pravda*, August 26, 30, and 31, 1930.

13. "The Red Trade Unions and IRA," *Rossiiskii gosudarstvennyi arkhiv sotsial'noi i politicheskoi istorii* [Russian state archive of social and political history] (RGASPI), f. 534, op. 1, d. 197, ll. 64–70 (quotation l. 69).

14. See, for example, *Trud*, August 13 and 14, 1930; and *Rabochaia gazeta*, August 15, 1930. For the headlines, see *Rabochaia gazeta*, August 11 and 13, 1930; and *Trud*, August 11, 1930.

15. George Padmore, "The Socialist Attitude to the Invasion of the USSR," *Left* 60 (September 1941): 193–99 (quotation on 196). On Padmore's expulsion from the Comintern in 1934, see James R. Hooker, *Black Revolutionary: George Padmore's Path from Communism to Pan-Africanism* (New York: Praeger, 1967); and Solomon, *Cry Was Unity*, 177–83.

16. "Obvinitel'noe zakliuchenie po delu izbieniia rabochego negra na Stalingradskom traktornom zavode" [Decision to indict in the matter involving the Negro

worker at the Stalingrad Tractor Factory], *Gosudarstvennyi arkhiv Rossiiskoi Federatsii* [State Archive of the Russian Federation] (GARF), f. 5469, op. 14, d. 382, ll. 15–18.

17. For the headline, see *Trud*, August 30, 1930. For a comprehensive analysis of the Stalingrad trial, see Meredith L. Roman, "Racism in a 'Raceless' Society: The Soviet Press and Representations of American Racial Violence at Stalingrad in 1930," *International Labor and Working-Class History* 71 (Spring 2007): 185–203. For the American perspective, see Barbara Keys, "An African-American Worker in Stalin's Soviet Union: Race and the Soviet Experiment in International Perspective," *Historian* 71 (Spring 2009): 31–54.

18. See, for example, *Trud*, August 18, 1930; *Rabochaia gazeta*, August 17 and 18, 1930. The trial was similar to the comrades-disciplinary courts and agitational trials of the early Soviet era. See Lewis H. Siegelbaum, "Defining and Ignoring Labor Discipline in the Early Soviet Period: The Comrades-Disciplinary Courts, 1918–1922," *Slavic Review* 51 (Winter 1992): 705–30. "Speaking antiracism" is a variation on Stephen Kotkin's "speaking Bolshevik." See *Magnetic Mountain*, 198–237.

19. *Prozhektor* [Searchlight] 48 (November 25, 1928): 12. On the qualities of the New Soviet Person, see esp. David L. Hoffmann, *Stalinist Values: The Cultural Norms of Soviet Modernity*, 1917-1941 (Ithaca, NY: Cornell University Press, 2003), 45–56; Karen Petrone, *Life Has Become More Joyous, Comrades: Celebrations in the Time of Stalin* (Bloomington: Indiana University Press, 2000), 1–5, 11–13, 66–69; and Peris, *Storming the Heavens*, 78–83.

20. *Rabochaia gazeta*, August 17, 1931.

21. For these reports, see, for example, *Mezhdunarodnoe rabochee dvizhenie* [International worker movement], 23–24 (August 1930): 32; *Trud*, August 20 29, 1930; *Put' MOPR'a* [The path of MOPR] 29 (October 1930): 9; and *Internatsional'nyi maiak* [International lighthouse] 3 (January 1931): 9.

22. On Soviet citizens' interest in "sadistic discourse," see Evgeny Steiner, *Stories for Little Comrades: Revolutionary Artists and the Making of Early Soviet Children's Books* (Seattle: University of Washington Press, 1999), 104–5.

23. U.S. authorities were disturbed by the sale of these postcards. See *National Archives and Records Administration*, RG 84, MLR no. 435, USSR Embassy, 1935, vol. 28, entry 60, 840.1.

24. See, for example, *Trud*, August 28, 1930; *Komsomol'skaia pravda*, August 28, 1930; *Ogonek* [Little flame] 17 (June 20, 1931): 13; and *Workers News*, May 17, 1931. On the Marion lynching, see James H. Madison, *A Lynching in the Heartland: Race and Memory in America* (New York: Palgrave Macmillan, 2001). On lynchings as "galas," see Amy Wood, *Lynching and Spectacle: Witnessing Racial Violence in America, 1890-1940* (Chapel Hill: University of North Carolina Press, 2009), 19–44.

25. *Trud*, August 10 and 23, 1930; *Komsomol'skaia pravda*, August 23, 1930; *Mezhdunarodnoe rabochee dvizhenie* 25–26 (September 1930): 10.

26. *Komsomol'skaia pravda*, August 30, 1930.

27. *Komsomol'skaia pravda*, August 26, 1930.

28. On *Pravda*'s depiction of U.S. leaders as responsible for U.S. racism, see Kevin

J. McKenna, *All the Views Fit to Print: Changing Images of the U.S. in Pravda Political Cartoons*, 1917-1991 (New York: Peter Lang, 2001), 35–42. On the standard image of capitalists, see Victoria E. Bonnell, *Iconography of Power: Soviet Political Posters under Lenin and Stalin* (Berkeley: University of California Press, 1997), 187–224.

29. Eight were sentenced to death, and the youngest defendant, who was only thirteen years old, was sentenced to life imprisonment. For the foundational texts on the Scottsboro case, see Dan Carter, *Scottsboro: A Tragedy of the American South* (1969; reprint, Baton Rouge: Louisiana State University Press, 1979); and James Goodman, *Stories of Scottsboro* (New York: Vintage, 1994).

30. See, for example, *Izvestiia*, March 26, 1932. For the phraseology, see *Pravda*, April 9, 1932.

31. *Komsomol'skaia pravda*, January 27, 1932.

32. "Vsem TsK natsrespublik, kraikomam, i oblokomam MOPR" [To the MOPR central committees of all national republics, and to all territorial and regional committees], GARF, f. 8265, op. 1, d. 41, l. 79; "Predvaritel'naia informatsionnaia svodka provedaniia kampanii po spaseniiu deviate negritianskikh iunoshei v skottsboro" [Preliminary informational summary of the campaign to save the nine Negro youth in Scottsboro], GARF, f. 8265, op. 1, d. 39, ll. 222–25.

33. See "Preliminary Informational Summary of the Campaign in Defense of the 9 Negro Youths in Scottsboro, USA, Measures Taken on the Part of the C.C. of the MOPR/IRA Section in the USSR," RGASPI, f. 539, op. 5, d. 127, ll. 105–8; and "Vsem TsK natsrespublik, kraevym i oblastnym komitetam MOPR," [To the MOPR central committees of all national republics, and to all territorial and regional committees] GARF, f. 8265, op. 1, d. 42, l. 45. On controversy in the Communist Party, U.S.A., surrounding the fact that the defendants were not "political activists," see Hill, *Men, Mobs, and Law*, 210–30.

34. For Soviet citizens' leading role, see, for example, "Tretii plenum TsK MOPR 7.4.32 g." [Third plenary session of the Central Committee of MOPR], GARF, f. 8265, op. 1, d. 45, ll. 236, 245; *Pravda*, March 8, 1932; *Internatsional'nyi maiak* 8–9 (March 1932): 6; and *Sputnik moprovtsa* [MOPR companion] 7 (April 1932): 1–2. On the international campaign, see James A. Miller, Susan D. Pennybacker, and Eve Rosenhaft, "Mother Ada Wright and the International Campaign to Free the Scottsboro Boys, 1931–1934," *American Historical Review* 106 (April 2001): 387–430.

35. "Vtoroi Plenum TsK MOPR SSSR" [Second plenary session of the Central Committee of MOPR USSR], GARF, f. 8265, op. 1, d. 31, l. 25; *Rabochaia gazeta*, June 23, 1931.

36. "Terror kapitalistov protiv negritianskikh rabochikh v Amerike" [Capitalist terror against the Negro workers in America], RGASPI, f. 539, op. 5, d. 76, ll. 252–53. For distribution, see "O khode kampanii protesta protiv kazni 9 negritianskikh iunoshei skottsboro v 1932 g" [On the progress of the protest campaign against the execution of 9 negro Scottsboro youth in 1932], GARF, f. 8265, op. 1, d. 57, ll. 68–79.

37. *Izvestiia*, July 8, 1931; *Workers News*, July 16, 1931.

38. Some protest rallies were held during the intermission of plays at Moscow

theaters. See, for example, "Operativnyi plan kampanii skottsboro" [Operational plan of the Scottsboro campaign], GARF, f. 8265, op. 1, d. 57, ll. 84–85; and *Rabochaia gazeta,* July 7, 1931.

39. "Linchevanie i presledovanie negritianskikh trudiashchikhsia v SASSh," RGASPI, f. 539, op. 5, d. 126, ll. 43–54, emphasis in original.

40. *Komsomol'skaia pravda,* July 10, 1931.

41. *Literaturnaia gazeta,* July 30, 1931.

42. "Svobodu uznikam skottsboro!" [Freedom for the Scottsboro prisoners!], RGASPI, f. 539, op. 5, d. 126, ll. 68–71.

43. MOPR deemed that this was the proper way for the Soviet masses to protest the Scottsboro death sentence. See "TsK MOPR SSSR no. 6050" [Central Committee of MOPR USSR no. 6050], GARF, f. 8265, op. 1, d. 42, l. 48; and n. 42.

44. *Komsomol'skaia pravda,* July 4, 1931. Overall, *Komsomol'skaia pravda* printed the most resolutions. See, for example, May 27 and June 8, 1931; and March 27, 1932. See also *Leningradskaia pravda,* July 10, 1931; and *Trud,* July 7, 1931.

45. On the disruption associated with collectivization and massive industrialization, see Sheila Fitzpatrick, *Stalin's Peasants: Resistance and Survival in the Russian Village after Collectivization* (New York: Oxford University Press, 1994).

46. Daniel Kowalsky makes a similar argument with regard to the domestic solidarity campaign on behalf of the Spanish Republic. *Stalin and the Spanish Civil War,* conclusion.

47. The terminology is from Vladislav Zubok, *Zhivago's Children: The Last Russian Intelligentsia* (Cambridge, MA: Harvard University Press, 2009). See also Jochen Hellbeck, "Speaking Out: Languages of Affirmation and Dissent in Stalinist Russia," *Kritika* 1 (Winter 2000): 71–96; and Kenneth M. Straus, *Factory and Community in Stalin's Russia: The Making of an Industrial Working Class* (Pittsburgh: University of Pittsburgh Press, 1997).

48. Maxim Matusevich, "Probing the Limits of Internationalism: African Students Confront Soviet Ritual," *Anthropology of East Europe Review* 27, no. 2 (Fall 2009): 19–39.

49. On America's disavowal of the connection between lynching and modernity, see Jacqueline Goldsby, *Spectacular Secret: Lynching in American Life and Literature* (Chicago: University of Chicago Press, 2006), esp. 9–27.

50. On these racial stereotypes, see George M. Fredrickson, *The Black Image in the White Mind: The Debate on Afro-American Character and Destiny, 1817-1914* (New York: Harper and Row, 1971).

51. This discussion is informed by Alrick Cambridge, "Black Body Politics," in *Where You Belong: Government and Black Culture* (London: Avebury, 1992), esp. 110–19.

52. On the internalization of this "vocation," see Maxim Matusevich, "An Exotic Subversive: Africa, Africans and the Soviet Everyday," *Race & Class* 49, no. 4 (April 2008): 67. African Americans' plight mirrored the official representations of the non-Russian nationalities. See Yuri Slezkine, "The USSR as a Communal Apartment, or

How a Socialist State Promoted Ethnic Particularism," *Slavic Review* 53, no. 2 (Summer 1994): 414–452; and Michael G. Smith, "Film for the 'Soviet East': National Fact and Revolutionary Fiction in Early Azerbaijani Film," *Slavic Review* 56, no. 4 (Winter 1997): 654–78.

53. *Komsomol'skaia pravda*, April 10, 1932.

54. On Soviet officials' rejection of the biological category of race (in favor of the sociohistorical categories of nationality and class) and belief that such rejection reflected their superiority over their Western contemporaries, see Francine Hirsch, "Race without the Practice of Racial Politics," *Slavic Review* 61 (Spring 2002): 30–43; and Amir Weiner, "Nothing but Certainty," *Slavic Review* 61 (Spring 2002): 44–53.

55. See, for example, Homer Smith, *Black Man in Red Russia* (Chicago: Johnson Publishing, 1964); Langston Hughes, *I Wonder As I Wander: An Autobiographical Journey* (New York: Hill and Wang, 1956); Paul Robeson Jr., *The Undiscovered Paul Robeson: An Artist's Journey, 1898-1939* (New York: John Wiley and Sons, 2001); Allison Blakely, *Russia and the Negro: Blacks in Russian History and Thought* (Washington, DC: Howard University Press, 1986); Joy Gleason Carew, *Blacks, Reds, and Russians: Sojourners in Search of the Soviet Promise* (New Brunswick, NJ: Rutgers University Press, 2008), 90–112; and n. 60.

56. The focus on black oppression in American proletarian literature often contradicted the Comintern theme of interracial solidarity. See Barbara Foley, *Radical Representations: Politics and Form in U.S. Proletarian Fiction, 1929-1941* (Durham, NC: Duke University Press, 1993).

57. Any revolution was depicted as needing the guidance of the Soviet Union to be successful. See Odd Arne Westad, *The Global Cold War: Third World Interventions and the Making of Our Times* (Cambridge: Cambridge University Press, 2007), 49–72, esp. 57–59.

58. "Soviet exceptionalism" is defined here as a synthesis of Marxist-Leninist ideology and Russian exceptionalism. For a discussion of how these two influences shaped Soviet leaders' understanding of the USSR's role in the world, see Westad, *Global Cold War*, 39–72, esp. 45–47.

59. Even the International Labor Defense, the U.S. affiliate of MOPR, had difficulty maintaining interest and participation in the campaign beyond 1932. Waldrep, *Many Faces of Judge Lynch*, 164.

60. In August 1932 Soviet leaders canceled production of *Black and White*, a film that had brought twenty-one African Americans to Moscow and was intended to expose the plight of African American workers. See Glenda Elizabeth Gilmore, *Defying Dixie: The Radical Roots of Civil Rights, 1919-1950* (New York: W. W. Norton, 2008), 128–47.

61. Norman E. Saul, *Friends or Foes? The United States and Soviet Russia, 1921-1941* (Lawrence: University Press of Kansas, 2006), 269–301; Hugh D. Phillips, "Rapprochement and Estrangement: The United States in Soviet Foreign Policy in the 1930s," in *Soviet-U.S. Relations, 1933-1942* (Moscow: Progress Publishers, 1989), 9–17.

62. See Eley, *Forging Democracy*, 266.

63. See, for example, *Trud,* July 14, 1936.

64. *Izvestiia,* June 17, 1936. On the targeting of Soviet territory in the Nazi Party's propaganda, see, for example, Mark Mazower, *Hitler's Empire: How the Nazis Ruled Europe* (New York: Penguin, 2008). On Moscow's belated recognition that fascism constituted the main threat, see sources cited in nn. 61 and 62.

65. See esp. Beth Holmgren, "*The Blue Angel* and Blackface: Redeeming Entertainment in Aleksandrov's *Circus,*" *Russian Review* 66 (January 2007): 5–22; and Richard Taylor, "The Illusion of Happiness and the Happiness of Illusion: Grigorii Aleksandrov's *Circus,*" *Slavonic and East European Review* 74, no. 4 (October 1996): 601–20. Similarly, the extralegal executions of African Americans is not a main theme in the work the Soviet satirists Il'ia Il'f and Evgenii Petrov penned after their travels through the United States by car in 1935–36. See Il'ia Il'f and Evgenii Petrov, *Odnoetazhnaia Amerika: Pis'ma iz Ameriki* [One-storied America: Letters from America] (1937; reprint, Moscow: Tekst, 2003); and "Negry," *Ogonek* 22 (August 10, 1936): 14–17.

66. On the primacy of race to Cold War politics, see esp. Mary L. Dudziak, *Cold War Civil Rights: Race and the Image of American Democracy* (Princeton, NJ: Princeton University Press, 2000); Thomas Borstelmann, *The Cold War and the Color Line: American Race Relations in the Global Arena* (Cambridge, MA: Harvard University Press, 2002); and Carol Anderson, *Eyes off the Prize: The United Nations and the African American Struggle for Human Rights,* 1944-1955 (Cambridge, MA: Cambridge University Press, 2003).

67. See, for example, *Izvestiia,* August 7 and 23, 1946; *Pravda,* August 22 and September 23, 1946; *Trud,* August 22, 1946.

68. See, for example, *Izvestiia,* August 1, 1946; *Trud,* August 2 and 7, 1946; and *Pravda,* August 3, 1946. The reports that the Soviet journalist Il'ia Ehrenburg wrote about America for *Izvestiia* in July and early August 1946 also reflect this change. On Americans' views of violence against blacks as "anachronistic" in the 1940s, see Philip Dray, *At the Hands of Persons Unknown: The Lynching of Black America* (New York: Modern Library, 2002), 338–64, 387–406.

69. On outrage, see Stephen J. Whitfield, *A Death in the Delta: The Story of Emmett Till* (Baltimore: Johns Hopkins University Press, 1991), esp. 24–47.

70. Instead they reported on the health of President Eisenhower, the "friendship" between the German Democratic Republic and the Soviet Union, the success of socialism among the Chinese, and a visit to the USSR by an American agricultural delegation and a group of U.S. senators.

71. Protest rallies were organized in the Soviet Union in the wake of the assassination of Martin Luther King Jr. in April 1968. See Ann K. Johnson, *Urban Ghetto Riots, 1965-1968: A Comparison of Soviet and American Press Coverage* (New York: Columbia University Press, 1996), esp. 115–18.

72. See esp. Kate A. Baldwin, *Beyond the Color Line and the Iron Curtain: Reading Encounters between Black and Red,* 1922-1963 (Durham, NC: Duke University Press, 2002), 149–251.

73. Maxim Matusevich, "Journeys of Hope: African Diaspora and the Soviet Society," *African Diaspora* 1 (2008): 53–85; Julie Hessler, "Death of an African Student in Moscow: Race, Politics, and the Cold War," *Cahiers du monde russe* 47, nos. 1–2 (January–June 2006): 33–64.

74. On the concept of two competing models of modernity, see Westad, *Global Cold War*, 8–72.

Contributors

WILLIAM D. CARRIGAN is Professor of History at Rowan University. He is the author of *The Making of a Lynching Culture: Violence and Vigilantism in Central Texas, 1836–1916*, which won the Richard Wentworth Prize. He is also the editor of *Lynching Reconsidered: New Perspectives in the Study of Mob Violence*. With Clive Webb, he is a coauthor of the forthcoming *Forgotten Dead: Mob Violence against Mexicans in the United States, 1848–1928*. Numerous newspapers and media sources have discussed, quoted, or cited his research, including National Public Radio, the *New York Times*, the *Washington Post*, the *Houston Chronicle*, and the *Philadelphia Inquirer*.

BRIAN P. LEVACK is John E. Green Regents Professor of History at the University of Texas at Austin. His books include *The Civil Lawyers in England, 1603–1641: A Political Study; The Formation of the British State: England, Scotland, and the Union, 1603–1707; The Witch-Hunt in Early Modern Europe;* and *Witch-Hunting in Scotland: Law, Politics, and Religion*. He is a coauthor of *Witchcraft and Magic in Europe: The Eighteenth and Nineteenth Centuries* and the editor of *The Witchcraft Sourcebook* and *The Oxford Handbook of Witchcraft in Early Modern Europe and Colonial America*. His book *The Devil Within: Possession and Exorcism in the Christian West* will be published in 2013.

JOËL MICHEL is a public official with the French National Assembly in Paris, France. He graduated from the École Normale Supérieure in Paris, wrote a doctoral dissertation on the comparative history of European coal miners, and has published books and articles on the subject. More recently his interests have extended to the comparative history of violence in Europe and in the United States and is the author of *Le lynchage aux Etats-Unis*.

RACHEL MONAGHAN is Senior Lecturer in Criminology at the University of Ulster. She is the author (with Colin Knox) of *Informal Justice in Divided Societies: Northern Ireland and South Africa.* and has been researching informal justice since 1998. She has published a number of articles on the subject of paramilitary "punishments" in Northern Ireland in the journals *International Criminal Justice Review; Space and Polity; Terrorism and Political Violence;* and *Journal of Conflict Studies.* She is Associate Editor for the journal *Behavioral Sciences of Terrorism & Political Aggression* and is on the editorial board for *Studies in Conflict and Terrorism.*

SCOTT MORSCHAUSER is Associate Professor of Ancient History at Rowan University. He has taught at The Johns Hopkins University and Princeton Theological Seminary. He is the author of *Threat Formulae in Ancient Egypt: A Study of the History, Structure, and Use of Threats and Curses in Ancient Egypt* and "Observations on the Speeches of Ramesses II in the Literary Record of the Battle of Kadesh," in *Perspectives on the Battle of Kadesh,* edited by Hans Goedicke. He has contributed to the *New Interpreter's Dictionary of the Bible* and has had articles on Egyptological and biblical subjects published in the *Journal of Biblical Literature;* the *Journal for the Study of the Old Testament;* the *Journal of the American Research Center in Egypt;* and *Studien zür Altägyptischen Kultur.* He is a coeditor of *Biblical and Related Studies Presented to Samuel Iwry.*

MEREDITH L. ROMAN is Associate Professor of Comparative Soviet and African American History at the State University of New York, Brockport. She is the author of *Opposing Jim Crow: African Americans and the Soviet Indictment of U.S. Racism, 1928–1937.* Dr. Roman's articles have appeared in such journals as *Race & Class; Critique: A Journal of Socialist Theory; International Labor and Working-Class History; The Historian;* and the *Journal of Communist Studies and Transition Politics.*

FUMIKO SAKASHITA earned her Ph.D. from Michigan State University and is Assistant Professor of American Studies at Kansai Gaidai University in Osaka, Japan. She has published several articles in Japanese and English, including "Witness/Spectator of Violence: The Politics of 'Looking' in the History of Lynching," *Kokujin Kenkyu* (Black studies); and "The Politics of Sexuality in Billie Holiday's 'Strange Fruit,'" in *Gender and Lynching: The Politics of Memory,* edited by Evelyn M. Simien. Sakashita has also translated several English essays and monographs into Japanese, such as Hazel V. Carby's "'On the

Threshold of Woman's Era': Lynching, Empire, and Sexuality in Black Feminist Theory," which appeared in *Critical Inquiry* and *Capitalism and Slavery*, edited by Eric E. Williams.

SARAH L. SILKEY is Assistant Professor of History at Lycoming College. She is the author of "Redirecting the Tide of White Imperialism: The Impact of Ida B. Wells's Transatlantic Antilynching Campaign on British Conceptions of American Race Relations," in *Women Shaping the South: Creating and Confronting Change*, edited by Angela Boswell and Judith N. McArthur. She received her Ph.D. from the University of East Anglia in Norwich, England, and served as a Carter G. Woodson Institute Fellow at the University of Virginia.

CHRISTOPHER WALDREP was Jamie and Phyllis Pasker Professor of History at San Francisco State University. Previously Professor of History at Eastern Illinois University, he is the author of *Night Riders: Defending Community in the Black Patch*; *Roots of Disorder: Race and Criminal Justice in the American South, 1817–80*; *Racial Violence on Trial: A Handbook with Cases, Laws, and Documents*; *The Many Faces of Judge Lynch: Extralegal Violence and Punishment in America*; *Vicksburg's Long Shadow: The Civil War Legacy of Race and Remembrance*; and *African Americans Confront Lynching: Strategies of Resistance from the Civil War to the Civil Rights Era*. His most recent book is *Jury Discrimination: The Supreme Court, Public Opinion, and a Grassroots Fight for Racial Equality in Mississippi*. The Supreme Court Historical Society's 2010 Hughes-Gossett Award for best journal article went to Professor Waldrep for his article "Joseph P. Bradley's Journey: The Meaning of Privileges and Immunities."

CLIVE WEBB is Professor of Modern American History at the University of Sussex. He is the author of *Fight against Fear: Southern Jews and Black Civil Rights* and *Rabble Rousers: The American Far Right in the Civil Rights Era*, as well as editor of *Massive Resistance: Southern Opposition to the Second Reconstruction*. With William Carrigan, he is the coauthor of the forthcoming *Forgotten Dead: Mob Violence against Mexicans in the United States, 1848–1928*. In 2004, he and Carrigan received the Arthur Miller Prize for their essay in the *Journal of Social History* entitled "The Lynching of Persons of Mexican Origin or Descent in the United States, 1848–1928." Dr. Webb has appeared on the BBC and in numerous other popular forums. He is on the board of editors of the *Journal of Southern History*.

ROBERT M. ZECKER is Associate Professor of History at Saint Francis Xavier University in Nova Scotia. There he teaches U.S. history with specializations in immigration, race, and ethnicity; urban history; and labor. He earned his Ph.D. in American Civilization at the University of Pennsylvania, where he was a University Dissertation Fellow. Dr. Zecker is the author of *Race and America's Immigrant Press: How the Slovaks Were Taught to Think like White People; Streetcar Parishes: Slovak Immigrants Build Their Nonlocal Communities, 1890–1945;* and *Metropolis: The American City in Popular Culture,* as well as several articles, including "'The Same People as Over Here': The Fluidity of Rusyn and Slovak Identity in Philadelphia, 1890–1945," in *Committing Community: Carpatho-Ruthene Studies as an Emerging Scholarly Discipline,* edited by Elaine Rusinko.

Index

world context of lynching, 6

World War I: atrocities commited during, 86; culture of war infusing Europe, 101; "race war" in U.S. during and after, 151

World War II: black troops in Europe in 1945, 99–100; French mobs attacking collaborators, 14, 100–101, 106–7, 111–12, 115n43; Japanese occupation of Manchuria, 226; Nazi policies impact on Soviet Union, 227; use of lynching as a foreign policy weapon, 7, 135, 181–207; "War Quiz for America," 201–4; wartime espionage among African Americans, 193–96

Wright, Cleo, 181, 201, 202

xenophobia and violence in the ancient Near East, 19, 28–29, 36, 41n48, 44n91

Yahweh (ancient Israelite deity), 32, 34
Yamato (newspaper), 196
yellow journalism, 149, 194
Yomiuri (newspaper), 183, 185, 188, 190–91
Yorozu Chōhō (newspaper), 184, 190–91

Zarate, Elias, 88
Zebediela, South Africa, 61
Zecker, Robert, 135, 137–53
Zemplín province, Slovakia, 145, 146